To Be Like Jesus

An Appraisal of Biblical Theology in Practice of Personal and Ministerial Spiritual Formation.

Daniel Mathano Mwailu PhD

WestBow Press books may be ordered through booksellers or by contacting:

WestBow Press
A Division of Thomas Nelson & Zondervan
1663 Liberty Drive
Bloomington, IN 47403
www.westbowpress.com
1 (866) 928-1240

ISBN: 978-1-9736-7260-9 (sc)
ISBN: 978-1-9736-7262-3 (hc)
ISBN: 978-1-9736-7261-6 (e)

Library of Congress Control Number: 2019914856

Print information available on the last page.

WestBow Press rev. date: 11/18/2019

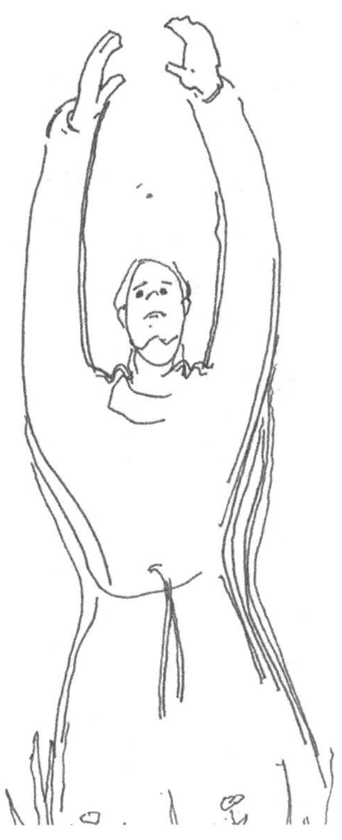

Image illustration by Douglas Barrett Wilkinson

The Bible says:

Romans 8:29 (TLB) "From the very beginning, God decided that those who came to him… should become like his son so that his son would be the First with many brothers."

FOREWORD

This unique book on personal and ministerial spiritual formation is both scholarly and practical. As an educator who has earned his Ph.D. and now lectures on spiritual formation at university, Dr. Daniel Mwailu has researched widely and documented extensively for this resourceful book. As a bi-cultural pastor and counselor for several decades (born in Kenya, educated and ministering in both U.K. and Kenya), Dr. Mwailu enriches the book with personal illustrations and applications from his rich life of diverse experiences. As a friend and mentor of Dr. Mwailu since the 1970s, I can vouch for his authenticity and integrity.

Dr. Richard Gehman, Former Principal, Scott Theological College, (now Scott Christian Univeristy), Machakos, Kenya.

ENDORSEMENTS

"Spiritual formation, upwards or downwards, is a process in the life of every believer. While the life of Christ serves as the ultimate model, His faithful followers of the past and present give to all of us hope that the upward journey is not impossible. In this work, and as he uses Scripture, lives of others and his own personal life, Dr. Daniel Mwailu makes a significant contribution to this subject. The drawing from the African context makes the contribution unique and invaluable for both personal study and academic work."

Professor Samuel Ngewa, Academic dean, Africa International University, Nairobi.

In this book *To Be Like Jesus*, Dr. Mwailu articulates a sound biblical theology of Christian formation. He weaves the teaching with vignettes of his own personal life, resulting in a very readable and cogent guide for both ministers and believers. His many years of experience in ministry and his biblical scholarship provide his readers with a reliable orientation for their spiritual lives. Due to the solid biblical material, *To Be Like Jesus* is a lamp to the feet and light to the path for those seeking guidance in the Christian life and ministry.

J. Russell Frazier (Ph.D.), Dean of the School of Religion and Christian Ministry and Coordinator of the DMin and PhD programs at Africa Nazarene University, Nairobi, Kenya

Dedication

To Margaret, my wife and a fellow sojourner in spiritual formation and our sons: Kyalo and Andrew the jewels in the crown of our marriage for whom I continue to pray for their continued spiritual formation.

To the faculty in the School of Religion and Christian Ministries in Africa Nazarene University for their colleagueship with thanks to heads of departments for giving me the opportunity to discharge the Wesleyan Heritage that God has bequeathed in me.

To my first doctoral students

To all the students who have sat in my lectures for your participation and positive feedback.

Acknoweldgements

Publishing a book is a project that involves the contributions of others besides the author. This book would not have been completed without the help of a few people who I would like to acknowledge.

Firstly, the Methodist Church for the gift of a sabbatical which gave me the time to concentrate and focus on writing this book. Special thanks to Rev Dr. Roger Walton, Chair of District, who made it possible through his support and encouragement. Thanks to Rev Mark Harwood and the sabbatical support group and especially for Mark taking on my workload during my sabbatical.

Secondly, Dr. John Job, a former lecturer at Cliff College, for painstakingly proof-reading the draft manuscript. Thirdly, Douglas Barrett Wilkinson, the artist and my long-time friend, who graciously drew up some images to illustrate and enliven the text of this book.

Fourthly and finally, Africa Nazarene University in Nairobi who gave me the opportunity to teach in their postgraduate and doctoral program during my sabbaticals and online when the lecture notes included in this book were researched and delivered. Special thanks to current Dean of the School of Religion and Christian Ministry, Dr Russel Frazier, for his colleagueship and friendship. Also thanks to Rev Gift Mtukwa, the current head of the religion department, for his pastoral care whenever I visited the department.

I also would like to acknowledge the encouragement from my publisher, Westbow Press, a division of Zondervan. I must admit, without your patient nudging encouragement, this book would still be draft notes in my computer, like four others that I started and never brought to completion. Thank you.

Contents

Preface xv
My Spiritual journey xix

Chapter 1 The Necessity for Spiritual Formation 1

1.1 Introduction 1
1.2 Raison d'être 3
Notes 12

Chapter 2 What is Personal and Ministerial Spiritual Formation? 13

2.1 Introduction. 13
2.2 Definitions of spiritual formation 15
2.3 Hindrances to Spiritual Formation 25
2.3.1 Original Sin 25
2.3.2 Psychological baggage 35
2.3.3 Witchcraft – An African challenge 48
2.3.4 The haunting Living Dead in African Spirituality 61
Notes 65

Chapter 3 Dynamics of Spiritual Formation 71

3.1 Circumcision of the heart 71
3.2 Baptism 78
3.3 Koinonia – Spiritual formation as a corporate journey 93
Notes 114

Chapter 4 Ministerial Formation 118

Notes 155

Chapter 5 Pillars necessary for personal and ministerial formation. 156

5.1 Introduction 156
5.2 Scriptures 158
5.3 Prayer 167
5.4 Fasting 176
5.5 Meditation 180
5.6 Journaling 191
5.7 Mentoring 202
5.8 Grace 260
Notes 281

Chapter 6 Spiritual formation in the Wesleyan –holiness movement 291

Notes 315

Chapter 7 Practical Application 317

Notes 361

Bibliography 365

Preface

This book started as lecture notes during my sabbatical and other teaching lectures online. As such, it has more extensive citations and Biblical references than usual. It is an academic book interspersed with the personal story of my spiritual journey, with added reminiscences to animate the text. As an academic scholarly document, it has numerous notes, citations, and references to facilitate further research. As I studied on the subject of spiritual formation, I felt it was an opportune moment to interweave my spiritual journey and development as a person and as a Christian minister to elucidate and illustrate the subject of Spiritual Formation. I offer my spiritual journey and reflection with the prayer that others would find the insights and experiences related helpful to enrich their lives, in pursuit of spiritual formation and their Christian ministries. It is my prayer also for those who might read this book, and have not started on their spiritual journey, and encounter with Jesus Christ that they may find this book an inspiration to begin their journey and that those who have already started, may find it encouraging and an inspiration to keep on. To those students who have just started on their personal and ministerial journeys, it is my prayer that you may take the seven pillars or disciplines (spiritual vitamins) suggested in this book seriously for, believe you me, using them will pay high spiritual dividends in your life's journey. Investing time to follow these disciplines would greatly enrich your experience. I highly commend these disciplines (spiritual vitamins) and the insights of this book to you, praying that God will use this book to bless you.

Image illustration by Douglas Barrett Wilkinson

Philippians 1:6 (NKJV) "He who has begun a good work in you will complete it."

My Spiritual journey

I grew up in an African village in the former British Colony of Kenya in Africa where there was no electricity, running water, the village church, or school. The nearest school was in the market town Ikutha, ten miles away from where we lived. That is where I started my education around the age of nine. Most children in my village never went to school at that time. I went through the chief's edict, established by the British Colonial government that decreed that every boy of a certain age, usually measured by their height, must attend school. My mother resisted owing to family poverty. For fear of the famous late chief James Matuku Muoka who was most revered by all people in Ikutha location, she allowed me to go to school, for which I am very grateful to God, as this marked the beginning of God's work of grace in my life. The story was more dramatic in that when the village elders called at our homestead, they explained why they had come, stating that I had been identified and chosen as one of the boys from our village who should attend school. My mother who was quite outspoken (my father was laid back and quiet and spoke with a little stammer) and objected to my attending school, stating that the family could not afford school fees, and that was going to be an extra burden to a family that lived from hand to mouth and found it had to make ends meet. The elders replied to my mother, politely that they understood her concern and apprehension. They then said to my mother; we could not face the chief without accomplishing his orders. Therefore, you come with us and explain to him yourself what you have told us. To which my mother replied, Okay, he might then go because she would not dare to face the chief herself to explain her objection. The chief's edict singled out three boys to attend a school that year, John, Kinyamasyo, and I from my village Mutomo, near Yatta Plateau in Kitui County. I recall the day as if it happened yesterday because of a comment made by our next-door neighbor who passed on, as we marched past her shamba (peasant's farm in Swahili) on our way to school on the first day; she made a demeaning, derogatory remark referring to me. I was deeply offended by her comment when she said in the vernacular "Yii ya Malee nayo noyo yimwe"- meaning, "Is this one of Malee one of them?" Malee is my mother's maiden name, and in the vernacular "yii –refers to a thing in a derogatory manner rather than to a person; its meaning implied that I was too thick to be included. What is more, in my original tribal culture, referring to a male after the mother's name is very demeaning and humiliating. In that culture, a male would take pride when referred to in the father's name, in this case, I would have been very proud if she had asked, "Is the son of Mwailu one of them?" The fact that I can remember this so vividly after more than half of a century perhaps affected me psychologically and made me apply myself harder in school. The other two boys never went beyond primary school, but by the grace of God, I was able to proceed further with my education. As the primary school was ten miles away from the village, we had to start walking at five in the morning to get to school by eight, when school started. The distance and the journey were arduous and hazardous, as we came across elephants, rhinos and other dangerous wildlife from Tsavo National Park, that was near our village. For this reason, my parents decided to relocate to a nearer village to the only school in the location. We initially relocated to Mavia village, and later to Ngwate village, each was five miles from the school. It was at Mavia village that my friend, Mikilo Sii, invited me to the local Missionary founded church, where I attended Sunday school for the first time. I can recall that first conversation that went something like this: "Would you come with me to Sunday School?" I replied, "What is Sunday School?" The answer I recall was, "Come and see." I enquired further by asking what I was supposed to do when we get there". His answer was, "if they ask for those who want to receive Jesus raise your hand." That sounded easy enough. I attended Sunday school for the first time, with him, and as my friend had predicted, the Sunday school teacher asked the question, and I raised my hand and pledged to receive Jesus. There was no further explanation given by way of discipleship than that; I could then count myself as a Christian, which I did. I continued attending church even when we moved to Ngwate village. I was the first in the family to become a Christian before the death of my father when I was about nine years of age. After his death, just as I started my second year at primary school, the family went through the animistic tribal ritual known as "kuusya kikwu" -appeasing the spirits of death. A renowned tribal medicine man performed the ritual to keep death at bay and not take any more members of the family. I tried to resist going through the ritual because I had become a Christian and told the family such beliefs were nonsense. I recall my older brother, who was eleven years older, coming to pick me from school on a bicycle that day to make sure I did not flee, for to do so meant that I might die. We went through the ritual, and after this ritual, my other siblings and my mother became Christians, possibly influenced by fear of my father's death so early in his life, hardly forty years old. I continued attending Sunday school and loved it so much that I became a Sunday school teacher. As I approached my early teens, I became rebellious and a challenge to my single widowed mother. At the same time, I started questioning much of what I had experienced in the church, in particular, what appeared to me to be the hypocrisy of attending church without any transformation of life. But just before I decided to abandon going to church altogether for what as a teenager I felt was meaningless, religious- ritualistic "Churchianity"- attending church without any meaningful spiritual change; God's grace apprehended me. As a Sunday school teacher, the church gave me the most precious present that was to make a lasting impact on my life, a Bible. My family could not afford a Bible, as my mother was an unemployed peasant living in one of the semi-arid parts of Kenya. The church gave me a Bible written in my vernacular language, Kikamba, as a gift for attending Sunday school and as a Christmas present. It was the most precious gift I needed but one that I could not afford at that time. I started reading my Bible, just randomly opening any passage without using any Bible notes. One day I opened the Bible, Revelation 20:15 (NLT) "And anyone whose name was not found recorded in the Book of Life was thrown into the lake of fire."

On that day, I had just taught Sunday school in the morning and concluded as always with an altar call, asking the children if any one of them wanted to commit their lives to Jesus Christ. It was a tradition in the church I attended at that time to conclude any service with an altar call. Later that day, I developed a strange feeling as if a voice was speaking inside of me asking, those children have registered their names in the Lamb's book of life in heaven, but have you? I tried to rationalize this out, arguing that I had once raised my hands to receive Jesus as they did and that I went to church and taught in the Sunday school. The voice searched deeper, making me reflect on the difference between my lifestyle and the rest of my peer group. It made me realize that I engaged and practiced the same youthful passions and sins as other youths did. The Holy Spirit convicted me. Although we did not have evening services, I recall walking back to the church at night, where I had taught Sunday school that morning all by my own; and knelt at the front of that muddy church and asked Jesus to come into my life for real and record my name in the Lamb's book of life. From that moment on, my life started to change, and the power of the Holy Spirit started to work in my life, helping me conquer peer pressure, my rebellious attitude at home changed. I felt a spiritual ability take control of my life and start breaking it slowly into a life of holiness. I remember abstaining from ungodly teenage life so much that my peer group ostracized and nicknamed me "kavonokya"- the redeemed or saved one. I felt quite lonely, but my relationship with God deepened, and I grew stronger and brave to shun the sins of youth. This change was so noticeable that I recall a comment from the senior pastor, the late Daniel Milu Kasaa, talking to other church members with the message that he was heard saying, "That son of Mwailu hates sin"! That was an excellent complement for the former pagan boy that I was, and it gave me the morale boost to stick to my newly found changed life. This change was so noticeable in the local church that I was asked to lead services in church and to preach when the local pastor did not turn up to take services. Thus in terms of my spiritual formation, my humble beginning started through attending school when I came into contact with Christianity planted in my location by missionaries from the West. It was also through a friend who invited me to attend Sunday school with him for the first time. Through attending Sunday school, the church gave me a Bible, and I later became a Christian in my late teens and committed my life to Jesus Christ on March 19,

1967, and I was then baptized by immersion on 13th August the same year. That Sunday evening on March 19 is as memorable to me as John Wesley's May 24 and although I cannot use the same words that I felt my heart strangely warmed, I can testify that day became a memorable beacon, a genuine, guiding lighthouse that directed my life in the start of my spiritual formation.

(Daniel Mathano Mwailu 2019)

One Chapter

The Necessity for Spiritual Formation

Introduction

Early childhood stories and nursery rhymes influence most of our personality. I never had Western nursery rhymes, but I remember two choruses that impacted my life in my early formative years at the start of my Christian journey. The first is:- "Let the beauty of Jesus be seen in me, All His wonderful passion and purity; O my Saviour divine, All my nature refine, Till the beauty of Jesus is seen in me."[1] I remember singing this chorus in Sunday school, and looking back on my Christian journey and the Christian ministries that I have been involved in, this chorus had a significant impact on my life. The second chorus is:- "To be like Jesus, to be like Jesus. All I ask to be like Him. All through life's journey. From earth to glory, all I ask to be like Him."[2]

It is this second chorus that influenced my life most in my late teens, especially as I was growing up in the Christian union movement under the auspices of Kenya Students' Christian Fellowship (KSCF) that I attribute the title of this book. In this chorus, I posit that we have a concise summary of the primary definition of personal and ministerial spiritual formation.

Although the author of this chorus is unknown, the verses added later[3] continue to embellish the principal meaning of spiritual formation; to be like Jesus.

This book deals with spiritual formation in the Christian faith and presupposes biblical teaching as its foundation. The reason for the use of the adjective *Christian* is to acknowledge that there are other spiritualities in other world religions. They, too, equally have their spiritual formations. The Bible is central to the Christian faith, and this is the prism and the lens through which we seek to explore spiritual formation. Christian spiritual formation is intricate. Ministerial formation and Christian spiritual formation like Siamese twins are intertwined. Although both, in essence, are divine initiatives, they require practical discipline and skills attained through spiritual exercises, that do not come naturally; are nurtured to develop. Spiritual formation begins with regeneration, is incepted by justification, and is nurtured through sanctification. Neither personal nor ministerial formation develops spontaneously without personal engagement with spiritual life exercises and Christian discipline. They both require the own resolve of the human will to allow divine power to establish them within each person. Ministerial formation is more than spiritual formation. It is a vocation, a calling in which Christian people respond to a call from God to a particular service, usually within the ordained (set apart, consecrated) ministry, and avail themselves to train to allow the necessary gifts and skills to develop in themselves for the work of Christian ministry. We will discuss this in-depth in chapter 4.

Spiritual formation is a lifelong process achieved through deliberately managed, planned, and intentional desire for spiritual growth superintended by the Holy Spirit.

Spiritual development and formation have been the subject of intense interest in recent years as scholars attempted to understand the ongoing relationship between the divine and human. Some scholars would trace this relationship to the creation of Adam and the fall, usually referred to as original sin. By original sin, we are referring to the propensity to the evil that is innate in all people, as articulated in Christian theology in the works of St. Augustine. According to some interpretations of the Bible creation narrative,[4] God created Adam's body first, but Adam did not become a "living being" until God breathed breath into him. The theory is that each human spirit was designed to share in and reflect God's holiness and love. According to this theory, original sin disturbed and destroyed the unique divine-human relationship between God and humanity, making it impossible for human beings to have an authentic natural relationship with God without regeneration. The theory makes it imperative for each human person to go through the process of spiritual rebirth and development. In this book, we will evaluate and appraise the various theological and biblical perspectives on spiritual formation, including how they relate to and impact the practice of personal and ministerial formation.

Raison d'être

The author believes this book will contribute immensely to the development of personal and ministerial spirituality and bring awareness to a largely neglected area of Christian development. Christianity lags behind other religions with respect to Christian discipline in discipleship and spiritual formation. Most major world religions have basic tenets and doctrines connected with their faith that define, differentiate, and exclude those who do not belong. In some religions, unless one is prepared to pledge and commit to their said religion's disciplines, one cannot be reckoned to belong to the said religion. For example, in Buddhism, there are four basic tenets: suffering, causation, cessation, and the eightfold path that include: right understanding; right thought; right speech; right action; right livelihood; right effort; right concentration and right mindfulness. For Buddhists, these tenets enable their spiritual formation. Buddhists are expected to adhere to them. For Islam, there are five principles that are commonly known as the five pillars of Islam: declaration of faith and belief in monotheism and Muhammad as the final prophet; daily prayers; almsgiving to charity and concern for the poor; fasting as means of self-purification and pilgrimage to Mecca. These pillars guide the disciples of Islam and are paramount to their religious formation into Islam. To be a Muslim entails adhering to these pillars of Islam.

When we come to Christianity, however, it is hard to discern any definitive fundamental tenets that define Christianity as a religion. Worse still is the lack of an all-embracing definition of the basics that make one a Christian. One wonders whether this is what Jesus Christ envisaged when he declared in the "manifesto of His kingdom" in the sermon on the mount: "Not everyone who calls me Lord will enter God's kingdom. The only people who will enter are those who do what my Father in heaven wants." Matthew 7: 21 (ERV). The Message translation puts this verse crudely in the context of the preceding and following verses,

> Don't look for shortcuts to God. The market is flooded with surefire, easygoing formulas for a successful life that can be practiced in your spare time. Do not fall for that stuff, even though crowds of people do. The way to life—to God!—is vigorous and requires total

> attention. Be wary of false preachers who smile a lot, dripping with practiced sincerity. Chances are they are out to rip you off some way or other. Do not be impressed with charisma; look for character. Who preachers *are* is the main thing, not what they say. A genuine leader will never exploit your emotions or your pocketbook. These diseased trees with their bad apples are going to be chopped down and burned. "Knowing the correct password—saying 'Master, Master,' for instance—isn't going to get you anywhere with me. What is required is serious obedience—*doing* what my Father wills. I can see it now—at the Final Judgment thousands strutting up to me and saying, 'Master, we preached the Message, we bashed the demons, our God-sponsored projects had everyone talking.' And do you know what I am going to say? 'You missed the boat. All you did was use me to make yourselves important. You do not impress me one bit. You're out of here.
>
> (Matthew 7:13-23 MSG)

For most Christians, this pertinent question remains: what does God the Father want? For some people, it is debatable even whether Christianity is a religion. Some Christians would posit that religion is man's effort to please God, which means earning salvation by doing good works. On the contrary, they argue that Christianity has to do with forming a loving relationship between God and humanity, mediated through the death of Christ on the cross, and that relationship is dependent on God's grace. In this sense, Christianity is a relationship and not a religion. Extreme Calvinism would emphasize the grace and sovereignty of God almost to the exclusion of human free will. This view, however, if extrapolated to the extreme, makes the Christian a zombie acted upon by grace and the Holy Spirit at the exclusion of human will and response. Although some would dispute defining Christianity as a religion when we view Christianity from phenomenological perspectives in the Heilsgeschichte Schule, it is classified and identified as one of the monotheistic religions of the world; it is a derivative from Judaism, which itself had specific tenets that defined it. Christianity, however, even when not presented as a religion for fear of being labeled legalistic, needs formal pillars or principles for Christians who take their faith seriously for spiritual formation to occur. That conviction provides one of the primary objectives of this book. These same formal pillars or tenets are also necessary for successful ministerial formation.

In my experience and observation over many years as a Christian minister,[5] those desiring to be ministers neglect these pillars at their peril and expose themselves to joining a legion of ministerial casualties, some by way of burnout and others discharged from ministry in disgrace. It is my observation, conviction, experience, and my contention that we could avoid most of these casualties if the spiritual and ministerial formation and the necessary disciplines (spiritual vitamins) were taken seriously and adhered to conscientiously, as is the case in other world religions. For instance, as I was working on this book, I was on holiday and had booked in at the East View Hotel in Kibwezi in Makueni County in Kenya. I had a few urgent errands lined up the following morning. At 5:00 a.m., I was woken up by the megaphone's loud call to morning prayer from the local mosque; this was repeated at 6:00 a.m. It was an appropriate call because I decided to use it for my devotions too. I turned into the devotional booklet that I tend to use while on holiday, *Word for Today*. The reflection that morning was based on Mark 14:8, with the title:- "Use What God Has Given You." The devotion was so useful that I wrote the article for the church magazine for that month using the thoughts I had gleaned from that Quiet Time. If that "Mosque Siren" had not waked me up, would I have done my devotions on that day? The chances are, being on holiday, lying in an elegant hotel room, I perhaps would have woken up late and decided to skip it as many Christians do.

The call to worship from the Mosque is a daily discipline, a form of "Islamic Spiritual Formation." My experience in the ministry has led me to believe that a good minister would of necessity need to be a good Christian, and a good Christian of necessity needs to adhere to specific disciplines, exercises, and spiritual habits. In this book, I have identified seven key disciplines that I would refer to as pillars and recommend as vital spiritual vitamins for spiritual formation and ministry development in the context of the church and the broader practice of Christianity. In this book, I would high- light the Biblical and Theological basis of these disciplines. Some of them form the "DNA" of early Methodism and subsequent Wesleyan holiness movement. Others are discernible from other strands of Christianity and practiced in their community outside the Wesleyan holiness movement. In this book, the basic thesis is that although Christianity base its faith on grace and not works, spiritual discipline is a God-given virtue to Christians to enable them to deepen and develop their confidence in God, and fellowship with him.

Paul exhorts the Christians as follows: "Therefore, my dear friends...continue to work out your salvation with fear and trembling, for it is God who works in you to will and to act according to his purpose." (Philippian 2:12-13 NIV) One of the hindrances to spiritual formation is "Christian zombiesm," in which the Christian attributes the state of their spiritual lives to God, a kind of Christian fatalism found in Islam under the Swahili expression. "Shauri ya Mungu"- it is all up to God. Whatever will be will be; I am just the way I am. It is against such laid back, laissez-faire attitude to Christian spiritual lives – a sort of, do nothing, God will do it all that I believe the entire thesis of this book addresses. It also requires balance on safeguarding the other extreme that over-emphasizes and even misinterprets, the biblical injunction, "work out your salvation," leading to salvation by works of which the same Apostle Paul cautions, "because of His kindness you have been saved through trusting Christ. And even trusting is not of yourselves; it is too a gift from God. Salvation is not a reward for the good we have done, so none of us can take any credit for it. It is God himself who has made us what we are and given us new lives from Christ Jesus." (Ephesians 2:8-9 TLB) Another translation puts it this way, "It is by grace you have been saved, through faith…it is the gift of God not by works so that no one can boast. For we are God's workmanship, created in Christ to do good works." Ephesians 2:8-9 (NIV)

What does "work out your salvation" mean?

Perhaps we might begin by stating what it does not mean. Firstly, the cumulative teaching of scripture seems to suggest that it does not mean that Christians can lose their salvation. Secondly, it does not mean living the Christian life nervously and anxiously in fear of getting it wrong. The original Greek words: φόβου καὶ τρόμου τὴν ἑαυτῶν translated "fear and trembling" in this text meant reverence or respect. Apostle Paul uses the same phraseology in other writings[6], and both cases; it does not refer to losing salvation or living nervously or anxiously. The debate about losing salvation is an age-long diatribe among Christians, in particular between ultra- Calvinists and Armenians. Suffice it here merely to state that salvation refers to sinful people coming to Christ, confessing their sins and forming a secure, eternal relationship with the Triune God, saved by the Son Jesus Christ, indwelt by the Holy Spirit and sustained by the power of God the Father through the indwelling Holy Spirit. This belief is supported by biblical passages that teach that once a person is justified, their salvation is guaranteed because predestination, justification, and glorification are divine acts of God, and they belong together.[7] The Bible strengthens this view by asking, "Who will bring any charge against those whom God has chosen" also the assertion that "nothing can separate us from the love of God in Christ Jesus in the same passages." Romans 8: 33-35 and 38-39 (NIV). It is also supported by the logic that just as one cannot "undo" natural birth, so it is with spiritual birth[8] implying the impossibility of being "un-regenerated"; hence, the new birth (salvation) cannot be lost. Believers, when they are regenerated (saved or born again), they get eternal life[9] and are indwelt by Holy Spirit[10]inferring that "eternal life" implies permanence, once saved, always saved leading to the conclusion that believers' salvation is eternally secure, sealed for the day of redemption.[11]This position is strengthened further by Jesus' assertion: John 6:39 (NIV) "I give them eternal life, and they shall never perish; no one can snatch them out of my hand." Jesus also went on to say, John 10:28-29 (NIV) "my father who has given them to me is greater than all no one can snatch them out of my Father's hand."

There are, however, those who argue for the possibility of believers losing their salvation according to this text. For the most part, this view relies on the translation of one Bible verse, Revelation 22:19, and in particular, the wording "blotting out or erasing from the book of life" as a result of tampering with God's word. The counter-argument against this view is that this verse does not refer to true believers. It instead refers to those who merely profess to be Christians; because true Christians depend on the Word of God rather than tampering with it. The second counter-argument relies on textual hermeneutics and the rendering "book of life" or "tree of life." Most translations[12]render "taking away any share in the tree of life and the Holy City." Textual studies reveal that only the King James translation uses the book of life. From the critical textual -semantic – perspectives, the hermeneutical explanation is that it is due to an error dating back to Erasmus. The error occurred when in compiling his Greek text from which KJV is translated, used the Latin Vulgate in which "the tree" was rendered "the book" because a scribe accidentally replaced Latin "ligno" (tree) with "Libro" (book). Hence all the translations that use the Latin MSS (Textus Receptus) such as KJV translate book instead of a tree of life.[13] The correct MSS would translate: "The one who corrupts (tampers with) the word of God will be deprived of access to the tree of life."[14]

In Paul's letters to the Corinthians[15], the phrase"working out" your salvation with fear and trembling," referred to being "mindful of the great and awesome nature of the work in which Paul was engaged. " In the second reference[16], it referred to the great humility and respect for Titus's position as a minister of the gospel of Jesus Christ. The sense in which we are to work out our salvation in fear and trembling, according to the Greek verb (κατεργάζεσθε) rendered "work out" refers to two things: Firstly, to continue working to bring something to completion or fruition." Etymologically, the same Greek word, was used for turning bullion into coins. From this etymological context, it means actively, obediently, and willingly pursuing obedience in the process of sanctification. Paul cites himself engaged in this process as "straining" and "pressing on" toward the goal of Christlikeness.[17] Trembling denotes the Christian attitude in pursuing this goal—a healthy fear of offending God through disobedience and an awe and respect for His majesty and holiness. Trembling can also refer to shaking due to weakness, implying a state of dependency on God. In another text[18], trembling refers to obedience and submission offered to God as reverence and respect also described as "reasonable service," which results in renewing hearts and minds of the Christian. This interpretation finds resonance in the Psalms: "Serving the Lord with fear and rejoicing with trembling."[19]

In light of this, spiritual formation is part of this straining and pressing on towards Christlikeness and is assisted by observing specific disciplines. This book will address the need for development in spiritual formation by suggesting seven (pillars or disciplines – spiritual vitamins) and explaining how each contributes to the dynamic process of spiritual formation. These are: - (Scripture; Prayer, Fasting, Lectio Divina; keeping a journal (journaling), mentoring, and grace). The thesis of this book is that these disciplines are essentials pillars (spiritual vitamins) for both personal spiritual formation as well as ministerial formation in light of current debates.

Chapter 1 Notes

1 "Let the Beauty of Jesus." Accessed July 23, 2018. http://hymnary.org/let_the_beauty_of_jesus_be_seen_orsborn/.,

2 "To Be Like Jesus." Accessed July 23, 2018.https://hymnary.org/text/to_be_like_jesus_to_be_like_jesus_my_des.

3 Later, 1st verse & music were added by Henry Slaughter 2nd verse by Gloria Gaither Copy right 1971 by Harvest Time Publishers. *Verse 1:* He lifted up the fallen man, He gave the world a helping hand, His heart was touched each time He saw a soul in need; Displaying kindness everywhere, Mercy and love was His to share, And like this Man of Galilee I want to be. Verse2: His look of love went everywhere, and lives were changed when He was there, Hungry eyes and hungry souls felt His embrace. He stooped to mend each crippled child, His healing touch was strong but mild, and like this Man of Galilee I want to be. 1st verse & music by Henry Slaughter 2nd verse by Gloria Gaither Copy right 1971 by Harvest Time Publishers.

4 Genesis 2:7

5 The author felt a call into Christian ministry and entered to train for the ordained ministry on 8th May 1974. He started his ministry as a church planter in Nairobi West with the Africa Inland Church. He was shortly transferred to AIC Ziwani (3000 member-congregation) where he served until 1979 when he got a scholarship to go to London University. He completed his PhD at Birmingham University in 1989. He has served with the Methodist Church in the UK for over 25 years; half of them as superintendent minister.

6 1Corinthians 2:3 (καὶ ἐν τρόμῳ πολλῷ ἐγενόμην) (and 2 Corinthians 7:15 (φόβου καὶ τρόμου ἐδέξασθε αὐτόν)

7 Romans 8:30.

8 John 3:3; Titus 3:5

9 John 3:15

10 John 14:17; Romans 8:9

11 Ephesians 4:30.

12 NIV; NASB, ESV, NLT, HCSB, ISV & ASV

13 Erasmus translated the last six verses of the book of Revelation chapter 22 using the Latin MSS.

14 Revelation 22:19

15 1Corinthians 2:3

16 2Corinthians 7:15

17 Philippians 3:13-14

18 Romans 12:1-2

19 Psalm 2:11

Chapter Two

What is Personal and Ministerial Spiritual Formation?

Introduction.

We start by defining what we mean by personal and ministerial spiritual formations. We would then later appraise how spiritual formation impinges on the pastoral formation and outline how the suggested seven pillars of discipline assist in achieving both. The word discipline is not in vogue in our modern and postmodernity egalitarian society. It is not "cool," to talk of discipline; the word is usually loaded with negative connotations in the post-modern community today. Modern people tend to view the word discipline with indifference as an antiquated Victorian concept, especially in postmodern Western society "where live and let live" seems to be the ethical signature motto of modern society. In this book, however, we use the word disciplines to denote tools (vitamins necessary) to foster growth and development in the Christian pilgrimage. Discipline understood as a tool is a necessity in all sport for athletes who want to succeed in their sport. It is remiss of us to expect to make a success in living spiritual lives without undertaking any exercise.

> "Discipline should work in concert with dependence since grace is not opposed to effort but to earning. The multiple benefits of the time-tested disciplines of the faith contribute to spiritual formation in the same way that training prepares us for the skillful endeavor."[20]

Spiritual formation entails resilience; the Christian life is not a walk in the park but a battlefield. Tony Horsfall, in his book *Deep Calls to Deep,* examines some Psalms that reveal honest insights into the reality of life with God, "those passing through the valley" as it were and "those who desire a deeper walk with God."[21] It expounds Psalms[22]that reflect deep emotions of human beings grappling with life in their spiritual pursuit with God and showing how God shapes Christian character and forms Christlikeness even in difficult times. Horsfall comments, "The book of Psalms taken as a whole provides us with a wonderful handbook for spiritual formation."[23]

He suggests,

> "As we read the Psalms, we are entering into the sanctuary, the place where God meets men and women in a special way. We will see that the conversation between God and his people is direct, intense, intimate, and above all, honest. Thus, the Psalms are a kind of literary sanctuary in the Scripture: the place where God meets his people in a special way, where his people may address him with their praise and lament."[24]

He cites a typical example from Psalm 69 that he entitles "The depths of unjust suffering,"[25] in which the psalmist uses the disturbing language of honest anger in his lament, feeling abandoned by God. He is expressing deep suffering, inner turmoil driving him almost to the point of being overwhelmed.

He normalizes Christian feelings of anger toward God by citing Timothy Keller, "We should not assume that if we are trusting in God, we won't weep or feel anger, or feel hopeless. The point is this: suffering people need to be able to weep and pour out their hearts and not immediately to be shut down by being told what to do.[26] Suffering is very much part of spiritual formation,

> unjust suffering is just one way by which God tests and refines our hearts, for the pain of it bring to the surface things that are hidden from view. Unhelpful attitudes and wrong beliefs are exposed: selfishness, self-righteousness, the need to be in control or always right, vindictiveness, impatience, self-absorption, pride, and everything symptomatic of a demanding nature.[27]

As these attitudes are exposed, God replaces them with humility, compassion, understanding, forgiveness, endurance, perseverance, trust, and dependence upon God, and in this way, our spiritual formation continues to take place. In this psalm, the suffering of Christ is prefigured, teaching us the lesson that when we suffer unjustly, we identify with the suffering of Christ in whose image we are striving to be conformed in our spiritual formation.

Definitions of spiritual formation

Some scholars are prescriptive and define spiritual formation as "the Spirit-driven process of forming the inner world of the human self in such a way that it becomes like the inner being of Christ himself."[28]

Augustine described Spiritual Formation as an inward journey to face our true selves in Christ, through the leading of the Holy

Spirit. "Away from the exterior of false self towards wholeness"[29]; an invitation to

> "Return to your heart (redi ad cor) and see there that which you may be thinking about God; for there (at your heart) is the image of God. In the "interiority" of your humanity, Christ dwells; there within, you are being renewed according to God's image. Recognize its author in the author's image."[30]

It is "a gradual process of being conformed to the image of Christ, a process of involvement with God's gracious work, moving us towards the wholeness of Christ." The spiritual life is an all-encompassing, lifelong response to God's gracious initiatives in the lives of those whose trust is centered in the person and work of Jesus Christ."[31]Howard Hendricks defines spiritual life as:

> Not a crisis but a continual process, not based on knowledge but on obedience, not external but internal, not automatic but cultivated, not the product of energy but of divine enablement, not a dream but a discipline, not an unusual experience but a normal experience, not a list of rules but a life relationship, not to be endured but enjoyed, not theoretical but intensely practical...it is the life of Christ reproduced in the believer by the power of the Holy Spirit in obedient response to the Word of God.[32]

Various metaphors in the Bible describe the spiritual life that develops in a believer. Ephesians, 4:22 (NASB) "Lay aside the old self, which is being corrupted in accordance with the lusts of deceit, and that you be renewed in the spirit of your mind, and put on the new self, which in the likeness of God has been created in righteousness and holiness of the truth." Also, Colossians 3:9-10 (NIV) "have taken off your old self with its practices and have put on the new self, which is being renewed in knowledge in the image of its Creator." Kenneth Boa refers to this as "the substitution of Christ's life for the self-life,"[33] "strengthening with power through God's Spirit in the inner man,"[34] also referred to as "an inside-out rather than an outside-in process… resting in what Jesus has already done for us,"…it is no longer I that live, but Christ lives in me[35]. Christlikeness is developed "through the Spirit, by faith."[36]There is a lot of literature on the work of the Holy Spirit in the Christian life. One of the most pertinent on the subject of spiritual formation is by Pamela Evans, *Shaping the Heart,* [37]in which she discusses how "God created the human heart to be worship-filled, a holy place with himself in residence, a garden in which the fruit of the Spirit may grow."[38]

In terms of Armenian theology that brings together divine sovereignty and human cooperation,

> "Once we understand spiritual formation as a process, all of life becomes spiritual formation. Consequently, cooperation with God's gracious work moves us towards the wholeness of Christ…the experience of being shaped by God towards wholeness."[39]

In this sense, spiritual formation is a mysterious dynamic divine-human synergy in which Christ transforms us in the very process of living in and through us. Spiritual formation in certain aspects is synonymous with sanctification in a sense that; it is a

> "Divine-human process that involves both dwelling in the power of his Spirit in our inner being and the gradual formation of Christlike character and behavior. It involves a balance of dependence and discipline, of divine sovereignty and human responsibility."[40]

According to Mark A. Maddix, "Spiritual formation refers to the transformation of people into what C.S. Lewis calls "little Christs,"...it begins with a focus on being "formed" and "transformed"...The human person being transformed (always present tense) into the image and likeness of Christ."[41] Other scholars define spiritual formation in "general terms," referring to all attempts, means, instruction, and disciplines intended towards the deepening of faith and furtherance of spiritual growth. It includes educational endeavors as well as the more intimate and in-depth process of spiritual direction."[42] In Christian spiritual formation, the focus is on Jesus, whose image of spirituality is the benchmark of our conformity. Richard Foster defines spiritual formation as

> The process of transformation, the inner reality of the self (the inward being of the psalmist) in such a way that the overall life with God seen in the Bible naturally and freely comes to pass in us. Our inner world (the secret of the heart) becomes the home of Jesus, by His initiative and our response. As a result, our interior world becomes increasingly like the inner self of Jesus, and therefore, the natural source of the words and deeds that are characteristic of him. By his enabling presence, we come to let the same mind be in us that was in Christ Jesus.[43]

It is a lifelong process as a believer desires to become a disciple of Jesus and become more like him made development possible by the divine grace of the Gospel and the empowering presence of the Holy Spirit. "Christian formation is not qualitatively distinct from Christian conversion, and we are never fully converted because we are never fully formed as followers of Jesus Christ."[44]According to Dallas Willard, it traces its fundamental premise on a belief in the fall of humanity and the doctrine of original sin. Meaning that spiritual formation entails growth but also dedicated discipline. The famous Reformation theologian John Calvin speaks of new life in Christ as "regeneration, a process, as a long-term, lifelong inculcation of a set of practices that do not come naturally." According to Calvin,

> This restoration does not take place in one moment or one day or one year, but through continual, sometimes even slow advance, God wipes out in the elect the corruption of the flesh, cleanses them from guilt, consecrates them to himself as temples, renewing all their minds to true purity that they may practice repentance throughout their lives and know that this warfare will only end in death.[45]

Other scholars have come to perceive spiritual formation as a lifelong process due to original sin so deeply rooted in our thinking and willing that only a lifetime of turnings, of fits and starts, of divine dislodgement and detoxification, can produce what God has in mind for us. In this sense, spiritual formation takes time, and Christians should be prepared to be committed for the long haul. Just like we cannot expect a baby to grow into an adult in one year, we should give time for spiritual growth. The last three years have been quite transformative in our family as we have been observing the growth and development of our first grandson, Zephyr. Since his arrival in June of 2016, we have watched him lying on his cot, to the first time, he started creeping and lately taking his first steps in walking and talking like a chatterbox! It would have been unreasonable when we went to pick up his mother from Derby Royal Hospital to expect him to walk home with us. Therefore, "spiritual growth is, in large measure, patterned on the nature of physical growth."[46] According to Gregory S. Clapper, "Christian conversion and spiritual formation must be non-negotiable features of the life of our church." Spiritual formation does not occur in a vacuum; it is continuously shaped and affected by various influences and responses to the world around us and the relationships we form or refuse to form. It entails going through stages of spiritual awareness and increasing depths of wholeness about God. Spiritual formation helps us understand that God is our highest good, the *summum bonum* of our lives, as it were, and drives us to become increasingly willing to renounce worldly aspirations to pursue God's pleasure. It creates a thirst within our souls described as follows: Psalm 42:1-2 (GW) "As a deer longs for flowing streams, so my soul longs for you, O God, My soul thirsts for God, for the living God. When may I come to see God's face?" It is a steady and constant struggle with our culture that infiltrates our attitudes unconsciously and makes us expect spiritual formation to happen instantaneously rather than through the steadiness progress of a process. Spiritual formation entails choices mentioned in scripture, Romans 12:2 (GW) "Don't become like the people of this world. Instead, change the way you think. Then you will always be able to determine what God really wants." Or, as other translations render it, Romans 12:2 (NIRV) "Do not live any longer the way this world lives. Let your way of thinking be completely changed." Romans 12:2 (NIV), "Do not conform to the pattern of this world, but be transformed by the renewing of your mind." Romans 12:2 (NLT) says, "Don't copy the behavior and customs of this world, but let God transform you into a new person by changing the way you think." Romans 12:2 (MSG) "Don't become so well-adjusted to your culture that you fit into it without even thinking. Instead, fix your attention on God. You'll be changed from the inside out."

We need to note that both verbs, conformed (συσχηματίζεσθε -syschēmatizesthe – translated conformed) and (μεταμορφοῦσθε -metamorphousthe –translated transformed) in the original Greek are in the second person plural passive imperative tense. In Greek, passive imperative tense is a way of telling people to be acted upon by some agent or instrument external to themselves. The use of passive imperative tense is a way of effectively telling people to submit themselves to a process or participate in a process in which external forces or instruments are playing a role in the process. The middle passive imperative in Greek also implies permissiveness in which the addressee is urged to cooperate with others performing an action upon them. The literal translation of μεταμορφοῦσθε is "be being transformed by the renewing of your mind." The second thing to notice is that the two verbs are offered as alternatives, as if to say, choose one or the other. In this respect, there is no neutral ground in spiritual formation. We are either "being transformed by the grace of God into the image of Christ, being shaped by the presence, purpose, and power of God in all things"[47] or continually being conformed into the worldly standards opposed to God's will. In this sense, there is no neutrality in spiritual formation; it is happening all the time whether we are aware of it or not. Human beings are spiritual beings and are always moving in one direction or the other. C.S. Lewis put it this way: "Each of us at each moment is progressing to the one state or the other." Mulholland aptly sums it up this way:

> "Spiritual formation is not an option! The inescapable conclusion is that life itself is a process of spiritual development. The only choice we have is whether that growth moves us toward wholeness in Christ or toward an increasingly dehumanized and destructive mode of being."[48]

My wife Margaret and I have two grown-up sons, Jonathan and Andrew, whom, by God's grace, we saw grow through Sunday school to university. Having grown up in a Christian home as ministers' kids, the time came when they wanted to assert themselves and express their opinions and chart out their lifestyles as all children do. I recall a conversation when one of them during his teenage years was challenging our way of life and castigating it as old-fashioned. I remember reminding him that as parents, we are aware that we are aging, and we have formed a particular way of living, which appears archaic to him. I then asked him, whether he could not see that, he too was imposing his newfound modern way of thinking and living to us, which equally felt strange to us. The point I was making was that my son's perception of the imposition of lifestyle works in two ways. It was not merely that we as parents were imposing our way of life on him, for that was all that we knew and had allowed forming in our lives. I wanted him to notice that also his new way of seeing and doing things that he had learned and allowed to develop in him at university and from his peer group, however new and valid for him was an imposition on us if he wanted us to change to his unique way of perspectives in life. What he had failed to realize was that in going through university, he had allowed a modern way of life at university; most of it, influenced by some New Age philosophy, to form in his life and that he was judging our spiritual formation using his new life lenses. The point is this: just as in spiritual warfare, there is no demilitarized zone, equally in spiritual growth, there is no standing still. We fail to realize that the process of spiritual shaping is a primal reality of human existence. Everyone is in the process of spiritual formation! Every thought we hold, every decision we make, every action we take, every emotion we allow to shape our behavior, every response we make to the world around us, every relationship we enter into, every reaction we have toward the things that surround us and impinge upon our lives – all these things, little by little, are shaping us into some kind of being.

> "We are being shaped into either the wholeness of the image of Christ or a horribly destructive caricature of that image – destructive not only to ourselves but also to others, for we inflict our brokenness upon them...The direction of our spiritual growth infuses all we do with intimations of either Life or Death."[49]

One of the significant hurdles in spiritual formation emanates from modernity and its DIY (Do It Yourself) philosophy, the desire to be in control of our lives and self– reliance encapsulated in the poet William Henley's saying " I am the master of my fate, I am the captain of my soul." Embedded in this modern philosophy is rebellion against God's grace, summed up in the famous words of Frank Sinatra, "I did it my way"- which has become the signature of the twentieth and twenty-first-century common folk philosophy in the Western World, unleashed by the Enlightenment. Self-reliance and the desire to control our lives has become the aspiration of modern living today. This philosophy depicts itself in its redefinition of being and doing, where what we do is driven by self- definition to meet other peoples' approval. Being and doing are integrally related. When correctly understood, however, spiritual formation, rather than doing things to be, the opposite is the case where our doing flows out of our being, our character controls our behavior. Modernity and postmodernity drive us to think that doing the right things brings about our nature. In spiritual formation, however,

> It is God, not we ourselves, who is the source of the transformation of our being into wholeness in the image of God...our part is to offer ourselves to God in ways that

> enable God to do that transforming work of grace. Our relationship with God and not our doing is the source of our being. In this respect, spiritual formation is the great reversal: from being the subject who controls all other things to be a person who is shaped by the presence, purpose, and power of God in all things.[50]

According to the Bible, 2 Corinthians 3:18; Ephesians 4:13 and Colossians 3:9-10; spiritual formation is not something that we do to ourselves or for ourselves, but something we allow God to do in us and for us as we yield ourselves to the work of God's Spirit transforming grace. Most of the definitions seem agreed that spiritual formation is a process that requires a lifetime in dealing with aspects of our lives that have unlikeness of Christ's image – those parts of our lives that are most alienated from God. It is also dependant on response to God's grace in our lives made possible by what Christ has done for us on the cross, "it is a process of being conformed to the image of Christ for the sake of others."[51]Spiritual formation is the agenda of the Holy Spirit. Jesus said, John 14:26 (GW) "The helper, the Holy Spirit, whom the Father will send in my name, will teach you everything. He will remind you of everything that I have ever told." Jesus added two other vital roles of the Holy Spirit, *convict* the world of sin, by showing the world what God approves and *convince* the world of judgment (John 16: 8-11). The Holy Spirit since taking his role of directorship in the church from the day of Pentecost is continually working in the world convincing and convicting humanity of its sinfulness and about the righteousness of God and the need for justification, regeneration, sanctification, and warning humankind on the final judgment and the promise of glorification. Before the process of spiritual formation even starts, the Holy Spirit is already at work and continues with the process for the rest of our lives. Sometimes Christians make the mistake of thinking that the Holy Spirit is Christians' private possession and forget the coming of the Holy Spirit was a Trinitarian cosmic assignment as the director of evangelism. The Bible affirms, Philippians 1:6 (NIV) "being confident of this, that he who began a good work in you will carry it on to completion until the day of Christ Jesus." The Holy Spirit starts and carries on the process of spiritual formation.

> When the Holy Spirit descended on the day of Pentecost, a new organism was created. This organism consists of all those who have received the gift of eternal life in Jesus Christ. The Bible describes it as a spiritual household or family. By virtue of both adoption and new birth. This organism is also called a holy temple. But its most frequently used metaphor for this new creation is the body of Christ.[52]

The concept of the Holy Spirit indwelling and imparting holiness in believers and building individual Christians into the body of Christ, is found in the following scriptures: Romans 8:14-17: Galatians 4:3-7; Ephesians 2:19-22; 1Peter 2:4-5; Romans 12:4-5; 1Corinthians 12:12-27; Ephesians 1:22-23; 3:6; 4:4-16; 5:23-30 and Colossians 1:18; 2:19

Hindrances to Spiritual Formation

Original Sin

Original sin in historical-philosophical perspectives:

The concept of original sin has remained a doctrinal hot potato, too hot to handle. It has been the subject of debate among philosophers and theologians over the centuries. It has the primary definition as the tendency to evil supposedly innate in all human beings, inherited from Adam and Eve, the first man and woman created by God in His image and placed in the Garden of Eden. That understanding alone holds sway in those who believe in creation but alienates those who believe in evolution. For those who hold the latter view, original sin is a non - starter and is ruled out a priori leaving evolutionists to find other explanations for the tendency to do evil common in all human beings.

For creationists, however, Adam and Eve disobeyed God, and this first disobedience is known as the original sin, also known as the Fall. In historical theology, the elaboration of the doctrine of original sin is in the writings of St Augustine in which it is most expounded and established in Western theology. There is a consensus among Christian theologians that the concept of original sin resulted from eating the forbidden fruit by Adam and Eve, which led to their expulsion from the Garden of Eden by God. Christian theology teaches that by this act, all humanity fell from divine grace. Through faith in Jesus Christ relationship between God and humankind is restored. The doctrine of original sin is one of the principal tenets of the Roman Catholic Church. It teaches that everyone is born sinful with a built-in urge to do bad things and to disobey God. Augustine explained it in-depth, the councils of Trent (1545 – 1563) ratified his teaching, and this became an essential doctrine of the Roman Catholic Church. Recent scholarship has watered it down to a condition, not something people do but the normal spiritual and psychological state of human beings, somewhat divorced from their evil thoughts and actions. The modern scholarship acknowledges it as a condition but remains puzzled how even a newborn baby who has not done anything at all is involved in the consequences of original sin.

Christian theology maintains that the ultimate effect of original sin is separation from God, the universal dissatisfaction of human beings, and inbuilt guilt in human lives. It manifests itself in inhumane, heinous acts like genocide, cruelty, destruction of human lives in warfare, and all forms of abuse. Even when atheists and humanists reject the Christian doctrine of original sin, they admit that the world and people, in general, are not as good as they could be and acknowledge that forces outside each individual's control influence individual behavior. There is a consensus among Biblical theologians that the only cure for original sin is through accepting the atoning death of Christ on the cross and accepting that only God's grace can cure sin through human confession of it and acceptance of forgiveness from God. The problem of humanity is not intellectual but lack of practical wisdom and will to do the right thing and conquer sinful urges. As a counselor, I was amazed sitting in front of very educated intellectual couples, where one of them would be engaged in unhelpful behavior that was destroying their marriage, and the number of times I heard the words "I cannot help it." Similar words were uttered by singles destroying their own lives and admitting to a force beyond them, driving them into the slavery of destructive behaviors.

Those who do not subscribe to this concept argue that it is unfair and unethical to punish or suffer for the wrong deeds of sin committed by someone else. The concept of original sin accounts for male chauvinism, misogynist, and views that blame Eve for tempting Adam and portray women as weak and easily deluded. Some theologians criticize Augustine for his bias against sexual love in developing his theory of original sin in his portrait of sexual passion as evil. Those who hold strong views on evolution reject the doctrine of original sin on the basis that life in the world evolves and changes contrary to the concept of original sin affecting all human behavior. Evolutionists perceive life on earth, evolving towards perfection as it adapts to its environment. There is also criticism of the concept of original sin because of inspiring excessive feelings of guilt. The 18th century philosopher Edmund Burke said: "Guilt was never a rational thing; it distorts all the faculties of the human mind; it perverts them, it leaves a man no longer in the free use of his reason, it puts him into confusion."[53]

About spiritual formation, the one most important thing the concept of original sin does is to demonstrate the fact that humanity is reliant on God's grace and His omnipotent moral goodness for human spiritual transformation to take place. The concept of original sin is summed up by St. Augustine in these words:

"Nothing remains but to conclude that in the first man all are understood to have sinned because all were in him when he sinned. Sin is brought in with birth and not removed save by the new birth, it is manifest that in Adam all sinned, so to speak, *en masse*. By that sin, we became a corrupt mass."[54]

The concept of original sin finds support in the major Christian denominations. In the modern Roman Catholic Church, Pope Paul VI in 1968, summarized its teaching in these words:

We believe that in Adam all have sinned. This means that the original offense committed by him caused human nature, common to all men, to fall into a state in which it bears the consequences of that offense, and which is not the position our first parents, established as they were in holiness and justice, where man knew neither evil nor death. It is human nature so fallen, stripped of the grace that clothed it, injured in its own natural powers and subjected to the dominion of death, that is transmitted to all humanity, and it is in this sense that every man is born in sin. We, therefore, hold, with the Council of Trent, that original sin is transmitted with human nature 'not by imitation, but by propagation' and that it is thus 'proper to everyone.' We believe that our Lord Jesus Christ, by the sacrifice on the cross, redeemed us from original sin and all the personal sins committed by each one of us so that, in accordance with the word of the Apostle, 'where sin abounded, grace did more abound.[55]

The words of John Calvin are representative of the Protestant church. He said;

> "We are lost, there is no means of help; and whether we are great or small, fathers or children, we are all without exception in a state of damnation if God does not remove from us the curse which weighs upon us, and that by His generosity and grace, without His being obliged to do so."[56]

In the Bible, Romans 7:14-15 (NIV) articulates this as follows "... I do not do what I want, but I do the very thing I hate." All humanity constantly struggles with the innately fallen nature endemic in human lives through emotional, psychological, physical, and mental states of the human persona. There is a common story told about D. L. Moody when asked why he kept urging Christians to be filled constantly with the Holy Spirit. "Well," he said, "I need a continual infilling because I leak!" He pointed to a water tank, which had sprung a leak. "I'm like that!" he said. "It's a fact that is living in this sinful world; we do need to be replenished by the Spirit." Moody's reply is consonant with the teaching of the New Testament regarding the infilling of the Holy Spirit. In Ephesians 5:18, the verb (πληροῦσθε - plērousthe) translated by most Bible versions as "be filled by the Holy Spirit"; is present passive imperative. In the original Greek text of this verse, there are two contrasts. The first contrast is between the effects of two nouns (οἴνῳ -oinō) wine and the effects of the πνεύματι –pneumati) the spirit. The second contrast is between two verbs (μεθύσκεσθε – methuskesthe) being drunk and (πληροῦσθε - plērousthe) being filled by the spirit. The second contrast on the verbs suggests that just as in craving for wine, one glass leads to two or three or possibly four and, eventually, the whole bottle or possibly bottles. The craving for alcohol (wine) is an ongoing addiction driven by deep psychological disturbances like anxiety, depression, or despair. Similarly, being filled by the Holy Spirit is not a punctiliar action or occurrence, but an ongoing action driven by the necessity to conquer and subdue the ongoing desires of the flesh. πληροῦσθε –being filled is a robust Greek verb that carries the meaning, to make full, to complete, to fill up, level up, satisfy, to be filled to the top so that nothing is wanting. The two translations that reflect the aspect of ongoing filling in the original Greek text are, The International Standard Version, Ephesians 5:18 (ISV) "Stop getting drunk with wine, which leads to wild living but keep on being filled with the Spirit."

Also, Complete Jewish Bible, Ephesians 5:18; (CJB) "Don't get drunk with wine, because it makes you lose control; instead, keep on being filled with the Spirit."[57]

The teaching in this verse resonates with some words I heard from my once principal Desmond Hales at college when I started my ministerial training over forty years ago, words that have lived with me since. He told us, "when we become Christians, we join Jesus' school, in which we never graduate in this life until we get to glory."[58] We can, therefore, conclude that spiritual formation is the life-long human transformation experience initiated by God through the prompting of the Holy Spirit in his holy word, the Bible and guided by the Holy Spirit that results in a person being more and more like Christ in character and action to the glory of God. This process is like a covenant; our part is to be available to God and make space in an intentional disciplined, and consistent way. God's role is to mold and shape us through His word and spirit to be His people, His creation, as we go through life's experience and the inner promptings of the Holy Spirit who firmly plants us and roots us in God's love. In spiritual formation, we need great discernment to juxtapose ultra-Calvinism where regeneration is perceived as God's sovereign responsibility almost to the point of fatalism but also guard against extreme Arminianism that extrapolates human cooperation to divine grace to its excessive leading to the danger of salvation by works. The truth is never in the extreme but in the balance between the two. One of a balanced view of spiritual formation states that:

> "A result of spiritual practices does not occur by direct human effort, but through a relational process whereby we receive from God the power or ability to do what we cannot do by our own effort. It requires intentionality and regularity with the goal of being formed into Christlikeness with the result (fruit) of growing in love for God and others"[59].

Mulholland appraises the human state as follows:

> In the face of a radical loss of meaning, value and purpose engendered by a largely materialistic, hedonistic,

> consumer society, human hearts are hungering for deeper realities in which their fragmented lives can find some measure of wholeness and integrity, deeper experiences with God through which their troubled lives can find meaning, value, purpose, and identity.[60]

He challenges the view of Christian spirituality as static possession and advocates "a dynamic and ever-developing growth towards wholeness in the image of Christ."[61] He further argues for dependence on God rather than on self in spiritual formation.

> The way to spiritual wholeness is seen to lie in increasingly faithful response to the One whose purpose shapes our path, whose grace redeems our detours (aberrations), whose power liberates us from crippling bondages of the prior journey and whose transforming presence meets us at each turn in the road. In other words, holistic spirituality is a pilgrimage of deepening responsiveness to God's control of our life and being. When the Apostle, Paul talks about "being conformed.[62]

He is addressing one of the great hindrances to spiritual formation, the innate desire in modern society to do rather than be. This current desire is illustrated by the story of a businessperson and a warehouse property he was selling. The building had been empty for months and needed repairs. Vandals had damaged the doors, smashed the windows, and strewn trash all over the place. As he showed the prospective buyer of the property, he took pains to explain that he would replace the broken windows and correct any structural damage and make it presentable. The buyer told the seller, forget about the repairs. When I buy this place, I am going to build something completely different. I don't want the building; I want the site! That sounds like what God is saying about our lives, compared with what He has in mind and our efforts to improve our own lives. It is as trivial as sweeping the warehouse that is ready for the wrecking ball! The coming of the Holy Spirit into human beings is not about renovating human beings but renewing them. Many years ago, the Prophet declared, Isaiah 64:6 (NIV) "...all our righteousness is as filthy rags." Our efforts to please God fall far short of His expectation. God invites all humanity to surrender to His Holy Spirit so that He can do the renewing and the cleansing Himself. When people come to Christ and receive His renewing Spirit, they become a new creation. Paul puts it succinctly, 2 Corinthians 5:17 (NIV) "...if anyone is in Christ, he is a new creation, the old has gone, the new has come." The risen Christ invites the weary and the burdened to come to Him and promises to give them rest. Rest from trying to reform their lives and allow God's Spirit to renew them. It is a call to rest in the mercy and the redeeming power of God; it is a call to spiritual, psychological, and physical rest.

Jesus said, Matthew 11:28 (NLT), "Come to me, all who are tired from carrying heavy loads, and I will give you rest." In another translation, it says, Matthew 11:28-30 *(MSG)*

> Are you tired? Worn out? Burned out on religion? Come to me. Get away with me, and you will recover your life. I will show you how to take a real rest. Walk with me and work with me – watch how I do it. Learn the unforced rhythms of grace. I would not lay anything heavy or ill-fitting on you. Keep company with me, and you will learn to live freely and lightly."

Spiritual formation is about handing over the property (human lives) to God and allowing Him to empower them to live lives that are pleasing to God. The humankind's role is to surrender and for the divine to empower.

In this sense, spiritual formation is the significant reversal, "from acting to bring about the desired results in our lives to being acted upon by God and responding in ways that allow God to bring about God's purposes…It is a journey of learning to yield ourselves to God and discovering where God will take us."[63]The grip of sin in fallen human nature is such that it needs rescue and redemption from a power outside human effort. Spiritual death does not require resuscitation but resurrection. Prophet Isaiah castigates human effort to please God as filthy rags. Isaiah 64:6 (TLB), "We are all infected and impure with sin. When we put on our own prized robes of righteousness, we find they are but filthy rags."[64] Another translation paraphrases it, Isaiah Isaiah 64:6 (MSG) "We are all sin-infected, sin-contaminated. Our best efforts are grease-stained rags." The Hebrew renders it as "men's trumps garments." Bob Gass illustrates this point beautifully in his devotional article, entitled *Keep your spiritual glasses clean,* in this story:

> One day a man was getting his windscreen washed at a petrol station. When the attendant finished, the man said, 'That's a terrible job. Re-do my windscreen - it's as dirty as when you started.' So the attendant wiped it again. The man looked it over and in frustration, said, 'That window hasn't changed a bit.' The man's wife was sitting next to him in the car fuming. She reached over, pulled off his glasses, wiped them, and gave them back to him. The attendant had been doing his job correctly. The man himself was the problem all along. Spiritually speaking, the glasses you're looking through determine what you see and how you see it. When you look through the lens of jealousy and envy, you become resentful of the blessings of others. When you look through the lens of judgementalism, you speak and act without mercy and grace. When you look through the lens of fear and

> unbelief, you limit God and forfeit what He can do for you. When you look through the lens of selfishness, you put yourself first, and your loved ones suffer. When you look through the lens of negativity and cynicism, people begin to avoid you because you're not enjoyable to be around. 'Be clean, you who bear the vessels of the LORD.' Just as your glasses need to be wiped clean from the contamination around you, so do your heart and mind. How does this happen? Jesus said, John 15:3 (KJV). 'Now ye are clean through the word which I have spoken unto you.' Through prayer and daily Bible reading, your perspective on life is kept right. [65]

Psychological baggage

After many years as a counsellor seeing over a thousand clients in a period of ten years,[66] I became convinced that most of the problems that surface in late life have their origin in early childhood. We spent several weeks exploring the difficulties facing one of my clients. We eventually traced it to his childhood when he was around the age of seven when at forty-eight years of age he could remember vividly how he was treated by his mother whom he described as discriminating against him by administering stricter punishment on him for minor misdemeanors while his sibling got away with less. As I probed him to relate the incidents further, he broke down and quipped, "I married my mother"! I asked him to explain what he meant by that, and he related how he used to get embarrassed walking with his estranged wife because she was an exact look-alike of his mother. The two, his wife and mother, used to get confused, he explained. He sobbed and said he had a wonderful wife that he mistreated before she left him. On exploring the problem further, I found out that psychologically during his marriage to this woman, he was continually revenging his mistreatment from his mother on his wife's unawares. By exploring his past as far as into his childhood, he was able to see how he had projected the bitterness he felt for his mother onto his relationship with his wife and so lost her. There is a sense in which we all walk on psychological crutches, and messed up by our early childhood experiences. There is a consensus among psychologists and pediatricians that "experiences between birth and age five matter significantly to children's long term emotional and psychological health and changing these experiences for the better pay great dividends."[67] In this book, we cannot delve into any details on child psychology, for it is outside the stated objectives of this book. What we would do, however, is to point the need to recognize the psychological crutches that people develop in early childhood from their families of origin and other initial childhood experiences. These experiences develop into great hindrances to our spiritual formation or even the desire to engage with it and much more so if people adopt the excuse mantra "that is my nature, that is the way I am." M. Farouk Radwan rightly points out that

> we develop certain traits as a result of the experiences we pass (have) through life. If a child was raised by an over protective family then he will develop fears and insecurities because of believing that the world is unsafe. Now when that child becomes an adult, he will have his fears and insecurities, but he will display them in a different way. So our childhood experiences affect our behavior and personality in adulthood even if we were not aware of the existence of this connection.[68]

In the counseling profession, the counselor tries to help clients recognize and understand the concepts of "Projection, Transference, and Splitting." Radwan makes the bold assertion that people's adulthood is just an extension of their childhood experiences and goes on to point out that

> Adults with all of their behavior and personality traits are just extensions to the childhood experiences they have been through long ago. 'The difference between men and boys is the size of their toys.' A person will try to fulfill his same childhood experiences when he becomes an adult in a way that is acceptable by his society and culture. Childhood experiences do not just affect adulthood, but they determine how the adult's personality and behavior will be like.[69]

The poem, *Children Learn What They Live,*[70] articulates this by pointing out that,

If children live with criticism, they learn to condemn, and if, with hostility, they learn to fight. The poem goes on to point out that each harmful exposure, fear, pity, ridicule, or shame produces a corresponding negative character trait in the child in later life. Similarly, if the parents expose the child to positive character traits, they grow up to show identical positive character traits in later life. For example, If children live with encouragement, they learn confidence; tolerance leads to patience, fairness help the child learn justice; praise to appreciation, approval lead to positive self -image, recognition drives to child learning to set goals while sharing lead to generosity and acceptance help the child learn to love in later life.

What this poem reveals is that no one starts his or her spiritual formation with a tabula rasa, whether born in a Christian home or not. All persons start spiritual formation with some psychological baggage, the difference is that some items of baggage are heavier and more complicated to carry around and to deal with, yet others are more hindering than others; but we all need to acknowledge that we all start our spiritual journey with some psychological baggage. The question we want to explore is whether some of this psychological baggage is in any way related to the reference in the passage of scripture that talks about the "sin that so easily besets us."[71]

The sin that so easily entangles/besets us – (Ευπεριστατον ἁμαρτιαν·)

The apostle Paul tells about "the sin that so easily besets/entangles us." This phrase containing six words is an English attempt to translate one word: Ευπεριστατον -"euperistaton" in the original Greek text, which only appears here in the New Testament. This one word in Greek carries within it three other words: (ευ (well); περι (about) and ἱστημι (I stand). Its literal translation implies the sin that stands well or is favorably situated, ever surrounding the person and soliciting his acquiescence. Over the centuries, scholars have wrestled with trying to understand the meaning of this text. What seems clear is that the context is "running the race with patient endurance fixing eyes on Jesus" and to achieve that goal one has to put aside or lay aside Ευπεριστατον -euperistaton that is to deal with the sin. The fixing of the eyes on Jesus in this context is pointing out to him as the prime example. The word "Ευπεριστατον -euperistaton" is made up of three Greek particles, "eu – good/well and περι – about; στατον –standing." It means, well standing around or well stood around," which is interpreted–entangle and might imply guarding against prevalent sin. Chrysostom took it to mean the sin that easily overcomes and gets the better of, while Theophylact understood it as the sin through which man is easily brought into danger. Erasmus thought of it as the sins that presses closely about to us to attack us, or which clings to us like an enfolding robe. Also, other scholars understand it as sin in general that is the obstacle to the race. Ευπεριστατον - translated clings, besets, entangles occurs only here in the New Testament and Moulton suggests four possibilities: easily avoided, admired, easily surrounding or besetting and dangerous from the sense of "having easy distress." The overriding evidence is that the writer to the Hebrews regards sin as a significant impediment in the spiritual race."[72] Vis – a'– vis spiritual formation.

The cause of disagreement on this text is whether "every weight" and "the sin that entangles us" refer to the same thing. The weight of evidence seems to point to two different distinguishable entities that have to be dealt with to run the race. First, there is "every weight- ὄγκον ogkon" and "Ευπεριστατον - the sin that easily besets." It is our strong contention that "so easily," imply propensity to particular sins, habits or tendencies particularly within each individual depending on each individual's cultural and psychological baggage, sins that chime with one's natural weakness in one's character. The distinction between "the weights" and "the sin that entangles us" is borne out by the fact that sin is sin and has its consequences while weights may be weights to one person while to another person they are no weights at all.

A prime example is in the story of David and Goliath. In which Goliath's armory (attire) is quite typical to him in battle while it is a heavy hindering burden put on David. Staying with the imagery of sport, we could say that the famous Athlete Usain Bolt, once the fastest man on hundred meters, could win his one hundred meters race competition wearing a tracksuit, but much more comfortable for him to reduce it to running trunks or shorts.

What is more important is his mental attitude; if he does not believe he can win, he is defeated before he even starts. The mental attitude in this comparison could carry the imagery of "sin that so easily entangles us" about weak or strong mental attitude while running shorts would take the representation of "the weights." People who take within their character trait of low self-esteem have an endemic defeatist attitude, as illustrated in one's family of origin, or through said experiences in the formative years like bullying. In such circumstances, such a mental attitude could become "the sin that so easily entangles." On the other hand, regular excise before a race to make sure of one's fitness represents the "weights" that need to be dealt with before a competition in this imagery; reducing unnecessary weight or wearing proper sports attire is also an encumbrance. It is important to note that in the context of running the race in athletics, both "the weight" and "the sin that easily entangles," must be laid aside and the focus on the goal maintained. The Greek verb ἀποθέσθαι -apothesthai (are to be put off) is used in Ephesians 4:22 and in the context of athletes it refers to laying aside every heavy or dragging article of dress and denotes throwing aside the clinging robe of habitual sin. In keeping with the theme of this book, to be like Jesus, to do so, we have to deal with sin. In context also is the amphitheater of public sport familiar for national festivals in Greece at that time and the severe discipline required of the competitors.

The central thesis of this book is that spiritual disciplines are like vitamins necessary for spiritual formation to take place in the life of the believer. In the context of original sin as a hindrance, the scriptures have much teaching on training up children and helping them in their spiritual formation. The Bible describes those who believe in Christ become children of God, not adults of God. John 1:12 (NIV) "to those who believed in his name, he gave the right to become children of God."1 John 3:2 (NCV) "We are called children of God, and we are." Also, 1 John 3:10. Apostle Peter goes an octave higher and describes Christians as babes, 1 Peter 2:2 (NIV) "Like newborn babies, crave pure spiritual milk, so that by it you may grow up in your salvation." This imagery describing Christians as children or even babies is paramount. God wants us to adopt the attitude of children so that we may continually be growing into the image of his son Jesus Christ. As George Bernard Shaw's famous saying goes, "We don't stop playing because we grow old; we grow old because we stop playing." Similarly, when the Christians feel that they are grown up, or old in Christianity, they stop growing into the likeness of Christ.

Spiritual formation in children

For this book, we would do a representative appraisal on three critical passages from three literary genres the OT, Gospels, and Epistles. From the OT, we will look at the advice of wise Solomon, Proverbs 22:6 (NKJV) "Train up a child in the way he should go: and when he is old, he will not depart from it." As another translation puts it, Proverbs 22:6 (NIV) "Start children off on the way they should go, and even when they are old, they will not turn from it."

In the Gospels, we will look at Jesus' dealing with little children in Mark 10:13-16; Matthew 19:13-15 and Luke 18:15-17. We will examine in the Epistles from Pauline letters on training children. Firstly Ephesians 6:4 (NKJV); "Bring them up in the nurture and admonition of the Lord." Secondly, 2Timothy 3:15 (NKJV); "From infancy you have known the Holy Scriptures." and 2Timothy 1:5 (ESV); "I am reminded of your sincere faith, a faith that dwelt first in your grandmother Lois and your mother Eunice, and now, I am sure, dwells in you as well."

OT on Training up a Child (Hanakh)

On reading the injunction in Proverbs 22:6 (NASB), "Train up a child in the way he should go, even when he is old, he will not depart from it." One might ask the question of why can't the child develop into adulthood, lead a good life, and do good things naturally. The answer to both these questions is apparent, left to their own devices and choices; children will always choose the wrong things. In wisdom literature and Proverbs, there are only two ways: the way of wisdom and life and the way of folly and death. In the context of the previous verse five and in the context of the whole book, Proverbs 22:6 teaches that unless trained in the way of wisdom and life naturally, the child will choose folly and death. According to Proverbs 7:7, children lack sense, and in 22:5, foolishness is bound in the heart of the child. A child left without training will bring shame to their mother (Proverbs 29:15). The Hebrew verb Hanakh- translated to train in English is in the imperative, and its ultimate meaning is "dedicate," educate implying focused, intentional, sustained action. The verb suggests that the parent's deliberate moral shaping of a child will have a permanent effect on the child. "Whatever occupation he is later to follow, it is necessary to prepare him for it in his early years because they are habits formed which influence his conduct in manhood."[73]The Hebrew verb hanakh – to train, means dedicate carrying the notion of narrowing or channeling the child's conduct into the way of wisdom. It mingles the concepts of "dedicate," "mouth," "make submissive," and "make experienced." In Semitic languages, it stems from a term related to the roof or lower part of the mouth. There is an Arabic verb close to hanakh that carries the thought of a midwife customarily dipping her finger into a pool of crushed dates to massage the palate and gums of a newborn to stimulate the baby's sucking instinct, thus encouraging beneficial behavior. The outcome of this training described by the Hebrew word "derek"- is usually translated way referring to literal way or road but also the manner of action. In Proverbs 22:6, however, it delineates the dictate's role of parenting; it does not necessarily guarantee the future choices of the child, which depend on the decisions made by the child on the training. What it also makes clear is the necessity of practice because of the Fall or Original sin that compels children to rebel against godliness. The cumulative teaching in Wisdom literature and Proverbs is that the way a child develops and behaves seems more negative than positive and without wisdom. This negative trait is explained and is traceable in the doctrine of the Fall and Original Sin. Hanakh implies molding into shape through discipline and practice, hence the necessity for spiritual formation. Bob Guss, put it this way:

> We keep being shocked by stories of children killing teachers and other children in school and then turning the gun on themselves. Two boys aged twelve and thirteen beats a man to death outside a convenience store just for the pleasure of watching him die. Another boy shot a man sitting in a car at a stop sign. When asked why, he replied, 'Because he looked at me.' What is causing this? Easy access to guns? Hours spent watching violent videos. Those may be factors. However, after extensive research, scientists are concluding that violent behavior is often related to early childhood abuse and neglect. When a baby spends three days or more in dirty

> nappies, or when children are burned, beaten, or ignored, their blood is filled with stress hormones – cortisol and adrenaline, among others. These hormones bombard and affect the brains of those children. Therefore, for the rest of their lives, they will not think and feel what others do. They actually lose the capacity to empathize with those who suffer. The same research has concluded that babies and young children are incredibly vulnerable between birth and three years of age. If their families don't protect them, love, and care for them, society will pay a terrible price for it in years to come. The Bible uses the word 'nurture.' It means to love, protect, encourage, compliment, and try to bring out the best in your child.[74]

Jesus' teaching on Children: In the Gospels, the most prominent passage on dealing with children is in the Synoptic Gospels.[75] We will look at Luke 18:16 (GW), "Don't stop the children from coming to me! Children like these are part of the Kingdom of God". The fact is that this passage appearing in the three Synoptic Gospels underscores its importance. Matthew reproduces precisely the words in Mark except for Mark's addition that Jesus was displeased-indignant at the forbidding of children coming to Him while Matthew adds, "and forbid them not." Most denominations that practice infant baptism refer to these passages and base their doctrine on them. They attribute their belief to covenant theology in which the faith of the parent is the faith of the child until the child reaches the age of independent decision when they confirm the faith of their parents by their own choice. This practice is based on Mosaic Law in which children were permitted into Judaism by the rite of circumcision and thus in New Testament terms into Christ's Kingdom. Those who do not subscribe to infant baptism argue that Jesus was referring to children's attributes of childlike-simplicity, innocence, and obedience as hallmarks of subjects of His kingdom.

The Syriac and Persic translations add "for of such is the Kingdom of God" meaning "who have been humble as these children." It is conjectured that Christ was defining the subject of His Kingdom to be like children: harmless, inoffensive, free from rancor and malice, meek, humble, without pride or self- conceit not ambitious or desire for superiority. Those who argue against infant baptism refer to these virtues as simply what Christ was implying rather than teaching infant baptism. Cultural context sheds some light on this passage in that perhaps what lies behind this text was the controversy in Judaism at that time whether children of wicked gentiles will go into the world to come. There was a dispute with some arguing that the children of the wicked nations of the world will not enter the kingdom to come. In context, also it was the practice of Jewish mothers to bring their babies to famous rabbis to bless the children. There is the argument that the disciples stopped the children from interference to show respect to Jesus' position as a rabbi, who did not need the bother of children. In this thinking, there is a sense in which Jesus would have been angry at the thought that He would be so dignified a teacher to be out of reach for children! This argument also highlights the social strata during the time of Jesus in which children and women occupied the lowest layer in society. First Century Jewish society was men dominated. There was the deliberate exclusion of both women and the children in the counting of people in the Feeding of five thousand, recorded in the four gospels, thus underscoring its significance.[76] An argument from silence is posed by way of a question in favor of infant baptism: "If they who are like little children belong to the kingdom of heaven, why should we for a moment doubt that the little children themselves belong to the kingdom."?[77] What is clear from these passages and even on the lips of Jesus is that involving and by implication, training children for spiritual formation should start as early as possible. Bob Guss succinctly summarizes this point as follows:

> There's a story about a woman who came to her pastor and said, 'How early should I start the spiritual training of my child?' The pastor asked, 'How old is the child?' She answered, 'Five.' He replied, 'Lady, get busy – you're already five years late!' Psychologists confirm that your child's capacity and hunger for knowledge begins at infancy. Therefore, while they are in the listening stage, you should be in the teaching stage. Take every opportunity to read the Bible to them. Use everyday experiences to teach them what God's Word has to say about the Golden Rule, how to be polite, how to forgive, and how to confess and repent of sin. Never underestimate God's ability to develop spiritual character and teach spiritual truths to your children, even at a very early age. While their heart is still young and tender, introduce them to Jesus. Some of the greatest Christians in history were saved at an early age. Jonathan Edwards, whose ministry shook New England for God, was saved at the age of eight. Charles Spurgeon, 'the prince of preachers,' was saved at the age of twelve. Matthew Henry, the great Bible commentator, was saved at the age of eleven. Timothy was an apostle by the time he was seventeen. Paul writes, 'From infancy, you have known the Holy Scriptures, which are able to make you wise for salvation through faith in Christ Jesus.' Yes, your child can understand the basic truths about salvation. And they can come to know Christ at an early age.[78]

Pauline writing on teaching children

The next text found in a Pauline epistle is equally significant about Timothy, one of the Apostle Paul's associates and perhaps his successor. In this text, Paul praised Timothy for his early spiritual formation taught by his mother and grandmother. Some argue from silence and conjecture that a single Christian mother assisted by his grandmother possibly brought up Timothy. This is an inferred argument from the silence because there is no mention of his father. The text in 2 Timothy 1:5 states that the genuine faith that was in Timothy dwelt first in his grandmother Lois and your mother, Eunice. Bob Guss sums this point as follows:

It's said Timothy became an apostle when he was seventeen. He was Paul's spiritual son and his designated successor. And it happened because of two women: his grandmother Lois and his mother, Eunice. Interestingly, his father and grandfather are not mentioned. So as a single parent, you can raise a winning child. According to a ten-year study conducted at Harvard Medical School, there are six factors related to the eventual intellectual capacity of a child: 1) The most critical period of a child's mental development is between eight and eighteen months old. 2) The mother is usually the most important person in the child's environment. 3) The amount of 'live' language directed to the child between twelve and eighteen months is absolutely critical. 4) Children given free access to living areas of their homes progressed much faster than those whose movements are restricted. 5) The family is the most important educational delivery system. 6) The best parents are those who excel at three key functions: they are superb designers and organizers of their children's environments; they permit their children to interrupt them for brief thirty-second episodes during which personal comfort and information are exchanged; finally, they are firm disciplinarians while simultaneously showing great affection for their children. In other words, they love their kids, talk to them, treat them with respect, expose them to interesting things, organize their time, discipline them fairly, and raise them in strong, stable families. It's a time-honored recipe for producing bright (and happy) children.[79]

Witchcraft – An African challenge

Spiritual formation is like a journey, and each person starts from a different place. Some are fortunate or perhaps unfortunate to be born in a Christian home. Some people born in Christian homes may never appreciate the privilege of living a sheltered Christian life from the cruel rigors of life outside the Christian Church where there is pig's food out there for the prodigal sons who rebel against their father's- all-embracing love.[80] There was a time in my pastoral ministry when I was forced to take extended compassionate leave because of stress. I was so miffed with the church at that time that I recall on Easter Day of that year preferring to read the story of the resurrection in John's gospel sitting on a bench in a cemetery near where I lived rather than on a bench in a church. I was profoundly hurting for an episode that had occurred in one of my churches that was cruel and loaded with hateful, racist overtones that I found difficult to cope with. My feelings were raw and painful. I felt like the woman in Philip Yancey's book, *What's so Amazing about Grace,* when she was asked whether she had thought of going to a church for help and her cry "Church! Why would I ever go there? I was already feeling terrible about myself. They'd just make me feel worse."[81] I knew my feelings were fleeting because I agree with Yancey when he observes from his own experience and says. "I rejected the church for a time because I found so little grace there. I returned because I found grace nowhere else."[82] I recall a conversation with one of my sons, who reacted negatively for being in the limelight as minister's kid (MK) or Pastor's kid (PK), and I recall asking him whether he would be happier if I were a coal miner who worked under the ground. My answer may have missed the point my son was expressing, namely the disgust of not being allowed to behave about the place like any other boy of his age because he was a minister's son. He was also expressing peer pressure and societal demands on him based on society's expectations and caricature. Our son is British born and raised, and he was expressing sentiments of typical British boys in modern post-Christian culture. If my son had grown up in Africa, however, his perception would have been different, where it would have been an honor and privilege to be in such a privileged position. In African primal societies, there are children born in animist demonic bondage, for who to be associated with Christianity, let alone in a minister's family is excellent emancipation that exudes joy. There are people born in Christian homes and experience the blessing of upbringing in a Sunday school, pampered and cared for. Such privilege is at times taken for granted, and such people overlook the joy of being prayed for and having parents and the church through Sunday school teachers looking after their physical and spiritual welfare and wellbeing. Spiritual formation in some places in an African context presents unique challenges in terms of demonic spiritual warfare and in particular, the essence and reality of witchcraft. Belief in witchcraft permeates every fiber of African society such that it is nigh impossible to develop into Christian maturity in Africa without encountering either belief in or fear of witchcraft in one form or another.

In this brief section, I would present some challenges that one encounters on their journey of spiritual formation in the African context. I would seek to highlight the challenge posed by witchcraft to Christian ministry in Africa Vis-a'-Vis spiritual formation. The section explores how African Christians practice their faith in light of their experience or the reality of confronting witchcraft. It poses the question of whether a true Christian needs to fear witchcraft and whether Western - imbued Christianity is fit for confronting witchcraft in spiritual warfare and engendering good spiritual formation. Practicing Christian ministry in Africa will always encounter the satanic Trinitarian beliefs in witchcraft, demonic possession, and exorcism within African tradition and spirituality. Any Christian mission that seeks to disregard this "trinity" is deemed by most traditional Africans to be devoid of power and benign to be effective. During and after the colonial era in most of the Western missionary instituted churches, the above African traditional Trinitarian beliefs were dismissed as primitive and superstitious. History has proved that "Missionaries from the West could not do away with witchcraft in Africa by "educating" the people out of their "superstitions." When I exercised ministry in Africa,[83] the denomination I served grew out of the missionary movement whose doctrine had leanings towards dispensational theology that relegated supernatural miracles and demonic exorcism to the first century for the initial planting of Christianity. The Enlightenment influenced most Western missionaries who planted churches in Africa, with the view that "belief in the supernatural is something which has no place in a world where most things can be explained or solved scientifically."[84] Many Western societies "view witchcraft, demonic possession, and exorcism as outdated superstitions that can be explained and even cured by the medical sciences.[85] The effect of the trivialization of witchcraft by Western missionaries was dire. The emerging African Christianity developed with a syncretistic- dualistic approach to faith and Christian practice. Some members worshipped God in Western-style in church on Sundays. When confronted by the witch and the evil eye and demon possession, which were real entities in the village, they felt the need to visit the village witch doctor or the traditional medicine man or woman to deal with the trinity of evil which the missionary or "white man's religion" as it was often referred to could not deal with. Even today, many Christians in Africa still face the same dilemma and challenges. This chapter seeks to highlight the challenge facing the Christian minister in nurturing Christian formation. Also, in confronting syncretism that ensues and the dualistic practices as well as pose the question as to whether Jesus Christ portrayed in the Bible engaging in the ministry of exorcism in the first century when He instituted the church on earth is the same today. The question is whether his followers should deal with witchcraft and exorcism in the same way that Jesus dealt with it and the Apostles in the Early Church[86]. Paul engaged in demon exorcism, and he was put in prison for doing so. The question is, "should Christians have the courage Paul had and exorcise demons when they encounter them in ministry? Are Christians bold enough to do so and bear the consequences, which Paul encountered? *To be like Jesus* suggests that like Jesus, we should confront witchcraft and other demonic forces and the fears of evil that ensue on our Christian journey. Our purpose here is not necessarily to provide solutions but to give awareness and provide a platform for African theologians, Christian workers serving the church in the African context to engage actively in contextual theological reflections, discussions and scholarly exchange on the subject of witchcraft and its impact on practical Christian ministry and spiritual formation in the African context today. My first encounter with demonic exorcism was as an eleven-year-old. I had started going to church and naively believed that the power of Jesus was greater than Satan's power. There was an evening village church fellowship at the homestead of my late maternal grandfather, Nguta Makali, who had decided to become a Christian and invited the church to his homestead to pray for him to become a Christian and burn his charms and other demonic paraphernalia usually associated with witchcraft. They gathered and sang Christian songs led by the local pastor, and when it came to the time of my grandfather renouncing animism and accepting Christianity, he brought out his charms and other demonic paraphernalia associated with witchcraft to be burned, as it was the tradition in those days. A bonfire was lit and re-enforced by adding more twigs and planks of wood to burn brightly and consume the charms; at that moment, I was very excited that my grandfather, like me, was becoming a Christian and that his charms were going to be burned! To my surprise, when that moment came to throw the charms into the fire, neither the pastor nor any of the church elders dared touch them for fear of the charms harming them! After waiting for some time, silence filled the crowd; no one dared to move. The fear was that some charms could jump out of the fire and hurt people and especially the person who touches them. Most of the people believed that touching charms could have long term demonic damaging effects on the one who touches the charms transferring deadly evil spirits in them. I then out of naivety volunteered, went and grabbed the charms, and threw them into the fire one by one until they all burned out. Although the crowd hailed me as a hero, in reality, naivety and excitement motivated me to try out the Christian teaching that Jesus is greater than Satan is.

There are two other incidences in 1975 that occurred on the same day, one after the other. I was in my second year of theological vocational training I was leading a group of students training for ministry from college for an evangelistic mission in two small villages in Kitui County. We were disembarking from the public coach in the afternoon with our PA equipment and guitar to set out for an open-air evangelistic meeting. A person scruffily dressed in tattered clothes and uncombed hair met us and started shouting obscenities at us without any provocation as we came out of the coach! This person has since died, but my encounter with him left lasting memories to this day. Judging by his appearance, he lived roughly around the small village town off the main road that we were trying to evangelize. He was well known and seemed to pull a crowd around him. We had arrived with an intercity coach. What amazed me most was that as we disembarked from the bus, he was not only shouting obscenities but also identified us as coming from the theological college and went on to name the college and all the main Christian mission stations in the country! It was our first time to be in that place, and there was no publicity beforehand. He spoke to us using the local vernacular language, Kikamba, and it was evident he had never traveled from his small native town. The local people in the small market town noticed that we were visiting them to do open-air evangelism. The man was confronting us to stop our evangelistic mission. People started gathering to watch the drama. Bemusement struck me for a moment before sensing in the spirit what was happening. It was a confrontation between the forces of darkness and the gospel. People were watching to see if the man would prevail in interrupting and stopping our mission. I was the group leader and felt responsible for taking charge of the situation. As my colleagues set up the equipment, the man continued taunting and casting insults at us, telling us to go away from that place. He said that he knew all the Christian mission stations in the country and that where we had come from Mumbuni in Machakos was not any higher as he listed all the mission stations! The crowd grew more extensive and more significant to witness the confrontation. I assessed the situation, and there were only two options, either silence the man or pack up our equipment and go back home because he was causing such a commotion with his heckling insults, making it impossible to preach any meaningful message. I felt compelled in the Spirit to confront him or silence him rather than recoil in fear and leave. I did not feel an urge from the Holy Spirit to attempt exorcism. I was aware that a person controlled or filled by evil spirits would never allow Christians to touch them, and so I boldly moved towards him telling him these words "I adjure you in the name of Jesus, to be silent or I will order you in the name of Jesus to come out of this man." I made a move towards him uttering these words, and every time I took one step towards him, shouting "in the name of Jesus," he moved backward away from me. I kept doing that until he had walked about a hundred yards from where we had pitched our PA system to a cleared patch on the ground that he claimed was his homestead and that he could not move any further. I contemplated whether to force exorcism on him or do a bargain with him. I felt moved in the spirit to do the latter. I recall telling him these words, "I adjure you in the name of Jesus, to keep quiet until I finish preaching, and if you utter one more word, I will order you to leave this man." To my shock and surprise, the man saluted in agreement and obeyed. He stood upright like a soldier on parade without a word or movement until we had finished our evangelistic mission that lasted nearly an hour to the amazement of the crowd in that town. As soon as we said our final prayers and ended the evangelistic crusade, the man resumed his chanting and entertainment of the crowd. What drove me to confront this man so publicly?

Humanly speaking, one could say it was the pride of youth because I was at the peak in the prime age of mid-twenties when one feels invincible. Another explanation could be that I am naturally courageous. Perhaps it was a combination of both.

Nevertheless, the real reason was spiritual prowess. I felt like young David in the Old Testament confronting the mighty Goliath[87]as I debated in my spirit how this one man controlled by evil spirits could make our Christian group cancel a planned evangelistic crusade and waste a whole afternoon. What message shall we be sending to this community watching the drama unfold about the gospel of Christ that we preach? As the leader of the group, I felt compelled and spirit - led to confront the man. Deep down in my heart, this verse kept ringing true: 1John 4:4 (NIV), "the one who is in you is greater than the one who is in the world."

I felt strengthened and courageous that God's Spirit, who is in me is greater than the devil who is in the world. I then went ahead to confront the man. I had witnessed exorcism of evil spirits before, but it was not something I felt gifted in to do as part of my ministry. On this occasion, however, I obliged to do it for the sake of the gospel. For a long time, I had read these words in the Bible, Mark 16: 17-18 (GW) "These are the miraculous signs that will accompany believers: They will use the power and authority of my name to force demons out of people. They will speak new languages. They will pick up snakes, and if they drink any deadly poison, it will not hurt them. They will place their hands on the sick and cure them." When I stepped forward to confront this man, I was not sure what was going to happen, but I felt that I should trust God to honour his word, and he did. This encounter significantly strengthened my faith. God is always faithful in vindicating His Word.

The second episode happened later that day in the evening in the town where we were staying. It was on a Friday our last day or last day but one before we ended that mission. The pastor, who was our host, told us that we needed to make a pastoral visit and pray with one of his members who had backslidden as a Christian. We went there straight after the exorcism encounter. The woman and her husband received us warmly and welcomed us to their home. We explained why we had stopped by, and the husband took me aside as the group leader and told me, please do pray but do not sing Christian songs because the wife reacts very violently to Christian praise and singing. Daring Daniel, I decided not to heed to the request and announced to the group to sing the chorus, "God is so good, God is so good to me." As I struck my guitar for the first line, the woman yelled with a very high-pitched tone with the sound of a goat, "meeh, meeh, meeh, and ran out of the homestead compound, shrieking like a goat! I turned to the husband and asked what happens when she runs like that, he explained: that is why I told you at the beginning not to sing Christian songs, she will not return to the home for three days or even more." I asked him where she would be staying. He said she would be living in the hills and bushes, avoiding the homestead! I was frightened that she may come to some harm, and prosecution ensues because the husband warned me not to sing Christian songs in her presence. Therefore, I removed my jacket, put down my guitar, and ran after her. As an athlete, I soon caught up with her before she had gone too far, still shrieking like a goat in such high-pitched tone that all in the village could hear. What happened next frightened me in encountering the power of evil spirits. She was a petite woman, barely five feet tall. In spite of my strength, I was at the peak of my strength as a young man; I had a great struggle to drag her back to her homestead. In her resistance, whenever she shrugged me off, I felt as if Mohammed Ali had pushed me. I had to enlist the help of the other men from the college, to help me hold her down while we prayed. The woman's voice changed from the high pitched voice of a goat to a deep male voice. And started speaking in Machakos, Kikamba dialect, rather than Kitui Kikamba where the woman came from saying: " ekai unthinya ndi mundu muthuku numite o vaa Katangi -do not torment me, I am not a bad person, I come from Katangi"; a town in Machakos County. At that point, I noticed that the woman was possessed by evil spirits, known as "jinni" quite common in Ukambani and Coast region of Kenya. I asked the male voice speaking through her, "what do you want?" The reply came back in a deep male voice, "nenda kumbatu"-I want tobacco, give me tobacco, and I will be alright." I replied, "devil, I give you no tobacco, but in the name of Jesus, I order you to come out of this woman." I asked the pastor to pray, while three of us held the woman. He prayed in a very calm, humble, and somewhat subdued voice as follows:- "Lord Jesus, you sent us this week to hold evangelistic crusades in this town, if you do not show your power now, the gospel we have been preaching will count for nothing." I was holding the woman's right hand, as the pastor finished his prayer, I felt a convulsion from the woman, and she lay down on the ground powerless, as if dead. I helped her up on to her feet and escorted her into the house. We were all frightened by the episode but felt that I had to be strong to calm it down because I felt morally obliged that I had caused the commotion by asking the group to sing Christian praise in spite of the husband asking me not to do it. The woman told me that once the "jinni, possessed her, she lost the memory of what happened; all she could remember was the start of the Christian chorus. In the private conversation that followed, first, she asked me what had happened after she came round, and I briefly explained to her. Then I asked her when did those troubles start? She told me that the jinni (demonic-evil spirits) entered her life while they lived in Mombasa in a public house selling alcohol where her husband either worked or was the owner, and the jinni remained in her even when they moved back from Mombasa which is nearly three hundred miles away. I was surprised that, before woman stormed out, she first entered the house and took a handful of hot ashes from the cooking pots and swallowed it then, drank hot water from a boiling cooking pan and it is when I tried to stop her from self -harm that she stormed out of the compound shrieking like a goat. On reflection, I realize that the jinni intended to destroy her. Therefore, as highlighted by these two incidents, evangelism and exorcism in Africa go hand in hand, and as such, when we think of Christian spiritual formation in the African context, it is in consideration of such milieu and horizon that we should seek to understand spiritual formation. Let us try to imagine a child or even a grownup person starting their spiritual formation from such a background compared to a person from a Christian home background.

What is witchcraft? The term witchcraft embraces a wide variety of phenomena. It derives from the Old English noun Wicca, "sorcerer" and the verb Wiccan," to cast a spell." The cardinal belief in African witchcraft is that it is "the habit of using supernatural means for illicitly destroying the interests, or even lives, of their fellows." Witchcraft is "the essence of evil, vicious and inscrutable, that whirls through the universe and seeks asylum in a sinful soul in which the germs of wickedness lie ready to be quickened into life." Witchcraft is the practice ("an act or instance), of employing sorcery, especially with malevolent intent…the exercise of supernatural powers, allegedly through intercourse with the devil"[88]. It is "the human exercise of alleged supernatural powers for antisocial, evil purposes. A female held to have such powers may be called a witch or sorceress, the male counterpart being named wizard, sorcerer, or warlock"[89].

The great importance of the phenomenon of witchcraft to the African church is reflected in the amount of literature on the subject over the last seven decades that ante-date the independence era in most African countries.[90] A review of this literature yields several points of consensus. Firstly, "Mediterranean and African cultures believe in evil spirits and Satan as actual beings that can cause serious harm and health problems to people." Akin to witchcraft is the belief in the evil eye. Extensive studies on the subject of the evil eye[91] have reviewed that "*the* basic belief in the evil eye consists of the notion that there are people, animals, demons or gods who have the power to cause harm to those of whom they are envious or jealous, just by looking at them. People may become ill, have accidents, misfortunes, or even die"[92]. Secondly, misfortunes and bad luck in most traditional African societies are, in most cases, attributed to witchcraft and the evil eye.

> "In the minds of many African people, there is no doubt as to the reality of witchcraft ... For many African people, it is an existential reality." Illnesses, misfortune, and disturbances are almost always attributed to evil spirits that have been caused to come upon the unfortunate person or family via a witch, wizard, or sorcerer."[93]

Thirdly the most common physical manifestation of anti-witchcraft and evil eye-protective devices is the wearing of charms and amulets. There is a considerable amount of fear observable in many African groups of people. Among the Akamba of Kenya, there are known fear for witchcraft."[94] Hill confirms the assertion made earlier that "missionaries ignored the problem of witchcraft." The inadvertent ignorance was passed on to the missionary instituted churches. In the Evangelical Presbyterian Church of Ghana,

> "the belief in the existence of witches is denied…and theologians and church leaders see it as superstition and belief in unimportant things, but for the majority of church members, however, witches and other evil spirits are very real."[95]

It must be noted, however, that not all Western scholars deny the existence of witchcraft and the occult. Unger contends for liberation and destruction of occult objects and asserts that.

> "Occult powers and mediumistic tendencies can be passed down from generation to generation. They run through the family tree of practicing sorcerers and magicians the third and fourth generation of people implicated in idolatry, and it's inseparable of people implicated."[96]

Koch echoes this and

> Lays down biblically-based procedures that lead to deliverance."[97] Koch claims to undertake the ministry of deliverance "to proclaim that there is a Victor, Jesus Christ…that people must be shown "the way to the great Deliverer…and warned of the imminent danger if and when they cross the borders and trespass into these areas, and *asserts that* God Himself has forbidden *meddling with the occult.*[98]

To be like Jesus in spiritual formation in the African context entails developing spiritually to be victors over demonic powers and exercise the ministry of deliverance and exorcism, which for some is life- long process.

The haunting Living Dead in African Spirituality

Akin to the subject of witchcraft as a hindrance to spiritual formation is fear of "the living - dead" in African primal societies. I was born and brought up in such a community. As mentioned earlier, I encountered Christianity when I went to school rather late at the age of ten. What I recall from my early childhood living in an African village in terms of spirituality are four things: Firstly, a ritual celebration of the harvest. I remember that as finger millet and maize ripened ready for eating the first fruits, we were not allowed to start eating them until the elders have done the ritual of celebration to the god of the harvest. It was a common belief that anyone who eats the fruits before the thanksgiving will become will and die. Rain season brought about a severe change of weather and disease, especially malaria, due to stagnant water, and indeed there was a lot of death associated with the time of harvest and rainy season. In most African countries, there are mainly two pronounced seasons: rainy season and dry season. After planting the crops, children took turns during the rainy season to protect the crops from invading animals, monkeys during the day, and swarms of birds trying to feed on the corn, millet, and finger millet. I recall salivating to eat the corn of millet; however, no one would dare before the elders at the harvest ritual celebration sanctified it. Secondly, there was daily libation and prayers to ancestors to bless the food before we ate it. I have a vivid memory of this because we only had one main meal in the day. It was usually the evening meal. I can remember waiting after mum finished cooking the meal and having to wait until she put a portion by the center post that supported the hut where we all lived, and then dad would pour a libation of some water or drink addressing the immediate ancestors to receive the food and bless the family. Thirdly, there were prayers offered to the ancestors to heal the sick. The prayers took the form of chanting pouring down water or some drink of alcohol to appease the ancestors and plead for their favors to cure the ill person in the home. The fourth thing that is most pertinent to the discussion in this chapter was naming a child after an ancestor, almost believed to be a mild re-incarnation of the ancestor. I remember my mother when I was growing up; mum associated me with an ancestor called Ikonze, who had passed on before I was born. I recollected that I was supposed to be a kind of Ikonze comes back! Thankfully, from very early in my life, my philosophical faculties were quite evident for I did not believe in that stuff, I was always skeptical thinking down deep in my heart such beliefs were a sort of nonsense, but I could not verbalize it. Now looking back, Psalm 139 was real in the way I formed spiritually, and I have come to believe it is nothing short of a miracle the way God got hold of my life and set me apart for His glory. Just imagine growing up being told that you are the spiritual reincarnation of a man you have never met, and whenever you fall sick, you see libation and prayers said to that person to keep you alive and protect you. In reality, these are challenges for spiritual formation in an African animistic society. If one used Google search engine for the term "living dead," a plethora of entries would appear, most of them musicals that bear that title. According to Wikipedia, "Living dead is a blanket term for various films, series, and other forms of media that all originated from and included the 1968 film Night of the Living Dead."[99]In African philosophy and traditional religions, however, the term means something different. My friend, mentor, and college principal, Dr. Richard Gehman, has written extensively evaluating the subject who are the living dead.[100] Professor John Mbiti developed the term "living dead" through his book on African religions and philosophy.[101] He is from my tribe, born and brought up in the same county of Kitui. He is one of the earliest African elite in terms of African religions and philosophical thinking; he is one of the first founding fathers of modern academic reflection on African religion and philosophy. Most modern African scholars cite his works and have remained one of the pioneering works on the subject. According to his theory and experience of beliefs of most traditional African tribes, after death, the spirits of the departed continue to interact and communicate with the living.

> For some Africans, the living-dead plays a very large part in their lives. The living dead appears to them in dreams, possess them during dances, punish them for disobeying them and help them in their need."[102]Gehman aptly points out that "the relationship between the living and the living – dead in Africa has been close. The living dead serve as the senior elders, bringing benefits and punishment t the living. The instead are required to obey the living dead, appeasing them when angry and having fellowship with them in food and drink.[103]

This summary resonates with my early childhood growing up and living in Akamba village in Kenya. Fear of the ancestors, living dead, and interaction with them in spiritual matters is widespread in most other tribes. For example among the Bantu, Giriyama tribe of Kenya,

> "The ghosts of the departed are feared, and it is to propitiate these that vigango and koma are erected, and a coconut bowl placed at their feet, into which tembo (beer) and the blood of slaughtered animals and fowls are poured. These offerings are made in order to prevent the ghosts of the departed from bringing ill-luck on the village."[104]

There are two most common obligations towards the living-dead: obedience and communion. For those who may want to delve in detail on the subject of the place of ancestors, in African traditional beliefs, I suggest the following literature[105] to help them do so. The object of highlighting this belief here is to show how the belief in the living dead among traditional African tribes impinges on spiritual formation as a hindrance. Most scholars present this belief in negative terms, and indeed, it is quite a challenge for an African starting the journey of spiritual formation from such a baseline. While I acknowledge the problem, I believe that taking cognizance of the issue should lead to finding a positive way of engaging with the problem and turning it into real preparation for presenting the gospel, turning it from setback into a springboard. In my doctoral dissertation, I suggested finding contextual Christological concepts that resonate with the African conceptual framework in expressing the idea of Jesus as Christ, the Messiah.[106] One of these concepts was as Mhondoro/mudzimu – divine ancestor. I pointed out, "this concept could be developed and serviced to communicate the Christological concept of Christ's pre-existence, his death and resurrection, and his apparent ever-abiding presence with the believer. In so doing, that would put to good use the African concept of the departed relatives, who are ever-present and real to the African mind, although Mhondor or Mudzimu cannot substitute for the work of Christ, nevertheless, it's a concept that enables the Shona people to understand and communicate the concreteness of the presence of Christ." In a similar vein, Kurewa, observes: "the incarnational presence and concreteness of God in human history, in Jesus, would be effectively proclaimed among the Shona People by pointing to Jesus as the Mhondoro or Mudzimu, by naming him, Mhndoro Jesus, or Mudzimu Jesus."[107] Bujo suggests "Christ as the proto-ancestor-unique ancestor who is the source of life and the highest model of Ancestorship."[108]Nyamiti has developed this further[109] for anyone interested in following up on its value in helping a young African Christian develop in his or her spiritual formation.

Chapter 2 Notes

20 Kenneth Boa, *Conformed to His Image: Biblical and Practical Approaches to Spiritual Formation*, (Grand Rapids, Mich.: Zondervan Publishers, 2009), 75.

21 Tony Horsfall, *Deep Calls to Deep: Spiritual Formation in the Hard Places of Life*, (Abingdon, U.K.: Bible Reading Fellowship, 2015), ad loc

22 The psalms identified in this book are Psalm30, 42, 43, 69, 88, 130 &145.

23 Tony Horsfall, *Deep Calls to Deep*, 8

24 Tremper Longman, *How to Read the Psalms*, (Downers Grove, Ill: IVP, InterVarsity Press, 2005), 11–12.

25 Ibid. *How to Read Psalms*, 84

26 Timothy Keller, *Walking with God Through Pain and Suffering*, (New York: Penguin Books, 2016), 242-45

27 Ibid. p. 89

28 Dallas Willard, *Renovation of the Heart: Putting on the Character of Christ* Colorado Springs, CO: NavPress, 2002), p. 22.

29 T. Martin OSA, *Our Restless Heart, The Augustinian Tradition*, (London: Darton, Longman and Todd, 2003), 42

30 Ibid. p.19 as cited in Rachel, Woods. *Into the Garden: Cultivation as a Tool for Spiritual Formation and Community Renewal*, (Cambridge: Grove Books, 2016), 12

31 Kenneth Boa, *Conformed to His Image*, 19

32 Ibid. p. 101-102

33 Ibid.

34 Ephesians 3:16-19

35 Kenneth Boa, *Conformed to His Image*. 103 citing Galatians 2:20

36 Galatians 5:5

37 Pamela Evans, *Shaping the Heart: Reflection on Spiritual Formation and Fruitfulness*, (Oxford: Abingdon, The Bible Reading Fellowship, 2011)

38 Ibid, on the blurb

39 Ibid p.16

40 Ibid. p. 122

41 Mark A. Maddix, "Living the Life – Spiritual Formation defined" in Diane Leclerc & Mark A. Maddix, Editors, *Spiritual Formation: A Wesleyan Paradigm*, (Kansas City: Beacon Hill Press, 2011), 11

42 Gerald G. May, *Care of Mind, Care of Spirit: A Psychiatrist Explores Spiritual Direction*. (San Francisco: HarperSanFrancisco, 1st HarperCollins paperback ed 1992), 6.

43 Richard Foster and K.A. Helmers, *Life with God, (London*: Harper and Stoughton, 2008), 10, citing Philippians 2:5

44 This assertion is made by Daniel PremkumarGnanadurai in his unpublished MA dissertation in Mission and Evangelism:"Exploring Conversion and Spiritual

Formation as an ongoing Conversion Process and its Implication to Mission", Cliff College (Manchester University), Calver, Hope Valley, Derbyshire, S32 3XG, p.1 citing R.V. Pearce, *Conversion in the New Testament: Paul and the Twelve,* (Grand Rapids: Werdmans 1999), 316

45 Ibid.

46 Robert M. Mulholland Jr., *Invitation to a Journey: A Road Map for Spiritual Formation*, (Downers Grove, Illinois: IVP Books, 1993), 21

47 Dallas Willard, *Renovation of the Heart: Putting on the Character of Christ,* Colorado Springs, CO: NavPress, 2002, p. 27.

48 Robert M. Mulholland Jr., *Invitation to a Journey.* 24

49 Ibid., 23

50 Ibid., 27

51 Ibid, p.12

52 Kenneth Boa,. *Conformed to His Image,* 301-302

53 Google, Accessed May 15, 2018. www.wiseoldsayings.com/authors/edmund-burke-quotes

54 Google, Accessed May 15, 2018. *St Augustine.* www.bbc.co.uk/religion/religions/christianity/beliefs/originalsin_1.shtml;

55 Ibid.

56 Ibid.

57 Ephesians 5:18; The *Complete Jewish Bible* (CJB) Copyright © 1998 by David H. Stern. Puts it this way: "Don't get drunk with wine, because it makes you lose control; instead, keep on being filled with the Spirit"

58 Desmond Hales, was the principal of Scott Christian University(then known as Scott Theological College), Machakos, Kenya in 1974. The College was named after Peter Cameron Scott, a Scottish missionary who founded the Africa Inland Mission, through whom I got scholarship for my undergraduate and graduate studies.

59 Daniel PremkumarGnanadurai in his unpublished MA dissertation in Mission and Evangelism:*Exploring Conversion and Spiritual Formation as an ongoing Conversion Process and its Implication to Mission*, Cliff College (Manchester University), Calver, Hope Valley, Derbyshire p.8 citing Tony Campolo and Mary Albert Darling, *The God of Intimacy and Action: Reconnecting Ancient Spiritual Practices, Evangelism, and Justice*, San Francisco, CA, Jossey-Bass, p.77

60 M. Robert Mulholland Jr., *Invitation to a Journey: A Road Map for Spiritual Formation*, Downers Grove, Illinois: IVP Books, 1993, p.11

61 Ibid. p. 12

62 in Romans 12:2

63 Mulholland, Ibid p.30-31;32

64 Isaiah 64:6 (The Living Bible Translation)

65 Bob Gass, The UCB Word for Today, 28 October 2017

66 I trained and worked as a Relate Counsellor in the City of York, in UK from1997-2008. Relate is the UK's largest provider of relationship support. It is a charity registered in the United Kingdom. It has adopted as its motto –The Relationship People. Its services include counselling for couples, families, young people and individuals, sex therapy and Mediation. It was co-founded in 1938 as the National Marriage Guidance Council, by the clergyman Herbert Gray and Dr Edward Fyfe Griffith after the clergyman, noted that the divorce rate was increasing. It changed to its current name in 1988 and in the 1990s; its public profile blossomed after the late Princess Diana became its patron in 1989. It sees over 150,000 clients a year, at more than 600 locations across the UK. In 2006, it opened the Relate Institute, the UK's first Centre of Excellence for the study of relationships, in partnership with Doncaster College and the University of Hull.

67 This is a according to an editorial and several reports in *Issue of Archives of Paediatrics & Adolescent Medicine, Sciencedaily.com May, 2010.* Accessed December 6, 2017

68 M. Farouk Radwan, *"How Childhood Experiences after adulthood."* Accessed December 6, 2017. 2knowmyself.com

69 Ibid

70 *Children Learn What They Live:* Poem by Dorothy Law Nolte, PhD. Accessed December 5, 2017. http://www.empowermentresources.com/info2/childrenlearn-long_version.html

71 Hebrews 12:1-2

72 J.H Moulton, *Grammar of New Testament Greek 2,* (London: T & T Clark, 1906), 282 cited in Donald Guthrie, *Hebrews, Tyndale New Testament Commentries,* (Leicester: IVP, 1988), 249

73 Cohen, A (ed). *The Soncino Books of the Bible,* (London: Soncino Press, 1983), 146

74 *Word For Today 16 November 2017, Nurture Your Children, "Bring them up in the nurture and admonition of the Lord" Ephesians 6:4; (*Stoke-on-Trent, Hanchurch Lane ST4 8RY : UCB Broadcast Centre, 2017)

75 Matthew 19:1-15; Mark10:13-16 and Luke 18:15-17

76 Mark 6:44 States "There were 5,000 men who had eaten the bread; Matthew 14:21states "About 5000 men had eaten, the number does not include the women and children who had eaten; Luke 9:14 stated "There were about five thousand men"; John6:10 states "There were about 5,000 men in the crowd".

77 Luke 18:16; Mark10:16

78 *The UCB* Word For Today. *'From infancy you have known the Holy Scriptures.'2 Timothy 3:15* Stoke-on-Trent: UCB publishers

79 *The UCB Word for Today - 13 Jul 2017,* Stoke-on-Trent: UCB:Publishers

80 Luke 15:15-16

81 Philip Yancey, *What's so Amazing about Grace?,*(Grand Rapids: Zondervan, 1997), 9.11

82 Ibid. p.16

83 I was a pastor of a 3000 membership congregation of Africa Inland church (planted by Africa Inland Mission) in Nairobi before I went to the UK where I have served with the Methodist Church as university chaplain, hospital chaplain, Relate Counselor, and for a period of ten years a tutor of lay preachers, circuit minister and superintendent for 13 years.. Since 2011 have been a visiting lecturer at Africa Nazarene University, Nairobi Kenya.

84 This is the central thesis in article by Anastasia Apostolides and Yolanda Dreyer, "The Greek Evil Eye: African Witchcraft and Western ethnocentrism" in *HTS 64 (2)*, 2008. See also, HTS 1995. *Powers of evil: A biblical study of Satan and demons.* (Grand Rapids, MI: Baker Books).

85 Keith Ferdinando, *The triumph of Christ in an African perspective: A study of demonology and redemption in the African context.* (Cumbria: Paternoster, 1999), 70.

86 In Acts 16:16-40 Paul engaged in demon exorcism and was imprisoned for it. The question is should the Christians have the courage Paul had and exorcise demons when they encounter them in ministry? Are the Christians bold enough to do so and bear the consequences, Paul encountered?

87 1Samuel 17:1-58

88 *Webster's Third International Dictionary, unabridged*, Chicago: 1986, 2525

89 *The New Encyclopaedia Britannica*, Chicago: Vol 12, 715

90 This is reflected in annotated list of the vast scholarly work on the subject of witchcraft appended in the Bibliography, starting with E.E. Pritchard, 1937 to the latest article in Wikipedia 2014

91 John Elliot has done studies on this subject of the evil eye: See, J H Elliott, "Paul, Galatians, and the evil eye". *Currents in Theology and Mission*, (Cleveland, OH: Pilgrim Press 1990), 262-273. Also J H Elliott, "The evil eye in the First Testament: The ecology and culture of a pervasive belief", in Jobling, D, Day, P L & Sheppard, G T (eds), *The Bible andthe politics of exegesis*, 1991, 147-159. Cleveland, OH: Pilgrim Press. Elliott, J H 1992." Matthew 20:1-15: A parable of invidious comparison and evil eye accusation", *Biblical Theology Bulletin 22*, 52-65. Also R Dionisopoulos-Mass,"The evil eye and bewitchment in a peasant village", in Maloney, C (ed), *The evil eye*, (New York: Columbia University Press, 1976), 42-62. Also F T Elworthy, *The evil eye.* (New York: Julian Press; 1958). See also N Finneran "Ethiopian evil eye belief and the magical symbolism of the iron working". *Folklore*, 2003, 114, 427-433; P B Gravel, *The malevolent eye: An essay on the evil eye, fertility and the concept of mana.* (New York: Peter Lang; M M Hardie, 1981). The evil eye in some Greek villages and the upper Haliakom valley in west Macedonia, in Dundes, A (ed), The evil eye: A folklore casebook, Vol 2, 107-123.

92 Ibid. Anastasia Apostolides and Yolanda Dreyer, *The Greek Evil Eye,* 1028

93 Ibid. p.1035 quoting M J Manala, Witchcraft and the impact on black African Christians: A lacuna in the Hervormde Kerk in Suidelike Afrika. *HTS Theological Studies 60(4),* 2004, 1491-1512

94 Mwalwa, Matthews Kalola, *The Power of witchcraft among the Kenyan Akamba,* unpublished MTh thesis submitted to Nairobi Evangelical Graduate School of Theology, Nairobi, June 2001

95 Ibid. p.8

96 Ibid p. 9 citing (Unger 1979), 158

97 Ibid. citing (Koch 1972, 9)

98 Ibid. p.10 citing (Koch, 1972,6) italics added for effect and grammar.

99 Living Dead, Accessed May 8, 2018 En.wikipedia.org/Living_Dead.

100 Richard Gehman, *Who are the Living Dead: A Theology of Death, Life After Death and the Living Dead, (*Nairobi: Evangel Publishing House, 1999)

101 John Mbiti, African Religions and Philosophy, (London: SPCK, 1969), 83

102 Richard Gehman, *Who are the Living Dead, 3*

103 Ibid. p.1

104 Barrett, W.E.H. "Notes on the Customs and Beliefs of the Wa-Giriama, etc, British East Africa." *Journal of the Royal Anthropological Institute, vol.41,* 1911, p. 20-39; Also cited in Gehman, Ibid. p.23

105 Among them are: Richard Gehman, *Who are the Living Dead: A Theology of Death, Life After Death and the Living Dead,* Nairobi: Evangel Publishing House, 1999, p.3; Barrett, W.E.H. "Notes on the Customs and Beliefs of the Wa-Giriama, etc, British East Africa." *Journal of he Royal Anthropological Institute, vol.41,* 1911, 20-39; Also cited in Gehman, Ibid. p.23; John Mbiti, African Religions and Philosophy, (London: SPCK, 1969),.83; Bascom, William. *The Yoruba of South Western Nigeria.* (London: Holt, Rinehart & Winston, 1969); Beattie, John. *Bunyoro, An African Kingdom.* (NY.: Holt, Rinehart & Winston, 1960); Carter, Jesse Bennedict. "Ancestor-Worship and Cult of the Dead (Roman)." *Encyclopaedia of Religion and Ethics.* Vol. 1:461-466. (Endiburgh: T & T. Clark, 1909); Champion, Arthur. The Agiryama of Kenya. Occasional paper No. 25, John Middleton, ed. (London: Royal Anthropological Institute of Great Britain and Ireland, 1967); W Crooke, "Ancestor Worship and Cult of the Dead." *Encyclopaedia of Religion and Ethics.* Vol. 1:425-432. (Endiburgh: T & T. Clark, 1909) ; J H Driberg, The Lango, (London: T.Fisher Unwin Ltd.,1923); Charles Dundas, *Kilimanjaro and Its Peoples,* (London: H.F.& G. Witherby, 1924); E E Evans-Pritchard, *Theories of Primitive Religion.(*London: Oxford University Press, 1965); Jack Goody, *Death, Property and the Ancestors: A Study of the Mortuary Customs of the Lodagga of West Africa, (*London: Tavistock Pub.,1962); C W Hobley, *Bantu Beliefs and Magic with Particular Reference to the Kikuyu and Kamba Tribes.* (NY.: Barnews & Noble Inc., 1938); E. Bolaji Idowu, *African Traditional Religion: A Definition,* (N.Y. Maryknoll: Orbis Books, 1973); J C D Lawrence, *The Iteso.* (London: Oxford University Press, 1957); Edward Lehmann, "Ancestor – Worship and

Cult of the Dead (Iranian)." *Encyclopaedia of Religion and Ethics.* James Hastings, Ed., vol. 1:454-455. (Edinburgh: T & T Clark, 1909); Gerhard Lindblom, The Akamba. (Uppsala: Apperlbergs Boktrycheri Aktiebolag, 1920); A Malandra, "The Ancestral Shrine of the Acholi." *Uganda Journal. Vol.7, No.1,* July 1939, pp. 27-43; B A Marwick, *The Swazi,* (London: Frank Cass & Co.,Ltd., 1966, 1st edition, 1940); John S Mbiti, *Akamba Stories,* (Oxford Clarendon Press, 1966); John S Mbiti, *Africa Religions and Philosophy,* (London: SPCK, 1969); John S Mbiti, *Concepts of God in Africa.* (London: SPCK, 1970); John S Mbiti, *New Testament Eschatology in an African Background,* (London: Oxford University Press, 1971); John S Mbiti, "Christianity and Traditional Religion in Africa." *Crucial Issues in Missions Tomorrow.* Donald McGavran, ed. (Chicago: Moody Press, 1972); Kivuto Ndeti,. *Elements of Akamba Life,* (Nairobi: East African Publishing House, 1972); E G Parrinder, *African Traditional Religion,(*London: SPCK. 1962); Okot P'Bitek, *Religion of the Central Luo.* (Nairobi: Kenya Literature Bureau, 1971); John Roscoe, *The Bakitara or Banyoro,(*Cambrige: Cambridge University Press, 1923) ; John Roscoe, *The Banyankole.* (Cambrige: Cambridge University Press, 1923); Charles S Salalah, "The Place of Ancestral Spirits in African Theology: Evaluated in the Biblical Teaching." M.A Thesis, Columbia Graduate School of Bible and Missions. 1981; I Shapera, *The Khoisan Peoples of South Africa, (*London: Routledge & Kegan Paul Ltd., 1930); Victor C Uchendu, *The Igbo of Southeastern Nigria,(*NY.:Holt, Rinehart & Winston, 1965); W C Willoughby. *The Soul of the Bantu.* (N.Y.:Doubleday, Doreen and Co., 1928); Monica Wilson, *Rituals of Kinship Among the Nyakyusa,* (Londond :Oxford Universty Press, 1957)

106 Daniel M Mwailu, *Christology in Africa: An investigation of the Encounter between Biblical and Indigenous Concepts with Reference to Missianism in two New Religious Movements in Kenya,* (Biringham: Birmingham University, unpublished PhD thesis 1989), pp.433-435

107 Zvomunodita J W Kurewa, "Who do you say that I am?", *International Review of Missions, vol. LXIX, No.2,* 274 (April 1980), 185

108 B Bujo, "A Christocentric Ethic for BlackAfrica" in *Theology Digest, Vol3. No.2,* 1982, 143

109 Nyamiti, Charles, Christ our Ancestor: Christology from an African Perspective, (Harare: Mambo Pres, 1984)

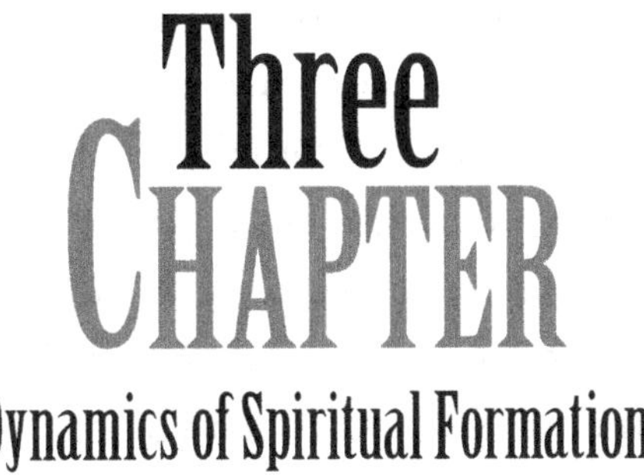

Three CHAPTER

Dynamics of Spiritual Formation

So far, in this book, we have been expounding the *raison d'etre'* and the need for spiritual formation. We have also tried to elucidate and appraise the various definitions from various scholars and sources. We now turn to the dynamics of how spiritual formation takes place. There are multiple imageries and examples used in the Bible to explain how spiritual formation takes place. For this book, I am going to highlight three examples: "Circumcision of the heart," Baptism and Body of Christ as a ((κοινωνία-koinonia) meaning fellowship.

Circumcision of the heart

The critical question is, how do we develop a spiritual heart?

Apostle Paul uses the concept of circumcision of the heart as a metaphor referring to how to develop a spiritual covenantal relationship with God. He asserts that circumcision is something that happens in a person's heart. It is spiritual, not just an outward ritual,[110] referring to the idea of having a pure heart consecrated to God. Paul uses this concept in the wider context of forming a relationship with God and draws from the Old Testament law making the point that a Jew is one inwardly and that circumcision is a matter of the heart by the Spirit not the letter of the law; only the Holy Spirit can purify the heart. Physical circumcision, he argues, cannot make a person right with God; outward obedience to the law alone is not enough. For a person to obey God's law, they need a change of heart. According to the Law, Deuteronomy 30:6 (NIV), "The Lord your God will circumcise your hearts and the hearts of your descendants, so that you may love him with all your heart and with all your soul, and live." Physical circumcision was a sign of Israel's covenant with God, but Paul points out that if the heart is sinful, it renders physical circumcision valueless. Paul is elucidating how Judaism relates to Christianity and the role of the Old Testament law in that relationship. When God initiated circumcision in the call of Abraham, it was meant to be a sign of the covenant between God and His people and had a place in the Law of Moses."[111] Paul's main apologia was against Judaizers – those who argued that to become a Christian one had to adhere to Judaism. Against this, Paul argues that Christ's death on the Cross was the equalizing factor between Jews and Gentiles and makes the point that a circumcised body and a sinful heart are a contradiction in terms and that rather than focus on external rites, the Christian should focus on the inside condition of the heart. In this case, Paul uses the circumcision as a metaphor to emphasize that only the Holy Spirit can purify the heart and set the Christian apart (sanctified) to God. In his argument for the circumcision of the heart, Paul is making the point that the law is not enough; a person's heart must change. In Heilsgeschichte (salvation history), God's desire has always been for a holy people; not people outwardly conformed to a set of rules, but with a loving heart, willing to follow and serve God willingly; out of intimacy, not intimidation. Such love sees the Bible as a love letter from a loving father to his children and not as a set of dos and don'ts. Such love manifests itself in the Christian, through a life of repentance and inward change (spiritual formation) to be right with God. It is important to note that in the Old Testament, it is God who took the initiative to institute this rite with Abraham as a sign of the covenant. The circumcision rite took place on the eighth day of the birth of a male child, indicating that the child was born into a covenant relationship with God. The use of this metaphor implies that there is a need for a new heart as a sign of authenticating the New Covenant with God in a Christian's life. Under the New Covenant, God is forming a new spiritual nation, ekklesia –the church, a called-out assembly, composed of all persons renewed and regenerated by His Holy Spirit irrespective of nationality. In order to understand the covenantal relationship with God, there is a need first to understand the distinction between a covenant and a contract. A covenant is not a contract. A contract is an agreement worked out between two parties. In the New Testament, however, a covenant, on the other hand, means a binding pact between God and God's people. A covenant is something that God initiates and stipulates all the provisions. In the Old Covenant, the pact was for each to keep their part. In the New Covenant, however, in Christ, God keeps both our part and His part through Jesus Christ's vicarious death on the cross. For the Christian to keep their part, they need the enabling of the indwelling Holy Spirit. The Christian needs some power to keep the covenant with God. The sign of the new covenant is a changed heart and a renewed mind. The mechanics of maintaining it is by relying on God's grace and the Holy Spirit. It is all by grace, God's unmerited favor. Paul put it this way: in Ephesians 2:8-10 (GW), "God saved you through faith as an act of kindness. You have nothing to do with it. Being saved is a gift from God. It's not the result of anything you've done so that no one can brag about it. God has made us what we are. He has created us in Christ Jesus to live lives filled with good works that he has prepared for us to do." The metaphor of circumcision of the heart implies a distinction between those who would allow circumcision to take place and those who would not. In the egalitarian ecumenical age in which we live influenced; by the Religiogeschichteliche Schule – the School of World Religions and the belief that all religions are the same leading to the same place, the metaphor of circumcision of the heart and the implied distinction comes as a great shock. In the Old Testament, circumcision had a national significance, distinguishing Israel from other uncircumcised nations. Typologically circumcision anticipates regeneration by the Holy Spirit and the removal of the old heart and replacing it with a new heart. In his Epistle to the Romans[112], Paul argues that circumcision was a seal – a confirmation of the righteousness that God had already imputed to the Christian through trusting God. In the Old Testament, both in Mosaic Law and in Jeremiah, circumcision implied the need for obedience. In Deuteronomy 10:16-17 (NIV), "Circumcise your hearts, therefore, and do not be stiff-necked any longer. For the Lord, your God is God of gods and Lord of lords, the great God, mighty and awesome, who shows no partiality and accepts no bribes." Prophet Jeremiah repeats the same injunction, Jeremiah 4:4 (NIV), "Circumcise yourselves to the Lord, circumcise your hearts, you people of Judah and inhabitants of Jerusalem, or my wrath will flare up and burn like fire because of the evil you have done—burn with no one to quench it."

Therefore, circumcision in the Old Testament is a type or model, a forerunner of what God wanted from the very beginning, having a close relationship with his people; made possible only through their change of heart –"circumcision of the heart." The exclusivity and distinction implied by the metaphor of circumcision come as a shock to those who espouse the theological notion that "all roads lead to Rome," meaning all religions lead to God. Jesus made this distinction of God's people explicit when he said, John 14:6 (NIV), "No one comes to the Father except through me." John 15:5 (NIV), "Apart from me, you can do nothing"- meaning –you can't produce fruit without me." And to sum it all, he added, in Matthew 7:21(NIV), "Not everyone who says to me, 'Lord, Lord,' will enter the kingdom of heaven, but only the one who does the will of my Father who is in heaven."

The English Puritan, John Favel discussed the concept of circumcision of the heart in the 17th century, he asserted that "the greatest difficulty in conversion, is to win the heart to God; and the greatest difficulty after conversion is to keep the heart with God. Heart work is hard work indeed."[113] As a student in a secondary school in my early years of Christian formation, the words of one of my teachers intrigued me [114] when he said; there are ingenious fools. The statement at first sounded like a misnomer until I became a counselor in psychotherapy many years later.[115] As a counselor, I was puzzled to come across quite intelligent people involved in what appeared to me to be foolish actions, but in the counseling, profession one takes care to be non-judgemental, and I engaged all my faculties fully to find out why there was such dissonance between intelligence and wise actions. There is one incident that stands out in my mind was when I counseled a couple, both of whom were doctors. The husband was the head of the science department in a reputable university, and the wife was the head of the gynecology department in a large district hospital. It is then that I came to respect the ancient Latin maxim: action sequitur esse - action follows essence meaning our response is always in accord with the inward reality of the heart. Human behavior does not necessarily dictate profound knowledge. What is paramount is our vital union with God and His wise counsel from God's word. The creation of new hearts in Christ and being fully controlled by the Holy Spirit, just as a natural branch connected to the vine produces grapes, so do our spiritual lives; once there is a connection to God through Christ; spiritual fruit becomes the expected produce: The Bibles puts it this way, Galatians 5:22-23 (MSG), "When we live God's way, He brings gifts into our lives, in much the same way that fruit appears in an orchard. Things like affection for others...a sense of compassion in the heart, and a conviction that a basic holiness permeates things and people...able to marshal and direct our energies wisely." Intellectual learning may swell our heads with knowledge and information, but that knowledge in itself without the enablement of the Holy Spirit of God is limited. It hardly yields any wise behavioral change without heart transformation. According to the wise man Solomon, Proverbs 4:23 (NIV): "Above all else, guard your heart, for everything you do flows from it." Proverbs 4:23 (NASB) "Watch over your heart with all diligence, for from it flows the springs of life." Proverbs 4:23 (NLT) "Guard your heart above all else, for it determines the course of your life." Bonaventure articulates the dissonance between human intellectual ability and God as follows:

> First, therefore, I invite the reader to the groans of prayer of Christ crucified, through whose blood we are cleansed from the filth of vice – so that he does not believe that reading is sufficient without unction, speculation without devotion, investigation without wonder, observation without joy, work without piety, knowledge without love, understanding without humility endeavor without divine grace, reflection... without divinely inspired wisdom.[116]

The current upsurge of emphasis on spiritual formation has its roots in the 16th century Pietism that reacted against Protestant scholasticism and emphasized personal renewal, individual growth in holiness, and religious experience. *Pia Desideria: Heartfelt desire for a God-pleasing Improvement of true Protestant Church* [117]argued for the renovation of the heart similar to the emphasis on spiritual formation.

Bob Gass, in his daily devotions, *Word For Today*, comments on Ezekiel 36:26 about the concept of "Christ in you" – and describes it as a form of a spiritual heart transplant. He gives an illustration of a skiing accident in 2010 of a thirteen years old girl of whom the parents decided to donate her organs. Her heart was transplanted to a heart patient whose heart had failed. The new girl's heart gave a fresh start in the life of the patient. When the parents of the girl were notified of the successful heart transplant, they made a journey to the patient into whose daughter's heart had been transplanted. They requested for a stethoscope, and they listened to the heartbeat of their daughter in the new person. The person functioned normally and lived a healthy life with the new heart transplant. Bob Gass succinctly puts it this way: "when they listened to the healthy rhythms, whose heart did they hear? Did they not hear the still-beating heart of their daughter? It indwelt a different body, but the heart was still the heart of their child."[118]

He goes on to make this application: "When God hears your heart, does He not hear the still-beating heart of His Son?" This is what it means when the Bible says, "it is no longer I who live, but Christ lives in me."[119]He also cites, "Christ in you, the hope of glory."[120]Bob then suggests that "The apostle Paul sensed within himself not just the philosophy, ideals and influence of Christ, but the person of Christ, Christ moved *in residence* and He still does."[121] He points out that in his writings, Paul refers to this union with Christ 216 times. John mentions it 26 times. They describe a Christ who not only woos us to Himself but actually "ones" that unites us with Himself. 1John (NKJV) says, "Whoever confesses that Jesus is the Son of God, God abides in him, and he in God." The logical conclusion is this, just as people may own the home they live in, so the Christ who lives in Christians owns them. And as, just as when people own their home, they may rearrange it the way they want it. Likewise, Jesus moves in and commandeers the Christian's hands and feet, requisitions the Christian mind and tongue. Bob Gass poses this question: "Do you sense things being rearranged in your life today? That's "Christ in you."[122] Eugene Peterson paraphrases Paul's' words this way: "He decided from the outset to shape the lives of those who love him along the same lines as the life of his Son." (Romans 8:29 MSG). Bob Gass concludes his thought-provoking devotion for the day this way: "Ever hear the old saying, "Making a silk purse out of a pig's ear"? That is what Jesus does when He takes up residence in your heart. He has a plan for your life, and He provides the power to fulfill it. And what's your part? To surrender and cooperate fully with Him."[123]

Baptism

It was fifty years in 2017 that I recall queuing for adult baptism by immersion in an outside dry pond on a rock filled with water from a nearby dam drawn by women all week carrying it on their heads! Before that date, my first name Mathano, now my middle name that I was given at birth by my mother, meaning droughts or English summer for I was born in August following two droughts, indicating that the long rains in February through

April had failed in that year. My baptism preceded two years of catechism at school that took place during lunchtime. The local minister conducted the catechism as a chaplain; I remember fleeing to take the oral test because I had not committed my life to the Lord, and baptism meant nothing at that time. What is more, as a teenager, I was inwardly critical of what I saw as the hypocrisy of attending church and carrying on the sinful life the same as those who did not attend church. Catechism used to take up to a year of teaching before one could take an oral test about the Christian faith, and once one passed, then one underwent adult baptism usually done by immersion. The following year, 1967, I committed my life to the Lord on 19th March, started to experience newness of life, following which I offered for baptism. I took the oral baptism test and passed. I recall being the first in the queue, went under the water as Mathano Mwailu, and I came out with a new name, Daniel Mathano Mwailu. It was the normal practice for Christian names to be given at baptism to symbolize new life in Christ, and once baptized, one used the newly acquired Christian name with pride making it known to all one's friends and relatives that one had become a Christian. It was important for most people who came from non-Christian families; it helped the new Christian to abstain from family animist religious ritual and to notify friends and one's peer-group that one would not be partaking in non-Christian partying and other sinful ways. My name was chosen for me by my classmates, Makovu Mutua, one of my peers, telling me that I was daring and that the name Daniel suited me best at baptism. Daring, I became as my classmates applied peer pressure to test whether I had truly changed, and by God's grace, I triumphed, singing the chorus "dare to be a Daniel dare to stand alone." I was ostracised by my peer group, giving me nicknames mostly calling me a bishop, but the one that stuck most was "kavonokya" – which in the vernacular meant, "the saved one." I was known by this name not only in my final year at primary school after I converted to Christianity, but it also remained my nickname through my secondary and high school days at St Charles Lwanga Secondary school and at Kabaa High School. My experience is that my baptism symbolized spiritual transformation that took place in my life, and my new name was its evidence. At first, after my conversion was quite trying with temptations of all sorts, particularly from my best friend, who was my cousin. We shared a room, and one night, he brought in a girl and spent the night with her in the room, tempting me to see if I had truly changed. By God's grace and by his spirit, I resisted and triumphed not only this one but on several occasions. I recall vividly some other similar occasions that surprised me to realize that power had entered my life, preventing me from youthful passions. The following year I started my secondary education in a Catholic secondary school. Peer pressure mounted, but God's grace was upon me not only by helping me triumph but also in helping start Christian Union in that Catholic school and becoming its first chairman. That was not a mean feat given the religious rivalry between Catholicism and Protestantism in those days. I recall two Catholic priests who were my maths teachers persuading me to change into Catholicism, and I refused. Nevertheless, God works in mysterious ways his wonders to perform. The principal of the school, a Catholic brother, had developed a deep love for me because of my Christian testimony and conviction. In spite of ridicule by others and the nickname kavonokya, he developed deep admiration, respect, and trust. I recall he used to trust me so much that once he forgot to bring some money with him to the school and he sent me to his bedroom explaining to me where to find his money and bring it to him. His name was Tony Woods, and as it turned out, he was God's angel sent to assist in shaping my life and career. St. Charles Lwanga was a secondary boarding school and had problems with finding a trusted stores' prefect. The school appointed prefects from the third year as they started their fourth and final year at school. As I started that year, Tony approached me, telling me that the school had a problem with the stores' prefects who ended up selling provisions meant for students, mainly soap and sugar, which they sold illegally to residents for pocket money. When he approached me, he told me that I know you will not steal anything from anybody, and as such, I would like you to become the store prefect and went on to say that he had to suggest my name to the staff meeting. At the staff meeting, he was vetoed because it is a Catholic school, and they cannot appoint a kavonokya, well known protestant religious fanatic as a prefect in a Catholic school! The deputy headteacher vetoed my appointment, and it is through him that I came to know the story. Tony overruled the staff and appointed me the store's prefect. For the full year, I was the store's prefect, none of the boys dared approach me to steal anything not so much for fear that, I would report them, but they were afraid I would start preaching to them about going to hell for stealing and asking them to be converted! In the same third and fourth year, I ran out of school fees even to pay for the examination fees. My widowed mother had sold all the five cows left by my father to pay for my fees, and so I had to drop out of school. In those days, the O level exams came from the UK, Cambridge Examination Syndicate to Kenya as a British ex-colony. The O levels certificate known as E.A.C.E (East African Certificate of Education) and the awarding board was known as East African Examination Syndicate in Collaboration with Cambridge University. The exam fees were paid in the summer before the exam year, the third school year. I recall it was in the 1970/71 school year in my final year; I had completely exhausted all means of finding money to pay for my school fees and exam fees. Tony kept me in the school a week longer than other students when he sent them home for a lack of school fees. He then called me to his office one afternoon, very apologetically and told me that he had to send me home because the board of governors would not allow me to stay in the school any longer without having completed my fees. I told him that is fine; I will go back to the dormitory and pack my bags and go home. My calmness in accepting the bad news surprised him. He asked me what I would do at home? I told him not to worry; I will look for a job now that my prospects had improved by having three years of secondary school education behind me. He muttered to himself and said, "what a waste of talent!" What he said next, astounded me, he said, "if I pay your exam fees from my pocket, will you refund me when you finish your schooling?" In a bit of shock, I replied, yes. He told me to go back to class, and he paid 320 Kenya shillings (UK£3.) for the eight subjects I took for my O level exams, forty shillings each subject from the Cambridge Examinations Syndicate in Collaboration with the East African Examinations Council. I always joke with Irish people and say, I owe my eight O levels to an Irish philanthropist. I was so bold and brave for my newfound faith; I would sacrifice anything for it. Moreover, the sacrifice I did. I graduated from St Charles Lwanga with two distinctions and six credits, and I started high school at Kabaa High School, another renowned staunch catholic school to study for my A levels and I registered for Maths, Biology, and Chemistry in preparation for my chosen career, to become a pharmacist. I organized a boys' choir among the protestant students within the first week and went singing in the local churches with a borrowed guitar from one of my teachers, Mr. Griffin. When the word reached the principal, he summoned me to his office at eight o'clock at night and gave me marching orders to leave the school immediately.

When I asked him what I had done, he replied, "I do not argue with boys," and he ordered the security guard to escort me to my dormitory and make sure I had left the compound! The security guard escorted me to the dormitory. When the other A level students learned that I was being expelled from the school, they decided to riot and demonstrate against my dismissal, stating that they are tired of the principal's autocracy! I implored them not to, and they listened to me. The security guard escorted me out of the school compound, followed by one of my protestant friends, Jeremiah Masila, who sought accommodation for me from his teacher friend known as John in the nearby primary school. I spent the night there, and in the morning, I reported to Education Head Office in Nairobi to explain the situation. The education officer reassigned me to go to Mangu High School, where I registered for Maths, Physics, and Chemistry, but without Biology, my chosen career as a pharmacist was in doubt. I stayed at Mangu High School for one term only, receiving hot letters telling me I was greatly missed from Kabaa High School, my first choice. I missed my friends here too. After one term, the principal met his commeuppance and took refuge in South Africa for an allegation of misappropriating school funds. My friends told me of the new changes, I paid a visit to the school and spoke to the acting principal Mr. Manube, and he admitted me back to my favorite school having missed a term of teaching which proved difficult to catch up. It was at Kabaa High School, where I witnessed God's hand in my life, such that I rate this period as the highlight of my Christian witness as a student. I was used by God to touch so many boys who became Christians through my witness. Some went on to become prominent Christian leaders, one in particular who referred to me as his father in the faith; it was a type of Paul and Timothy type of relationship the late Anthony Muange Kathima, former deputy director of education in Coast Province of Kenya. At this high school, God used me to found the Christian Union, becoming its first chairperson. It was the first protestant Christian organization in that school. The protestant group grew from under ten students to fill the classroom we used to meet for Sunday services with over thirty students who had professed or confirmed their faith in Christ. During that time the school, though Catholic, the Christian union hosted its first Christian rally organized through Kenya Students' Christian Fellowship (KSCF); also its first weekend Emphasis (Friday to Sunday), enhanced Christian teaching coming from the local protestant theological college that provided chaplaincy for the protestant students at this Catholic school. Through my encounter at Kabaa high school and the difficulties that ensued unexpectedly, I witnessed God turning disappointment into appointments. It was through contact with Scott theological college that provided chaplaincy to the protestant students at Kabaa High School that God through Dr. Richard Gehman, whom God used to encourage me to discern my call into the Christian ministry and through him and his wife Florence, I got a full scholarship to study for ministry at the college. I could not afford to pay for fees; neither could my local church. It is through this encounter that I started my ministerial formation in a mysterious way of God's provision. I remember meeting Dr. Gehman at St Charles Lwanga, where I taught maths. I spent the weekend with him, he preached at St Charles Lwanga Christian union, Mulango girl's Christian union, and on Sunday, I translated for him when he preached at Kitui Town Africa Inland Church. We went for lunch at my friend, the late Timothy Munywoki. Dr. Gehman took me aside for a conversation under a mango tree, and he introduced the subject of my call to the ministry based on his discernment of my Christian witness at Kabaa and now as a teacher. I resisted and told him that I could not afford it; neither could my local church, but I will ask my local church again, and if they do not, I will continue working as a secondary school teacher until I had saved enough money to pay for my fees. After a short while, I received a letter from Desmond Hales, the principal of Scott Theological College, telling me that the college had learned of my call into the ministry and that subject to confirmation by my local church, an anonymous donor had offered to pay my college fees and expenses to train for the ministry. When I shared this news with one of my friends Timothy Munywoki, his response stunned me. He told me that God is calling me to the ordained ministry, and I am resisting like Prophet Jonah in the Old Testament. He went on to say; the only problem is that Kitui is so dry, there is no water source for God to send the same fish he sent for Jonah! With that affirmation, my ministerial formation started.

Following my conversion and baptism; spiritual transformation evidenced itself in my life and drove me to start witnessing to others with the unusual positive response, and subsequently, I started preaching publicly. From very early on after my baptism, I never looked back, and God's grace upon my life manifested itself in the gift of evangelism and preaching, leading to my call into full-time Christian ministry in my early twenties. I started training at Scott Theological College, now Scott Christian University, for my vocational in the Christian ministry on the 8th of May 1974. In this book, I have presented my experience of baptism about my spiritual formation and by no means suggest this to be normative for all Christians. For this book, I will give a brief appraisal of historical and the biblical meaning of baptism as a perfect tool for spiritual formation. Biblical and theological discussions on baptism are quite extensive[124], and the assessment given in this book is pertinent to the subject of spiritual formation.

What is baptism?

Definitions: According to *The Encyclopedia Brittanica*, baptism is "Christian sacrament of admission and adoption, almost invariably with the use of water, into the Christian Church generally."[125] Baptism comes from the Greek neuter noun βάπτισμα (baptisma) or masculine (baptismos) both nouns implying ritual washing. The verb (bapto) means to dip. As a noun, its primary meaning as defined in the dictionaries and encyclopedia is:

The Christian religious rite of sprinkling water on to a person's forehead or of immersing them in water, symbolizing purification or regeneration and admission to the Christian Church...a person's initiation into a particular activity or role, especially a role that is perceived as difficult....the ceremony of initiation into Christianity...the Christian religious rite of sprinkling water on to a person's forehead, or of immersing them in water, symbolizing purification.[126]

According to *Webster's New World College Dictionary*,

Baptizing or being baptized specify the ceremony or sacrament of admitting a person into Christianity or a specific Christian church by immersing the individual in water or by pouring or sprinkling water on the individual as a symbol of washing away sin and of spiritual purification...any experience or ordeal that initiates, tests, or purifies.[127]

According to Ray Pritchard, "If the meaning of baptism could be boiled down to one word, that word would be *identification*. Baptism speaks primarily of personal, public identification with Jesus Christ."[128] This understanding of baptism in Christianity resonates with the Old Testament understanding. In Judaism, it implied and was a requirement for conversion into Judaism.[129] According to most contemporary lexicons, the primary meaning is "to dip, plunge, immerse." The secondary meaning is to "bring under the influence." According to Tenney, "after making allowances for certain occasional exceptions, such as passages where washing is implied, the etymological meaning indicates that baptism was originally by immersion."[130]

My experience of baptism resonates with Pritchard's observation on baptism as a public identification with Jesus Christ. Having been brought up in the first ten years of my life as a non-Christian in the context of tribal identifications[131], becoming a Christian was a conscious decision to belong to something other than what I was. Baptism made sense as identification with something new, a sign of new a beginning and belonging. I came to perceive baptism, not as ritual but a dynamic sign of transformation that signified change and new status in Christ; it meant I had turned away from the old life of sin to a new life in Jesus Christ; it felt as if I had gained new impetus and determination to pursue personal holiness daily. In the words of the Apostle Paul, it meant living a new life. [132] As I emerged out of the water, there was the anticipation of a new life, but also the expectation of suffering on behalf of Christ. It was clear in my mind that I was "leaving and cleaving." I was leaving the sinful life I enjoyed with my peer-group and cleaving to God and the minority few committed to him - mainly older people because, in those days, there were not many Christian youths in the local church. Religion and church attendance belonged to older people who had passed life enjoyment and responded to the call into full-time Christian ministry. When I responded to the call into full Christian ministry, I had just finished my A levels where I had studied science: Maths, Physics, Biology, and Chemistry. I was temporally teaching maths my favorite subject in secondary school. I recall one church elder, in particular, the late Samuel Kasimbu Ndumbali, who had been my school teacher, asking me why I was wasting such a valuable science education. I was shocked, but he was referring to the fact the perception in those days was that those who had no other career prospects were the ones who offered for the ordained ministry, usually older people and ministry at that time was associated with poverty and living on handouts. For me, however, it meant that I was publicly identifying with those who believe and belong to Christ and are prepared to serve him at whatever the cost. It was an important decision consonant with the imagery used by the apostle Paul: "I died with Jesus Christ, I was buried with him, and now I am raised with Christ to a brand-new life."[133]

Baptism: an appraisal in Biblical and historical theology

My experience of baptism only tells part of the story of baptism in historical theology. As noted earlier, the Webster's New World College Dictionary defines baptism as "sacrament of admitting a person into Christianity or a specific Christian church." What do we mean by sacrament? St Augustine, in the 5th century, described a sacrament as 'an outward and visible sign of an inward and invisible grace.' I came into Christianity from a non-Christian background, having lived the first ten years of my life outside the church. I experienced baptism as a means of grace that helped in my spiritual formation after my conversion to Christianity. Such an experience, as described in my testimony about baptism, has remained a bone of theological contention in many denominations throughout Christendom. In the early history of the church, the Donatists started practicing re-baptisms. The Catholic Church took a hard line and stated that baptism imparts an indelible seal upon the soul of the baptized; hence a person who is already baptized cannot be validly baptized again...according to the Catholic Church understanding of baptism, the grace received in baptism is believed to operate "ex opera operate" literally meaning as the result of the dead having been done and as such it does not matter even if administered in heretical or schismatic group.[134]

The debates and discussions on the rite of baptism are quite divergent and extensive. The bulk of the debates hinge on whether the rite of baptism is for adults who confess faith and who can answer for themselves or for infants who cannot answer for themselves, and the parents or guardians request it simply as a rite of passage in a given culture. Tracing the historical development of the sacrament of baptism is out of the remit of the objectives of this book. In this book, we would focus on baptism and about spiritual formation as an appraisal to identify its role in the dynamics of spiritual formation. My experience of baptism described in this book resonates with non-conformist churches in which there is a wide divergence of views. The Reformed Protestant traditions, the Anglicans, Lutherans, Methodists, Wesleyans maintain a link between baptism and regeneration but also maintain that it is not automatic or mechanical and that regeneration may occur at a different time after baptism possibly at Confirmation which is why they feel at home to administer infant baptism. It is a sign of regeneration or the new birth, a sign of adoption into Christ by the Holy Spirit. The mentioned churches above administer baptism to infants, anticipating their profession of faith through confirmation in later life through God's grace and prayer. In these denominations, baptism is the entry sacrament into the church administered to both adults and infants alike by sprinkling or pouring water or by total immersion. In the church of Nazarenes, baptism for adults signifies the acceptance of Christ Jesus as Saviour and willingness to obey him and to pursue a life of righteousness or holiness. The Catholic Church, Lutheran, Anglican, and Methodist churches acknowledge and accept baptisms performed by any of the churches in this named group of churches. Reception into membership from any of these churches is by transfer rather than by baptism. Historically throughout the Early Medieval Ages until the Reformation, the church administered infant baptism as a sacrament necessary within the journey of spiritual formation. After the Reformation, however, Huldrych Zwingli had a paradigm shift perceiving adult baptism as necessary for salvation; he came to see it as merely symbolic.[135]Another major shift also after the Reformation regarding baptism came from the Anabaptists, who developed a hard line that rejected infant baptism altogether and started re-baptizing converts in later life. As their name implies, Anabaptize means to baptize again. The majority of Anabaptist Churches considered baptism essential to Christian faith but not to salvation, almost in line with Zwingli; they consider baptism as an ordinance. There is a need to understand their stance in their context. Anabaptists stood against infant baptism at a time when the Church and State were united and when people were made citizens of the state through baptism into the officially sanctioned Church, either Reformed or Catholic[136] The Roman Catholic, Orthodox, Anglican, and Methodist churches perceive baptism as a sacrament, an outward sign with inward meaning. They see baptism as having a role to play in spiritual formation, and as such, they legislate who could perform it, usually by an ordained person. Historical theology reveals that in Roman Catholic, Eastern Orthodox, Anglican, Lutheran, and Methodist churches, the rite of Christian baptism has its antecedents in Jewish purification rituals.

The Greek verb baptzein – baptize has an allusion to other meanings like the sink, disable, overwhelm, go under, overcome and drown from a bowl. In all the symbolism cited in the dictionaries and encyclopedias, the most pertinent in terms of significance to spiritual formation is that the importance is not so much on the person doing the baptism but on the Holy Spirit working through the sacrament and producing the effects of the ritual to the believer. The primary symbolism is threefold: a sign of rebirth, putting off the old man and old deeds, and the renewal of innocence or reversal of the Fall in the individual being baptized. Martin Luther equated baptism with salvation: "to put it most simply, the power, effect, fruit, and purpose of baptism are to save. No one is baptized to become a prince, but as the words say, "to be saved," to be saved, we know, is nothing else than to be delivered from sin, death, and the devil and to enter into the Kingdom of Christ and live with him forever."[137] Some Methodist theologians view baptism as a covenant and argue, "since God never abrogated a covenant made and sealed with proper intentionality – rebaptism was never an option unless the original baptism had been defective through not having been made in the name of the Trinity."[138] The second World Conference on Faith and Order met in Edinburgh in 1937, seeking fresh expression and understanding of the sacraments. Its initial statement regarding baptism stated:

> "Baptism is a gift of God's redeeming love to the Church; and administered with water in the name of the Father, the Son, and the Holy Spirit, is a sign and a seal of Christian discipleship in obedience to our Lord's command. It is generally agreed that the United Church will observe the rule that all members of the visible church are admitted by Baptism."[139]

Although most of the scholars in this conference were from the Baptist church, the statement would find acceptance in most other Christian traditions. For the Baptist tradition, a footnote was added, stating that this statement only applies to "those capable of making a personal confession of faith."[140]According to Emil Bruner, "Baptism is not only an act of grace but just as much an act of confession stemming from the act of grace....the contemporary practice of infant baptism can hardly be regarded as being anything short of scandalous."[141]

How does my experience of baptism and my spiritual formation relate? I received assurance of faith and forgiveness when I accepted Jesus Christ as my Lord as Saviour on 19th March. Between then and my baptism on 13th August of the same year, I did not doubt in those intervening months that God's love had permeated my life and wrought an incredible change, I was sure that I was born again and that the Holy Spirit was resident in my life and effecting change in it. What I was seeking when I asked for baptism was to make a public declaration for all who knew me to know that I was a new creation. I perceive both incidences to be the work of the same Holy Spirit for the same ultimate goal, my sanctification to be like Jesus. I recall moments during my early days of evangelism we used to talk about "dry and wet sinners," referring to those who undertook believer's baptism but had no visible fruit of the spirit to show for it. We used to tell them that they went underwater as dry sinners and came out as wet sinners. It was a way of challenging them to live up to their new names acquired at baptism. A challenge to allow the Holy Spirit to work in their lives to apply God's grace evidenced by changed life through the power of the Holy Spirit.

(Κοινωνία –koinonia - fellowship): Spiritual formation as a corporate journey

Acts 2:42(NIV), "They (early disciples) devoted themselves to the apostles' teaching and fellowship."

So far, most of the discussion in this book has emphasized personal aspects of spiritual formation and may have painted the picture of spiritual formation as a journey of a lone ranger. Spiritual formation, however, is like a two-sided coin. There is the individual –personal journey of intimacy with God that needs to be cultivated individually, but the other side of the coin is that we also walk with God and are formed spiritually assisted by and with others. This dual journey development finds validity in the way Jesus summarized the greatest commandment: Love God, love fellow human beings[142]. There is a corporate aspect of spiritual formation that is equally important and must develop concurrently. "Spiritual formation involves both personal and corporate dimensions."[143] God created human beings in his image, and God exists in a trinitarian relationship: Father, Son, and Holy Spirit. The Trinity is the blueprint for our spiritual formation; humankind consists of relational beings that thrive best in communal relationships. Although Jesus called his disciples individually, right from the start, he made his intention clear that he intended them to build a fellowship. When they started to argue among themselves on who was the greatest, Jesus rebuked them.[144]He commanded his disciples to love one another, adding that it is by loving one another and fellowship they would vindicate their discipleship when he told them: John 13:35 (NLT), "Your love for one another will prove to the world that you are my disciples." In his farewell recorded in the Gospel of John, usually referred to as the farewell discourse and in which

Jesus instituted the sacrament of Holy Communion, Jesus prayed that his disciples would live in fellowship.[145] The psalmist praises the importance of living in unity and brotherhood.[146]Fifty days after Jesus' resurrection, when the Holy Spirit was manifested at Pentecost, the disciples were gathered in fellowship Acts 2:1 (KJV), "they were all with one accord in one place." After the day of Pentecost, the disciples continued living in fellowship.[147]

What is κοινωνία (koinonia)?

Koinonia is a robust Greek word that translates in Modern English as communion, joint participation, sharing, or intimacy. The Merriam-Webster dictionary defines koinonia as

> "the Christian fellowship or body of believers; an intimate spiritual communion and participative sharing in a common religious commitment and spiritual community; the fellowship of the disciples with each other and with the Lord."[148]

Fellowship with God and other Christians defines what it means to be in the body of Christ. Fellowship was one of the characteristics of the early church expressed in the apostles' teaching and in breaking bread together. The Holy Communion has its roots in the Jewish Passover, and when Jesus instituted it, the three synoptic gospels record it to underscore its importance.[149]The apostle Paul traces the practice of sharing communion in the early church to Jesus himself and the institution of the Last Supper. 1Corinthians 11:23-26 (NIV), "For I received from the Lord what I also passed on to you: The Lord Jesus, on the night he was betrayed, took bread, and when he had given thanks, he broke it and said, "This is my body, which is for you; do this in remembrance of me." In the same way, after supper, he took the cup, saying, "This cup is the new covenant in my blood; do this, whenever you drink it, in remembrance of me." For whenever you eat this bread and drink this cup, you proclaim the Lord's death until he comes." Koinonia in the church implies agreement and unity of purpose in serving God alongside each other. There are about twenty references to the concept of koinonia (κοινωνία) nine times; (κοινωνίαν) seven times; (κοινωνίας) three times. In the New Testament the idea of koinonia is expressed in various phrases like: "devoted to one another;"[150] "accept one another;"[151] "honour one another;"[152] "Be kind and compassionate to one another;"[153] "harmony;"[154] "spur one another to love and good deeds;"[155] "admonish one another;"[156] "serve one another in love;"[157] "offer hospitality;"[158] "love one another;"[159] "encourage one another."[160] Koinonia, in modern terms, is a partnership for the mutual benefit of those involved. The Old Testament proverb "as iron sharpens iron"[161] sums the core meaning of koinonia, Christians sharpening one another, stirring one another to faith and good deeds by the grace of God.

While the Enlightenment may have unleashed the spirit of self-determination, self-reliance, the supremacy of reason, and pursuit of autonomy giving rise to modernity and postmodernity social culture focused on individualism, the word community in recent decades has crept back into the Western vocabulary. There are many reasons for this, not least the recognition that individualism, the quest for independence, self-preservation, privatization, avoidance of accountability, superficial relationships, and alienation contribute to the growing plight of social instability and tensions. The Western cultural overemphasis on individualism has failed to deliver the envisaged dream of human utopia. An alternative view involves recognition and awareness that have dawned calling to seek the utopian ideals elsewhere and jettison the status quo. In such time as this, we suggest that the Biblical World View comes to our aid giving the vision of unity in diversity starting with the Trinity: Father Son and Holy Spirit. "This Trinitarian vision of the One and the Many, the Unity in diversity, the Three in one is found only in the Bible... The Old Testament lays the foundation for the fuller expression of the three-personed God of the New Testament....mystery of God as one essence who subsists as three eternal and co-equal persons."[162]The Biblical view is that God created humankind to live and develop as a community. Christians are called to become members of a new covenant community called to reflect the glory of the Godhead in its corporate unity."[163] As pointed out at the beginning of this book, the original sin and the fall of Adam and Eve necessitates the need for Spiritual Formation. Therefore,

> God's redemptive plan is to restore relationships on every level with God, self, others, and creation – so that *humanity* will experience and express shalom (peace, love, unity, and harmony) of the Trinity...we have been transferred from a hypostasis (substance or essence) of biological existence to a hypostasis of ecclesial existence. In the new birth, we are no longer identified with natural necessity but with the freedom of the life of Christ in communion with God and with the community of faith.[164]

One way to understand spiritual formation is, "The personal inside-out transformation that is realized through the presence and action of Jesus meant to reconcile and renew our relationships with others."[165] Dietrich Bonhoeffer articulated the corporate aspect of the spiritual formation when he said, "Let him who is not in community beware of being alone. Into the community you were called, the call was not meant for you alone; in the community of the called you bear your cross, you struggle, you pray. You are not alone, even in death, and on the Last Day, you will be only one member of the great congregation of Jesus Christ. If you scorn the fellowship of the brethren, you reject the call of Jesus Christ, and thus your solitude can only be hurtful to you."[166]After regeneration, the believer soon embarks on the journey of spiritual formation. To aid that journey, the believer needs to embrace the fact that God calls the believer to a

> "vital organism of others-centered people of which Christ is the head...the creative interplay of the vertical and horizontal dimensions of our love for God and our love for his people...The corporate life of the body of Christ is not optional...our personal life together with Christ should both support and be fed by our corporate life together in Christ."[167]

The corporate aspect of spiritual formation is enhanced further by the realization that new believers are born into and baptized into the body of Christ, the church. The New Testament uses various metaphors to describe the church, and each of them indicates that the church is more like a living organism than an organization. There has been a shift in the perception of the church as a living organism. Richard Halverson articulates it as follows:

> "In the beginning, the church was a fellowship of men and women-centered on the living Christ. Then the church moved to Greece, where it became a philosophy. Then it moved to Rome, where it became an institution. Next, it moved to Europe, where it became a culture. And finally, it moved to America where it became an enterprise."[168]

To appreciate the corporate nature of the spiritual formation, one needs to understand the meaning of the church as an organism made up of baptized believers into Christ's body. The idea of the church as a building or place of worship does not find its origin in the early church since the early church had no such facility for their meetings. What existed then was either synagogue or "house churches" (meeting in people's houses). The usage of church referring to a building came much later than the New Testament period. The word church (Ekklesia) appears three times in the Gospels; both are in Matthew[169] The word Church in the original language in the LXX (Greek Septuagint) resonates with the Hebrew word "qahal" meaning the congregation of Israel standing for the community of God's people. Guthrie[170] suggests that Jesus, by using Ekklesia in the LXX sense of qahal, ekklesia refers to God's people conceived as a community, especially related to the Messiah hence the expression "my church" used by Jesus. An article by Howard Marshall [171] gives details of the New Testament meaning of the term ekklesia in relation to its original meaning in the LXX. It gives special attention to its probable Hebrew and Aramaic equivalents. The article is a lucid appraisal and concludes that in the New Testament, the doctrine of the ekklesia owes little to the theological use of corresponding terms in the Old Testament. The reference to the word church in Matthew's texts would in the context fit the metaphor of a people of God[172], J.J. Jeremias[173]asserts that Jesus frequently spoke in terms of a gathering of the people of God, and points out that Ekklesia must be understood in the same sense. P.G.S. Hopwood[174] interprets the Ekklesia in Matthew's statements to refer to Israel. According to Hopwood, when Jesus said, "My church," He meant "My Israel." The cumulative evidence seems to suggest that by Ekklesia, Jesus is not referring to an organization, but to a group of people whom He considered to belong to him and of who the disciples were in some way representatives. Guthrie points out that "There is no reason to suppose that the Ekklesia of Jesus did not form the embryo of the church in the book of Acts and New Testament epistles...it should further be noted that the word ekklesia could also represent a particular assembly as well as be used as a generalized form for the people of God."[175] There is a division of opinion among Scholars on the use of Ekklesia and its usage in Matthew. There are two extremes. The first extreme is championed by Rudolph Bultmann, who is one of the leading German scholars on New Testament Criticism. He rejects the view that Jesus thought of founding a church because he considers that Jesus spoke only of a coming Kingdom;[176]he denies ekklesia linkage to the LXX and argues that the word was taken over from secular Greek by Hellenists to express their rejection of the Law. Other scholars[177], also deny that the word Ekklesia was borrowed from the LXX to express the view that the church was the true people of God. This view asserts that the Christians first used the word to describe simple meetings, and later to describe local congregations. This view pays no attention to its possible origin in the teaching of Jesus. Ekklesia is used in the Epistles of Paul more extensively, and the basic meaning that it carries is "that of a group of citizens gathered together for some public purpose... "the called out" or called together to form an assembly. In Greek literature, the term has only a secular meaning"[178]Ekklesia is used in this secular sense in Acts 19:32, 39, 40, and Chapman points out that "elsewhere it speaks of those who are gathered together because they belong to God." He also notes the important phrase "of the Lord" in connection with the use of Ekklesia. Due to the scarcity of the usage of Ekklesia in other Gospels, some scholars have questioned its authenticity and whether Jesus intended to found the church. The cumulative evidence from Scripture, however, is that Jesus did intend to found the church. It did not grow in His lifetime as the organized institution that represents it today, but as Emil Brunner puts it, "Jesus wills to have a people… but certainly not an institution."[179] The cumulative evidence points to the fact that Jesus brought together a people, who found their meaning and their fellowship in relationship to Him as they, in faith, claimed Him as Lord and Saviour. The story of the Bible, both OT and NT, is the story of God's search for people who will respond to Him in faith and obedience. It is fair to surmise that there is no specific date that marks the founding of the church; the Day of Pentecost marks its empowerment for mission through the outpouring of the Holy Spirit. A balanced view on when the church began is found in Chapman's assertion that it "began in those who were responsive to Jesus' call to repentance because of the imminence of the Kingdom of God."[180]In summary, according to *Encyclopaedia Britannica*, The church refers to the Christian religious community as a whole or a body or organization of Christian believers. The Greek word Ekklesia, which came to mean church, originally in the Classical period applied to an official assembly of citizens. In the OT between 3-2nd Century BC, the term Ekklesia referred to the general assembly of the Jewish people, especially when gathered for a religious purpose such as sharing the Law[181] In the New Testament, it refers to the entire body of believing Christians throughout the world. This is the usage alluded to in Matthew 16:18. It is also used to refer to the believers in a particular area as referred to in Acts 5:11 and of the congregation meeting in a particular house, "the house- church," as referred in Romans 16:5. There are four distinguishing marks of the church, formulated in the Nicene Creed: **One** through the rite of Baptism. "It has been held that since Baptism is the rite of entry into the church, the church must consist of all baptized people, who form a single body irrespective of denomination."[182]Secondly, **Holy** – made through the work of the Holy Spirit. "The holiness of the church does not mean that all its members are holy but derives from its creation by the Holy Spirit."[183]Thirdly, **Catholic** - originally meant universal church as distinct from denominational congregations. Fourthly and finally, **Apostolic** – implies that, in its ministry, the church is historically continuous with the teaching of Apostles and thus with the earthly life of Jesus. St. Augustine, when addressing the nominal beliefs and contradictions in some Christians who profess Christianity but not acting as pointed out that, "the real church is an invisible entity known only to God."[184] Martin Luther held the same theory in addressing the division of the church during the Reformation. He maintained, "the true church has its members scattered among the various Christian bodies but that it is independent of any organizations known on earth."[185]When we turn to the current world scene, the church seems to split into two: on the one hand, Ecumenical movement comprising of Christians who strongly believe that Jesus intended to found one visible church here upon earth and are committed to working hard to restore the unity of the church. On the other hand, we have the Evangelical movement comprising Christians who believe that for church unity to occur, the church must restore fidelity to apostolic doctrine and practice. There are scholars in between these two views. When we try to trace the meaning of the church from scripture, and as we move outside the Gospels into Acts and Pauline Epistles, the first explicit reference to Ekklesia occurs in Acts 5:11. Other metaphors emerge to describe what then constituted the Church: terms like believers, disciples, brethren, etc. In Acts (ekklesia) occurs 27 times, but 3 of these seem to refer to the civic assembly in Ephesus[186] In the book of Acts, the word church is used to refer to a specific congregation.[187]There are other general references like, "they appointed elders in every church,"[188] or went strengthening the churches.[189] The term Brethren became prominent[190]such that as Hanson suggests, "it is likely that this word was, in fact, the earliest Christian word for members of the Christian Church."[191] The word Brethren as a definition of the church is much richer because the "term is expressive of the sense of new horizontal relationships to persons that came along with the sense of a new vertical relationship to God, and it expresses the idea of community and belonging."[192].

The church as ekklesia is an assembly, congregation, or community.

> Believers who meet together for edification in various places as part of a single body whose head is Christ. The church is a spiritual family of brothers and sisters whose personal and corporate identity are rooted and grounded in the love of Christ...*they* minister to one another through teaching, fellowship, sharing, prayer, mutual service, and encouragement.[193]

One of the most vivid renderings of the corporate aspect of spiritual formation is, however, expressed in the imagery metaphor of the church as a body. Ephesians 4:16 (NIV) "From him the whole body, joined and held together by every supporting ligament, grows and builds itself up in love, as each part does its work.". For the church to thrive, the cells must work together to form organs, the organs must function together to create systems, and the systems must operate in synchrony through the directives of the brain. Just as the cells serve the body, so the body, through its vascular capillary system, nourishes and sustains the cells. The church is a dynamic and synergistic community in which the total is greater than the sum of its parts."[194] Therefore, as each

Christian develops in spiritual formation, the whole body, the church grows more into Christlikeness. Rachel Woods argues a case for spiritual community formation patterned after monastic spirituality. She does so by evaluating the Anglican Rogation season [195]and sees the *raison d' etre'* for this appraisal. She argues that it is rooted in

> "The complex cumulative effects of physical and spiritual disconnection from our agrarian roots upon humankind and creation, and upon our relationship with God. She also finds this in reaching out to our fragmented, distracted, secular society in fresh ways and ministering into the hearts and lives of the spiritually hungry."[196]

She reviews ways in which Biblical imagery focuses on agriculture and communal development of spiritual formation understanding of God based on nature. She observes that "relating our journey in Christ to the redemptive journey of wider creation helps to contextualize the distinct ways that aspects of gardens and cultivation have been and are being reclaimed as sacramental spiritual disciplines for Christ-centred spiritual formation."[197]She sees connectedness with creation as an aspect of corporate spiritual formation. She credits this to growing awareness in the last three decades pioneered and championed by ECO church, in which "churches find their own ways of including creation care with discipleship;"[198]and perceives this as a corrective measure from pulling away from direct physical connection with creation and the interconnectedness that God intended for wellbeing, and she speaks of "the need to reprioritize and retrain ourselves "to take note of the world around us and let its grandeur and majesty speak to us of the greatness of God"[199] Rachel perceives gardening and physical cultivation as an essential metaphor for spiritual formation in the sense that in gardening there is constant physical transformation in growth, death by pruning and renewal as helpful reminders of spiritual cultivation and healing of our souls."[200]She perceives further parallels between the garden of the soul and physical cultivations and defines Christian spiritual formation as a focus "on a heart relationship with Jesus as a lifelong redemptive process "forming the inner world of the human self in such a way that it becomes like the inner being of Christ himself."[201]Corporate spiritual formation embraces more than the individual Christian growing spiritually in fellowship with other believers; it encompasses the whole of creation. According to Rachel, "The DNA of Christ incarnate and the narrative of our redemptive journey in relationship with him constantly echo throughout creation, within and through cycles of birth, growth, death, and renewal, which are regularly recurring. Without physical encounter with nature and the accompanying spiritual literacy of how God speaks through it, we lose sight of Christ's redemptive narrative shouting out to us through every living thing, and we miss the opportunities that God has set up for speaking his word directly to our hearts and into our relationships, communities, and world. Cultivation and its metaphors and connectedness with creation's seasons and cycles are a God-given spiritual framework, set into the heart of humanity right at the outset, a strategic resource from the head gardener's heart, to help us make the journey back home to him.[202] In this sense, spiritual formation as a process is a journey of faith lived out in deep connection with God and his creation. Teresa of Avila, the 16th century mystic, further developed the analogy of spiritual formation interconnectedness with nature. Her thinking was not original; Augustine greatly influenced her thinking. She saw a connection between the human heart and gardening. She understood the human heart as a garden and gardening as a spiritual discipline. She maintained that

"The beginner must think of himself as one setting out to make a garden in which the Lord is to take his delight, yet in soil most unfruitful and full of weeds; His Majesty uproots the weeds and will set good plants in their stead. It used to give me great delight to think of my soul as a garden and of the Lord as walking in it."[203]

Therefore the aspect of spiritual formation as a corporate act is enhanced by horticulture in the sense that the discipline of designing, planting, nurturing, and caring for a garden is a useful resource for reflection on personal spiritual formation. Going through the season of nature continually reminds us to learn to discern the season we are in on our spiritual journey and perhaps lead us to pray with the psalmist for God to "teach us to live as if on borrowed time."[204]The season and exercise of weeding our gardens form a good analogy on the discipline of weeding sinful desires and passion that seek to grow in our lives also the fact that gardening is a form of ritual, and so is spiritual formation a form of disciplined routine achieved through spiritual disciplines. Interconnectedness with God, with one another and with creation, builds our faith, nurtures our human spirit and strengthens "our sense of belonging where we are placed."[205] Corporate spirituality finds its roots in the Wesleyan spirituality and the Class meetings. The genius of John Wesley was the discovery that people in church relate as if to an organization, but in the class meetings, they tied together as if in an organism, in a body expressing mutuality and accountability. The class meeting fostered connecting with God, with others and with oneself and instilled the discipline of accountability. The class meeting principle is one of the most exceptional contributions of Wesleyan thinking to the broader church. In the West, some of the Wesleyan churches, by abandoning the practice of class meetings, have consequently struggled to grow. Most have much struggled with decline. At the same time, the modern church movement has adapted to good use of the value of the class meeting. Some of the churches who have adopted the class meeting philosophy and seen considerable growth are The House Church Movement, the Alpha Course Movement, and the Cell Church Movement. It has become evident that the gathered church on Sunday is not conducive to individual spiritual growth, but the small group is. Bill Hull, in his book, *The Disciple-Making pastor and The Disciple-Making Church,* developed this concept in which he highlights four aspects of the church: Celebration, Congregation, Cells, and Cores. In the celebration, the whole church gathers for worship, preaching, and prayer. While such a meeting is useful for inspiration and general teaching, it is not conducive to Christian nurture and spiritual formation. The church then congregates in small group meetings either on Sunday or mid-week for fellowship and in-depth learning. This type of meeting may be conducive to spiritual growth but could still be daunting for new Christians. The church further divides into cells or cell-groups where support, in-depth instruction, prayer, and accountability take place; this is the equivalent of the Wesleyan class meetings. The church may then encourage even smaller units, cores that function like family units, sometimes-in fours or twos, where mentoring for spiritual formation takes place. "Corporate spirituality affirms that growth involves the whole person and that it is enhanced in relation rather than in isolation. Growth in spiritual maturity is a gradual process of formation into the image and character of Jesus Christ; that is fostered by the power of the Spirit, by spiritual disciplines, and by the loving support of the genuine community."[206]

The following two dynamics illustrate spiritual formation as a corporate journey. The first is cycling in a single file when facing a headwind, and secondly, Geese flying in V formation.

Image illustration by Douglas Barrett Wilkinson

Galatians 6:2 (GW)

"Help carry each other's burdens.

In this way, you will follow Christ's teachings."

Single file cycling facing a headwind: In 1995, the late Dr. Brian Loy introduced me to cycling for Charity when I served as the minister at Menston Methodist Church, where he was the senior church steward. I was a complete novice in cycling; I did not even own a bicycle; I had to borrow his wife Elizabeth's for my practice to gain stamina. I raised enough sponsorship for my first charity bike ride in Israel for EMMS (Edinburgh Medical Missionary Society) in November 1996. I had to delay the actual cycling for a year due to the sudden death of my mother in October of that year. I paid in the sponsorship and took part in cycling the following year after I had moved to Poppleton Methodist Church in York. My first ever charity bike ride took place in November 1997 in Israel; its theme was "Into Galilee." The cycling was a challenging feat covering 250 miles through hilly parts of North Galilee starting from Mount Carmel, down to the Mediterranean, climbing up along the Lebanon border to the Golan Heights, then descending to Lake Galilee before cycling up the hills leading to Nazareth EMMS hospital in five days. One hundred and eighteen cyclists took part in the challenge. I had underestimated the difficulty, I recall after climbing a few hills going panting to the organizer, Dorothy Mackenzie, and telling her, I may have to use the empty tomb that I read about in scripture; that lies empty in Israel. She smiled and cheered me up, saying, you can do it, Daniel keep going. On the fifth day, as we celebrated and cheered the completion in Nazareth, Dorothy walked to me and teased me, saying, Daniel, do you still need that empty tomb, and I remember telling her, "No thanks keep it for the tourists"! Since then, I went on to complete 17 international bike rides for the same charity, ten in Israel and six in Malawi, one in Zambia, also two national bike rides, Manchester to Blackpool, and raising over forty-five thousand pounds for charity.

I entered into cycling as a novice, and in the years, I have learned many lessons from the experienced cyclists, mainly from Scotland. One of the experiences was a single file cycling facing a headwind. When I observed it the first time, we were facing headwind cycling from Salima along Lake Malawi and covered over 100km on that day. At first, I thought it was just a fad, then I decided to try it, and amazingly, I found out that it works. It is much easier to cycle single-file regularly exchanging the lead when facing a headwind than cycling alone. My problem was that I could not keep up with the speed because the other cyclists were faster and more experienced than I was.

Image illustration by Douglas Barrett Wilkinson

"We are each of us angels with only one wing,

And we can only fly by embracing one another."

(Luciano De Crescenzo)

Geese V Formation

The way Geese fly in V formation. A U.S.A scientist researched the way geese fly. He discovered that geese could fly 71% farther and longer by flying in V formation. It seems that as the geese position themselves in the V formation, the motion of the wings of the goose in front of each one provides an uplift that makes it easier for the following goose to fly 71% farther and longer by flying together. Occasionally, an independent goose strikes out on his own, but it soon gives up and has to stop or get hopelessly behind and maybe risk the buckshot of goose hunters hiding in the reeds. Christians are like that too. On our own, we soon grow faint, give in to temptation, or get too discouraged to go on. We do need each other. What happens to the lead goose? He has no bird to provide the uplift for him, one may ask. The answer is simple and practical. When the lead goose gets tired, it falls out and takes its place at the end of the formation where it is easier to fly. Another goose moves up and leads. On the question, why do geese fly in a V? "Scientists have determined that the V-shaped formation that geese use when migrating serves two important purposes: First, it conserves their energy. Each bird flies slightly above the bird in front of him, resulting in a reduction of wind resistance. The birds take turns being in the front, falling back when they get tired. In this way, the geese can fly for a long time before they must stop for rest. The authors of a 2001 *Nature* article stated that pelicans that fly alone beat their wings more frequently and have higher heart rates than those that fly in formation. It follows that birds that fly in formation glide more often and reduce energy expenditure. The second benefit of the V formation is that it is easy to keep track of every bird in the group. Flying in the formation may assist with the communication and coordination within the group.

Fighter pilots often use this formation for the same reason."[207]In this chapter, we have identified and discussed at length the three-fold dynamics of spiritual and ministerial formation. The Circumcision of the heart: This highlighted the necessity of spiritual heart plant through regeneration. The sacrament of baptism understood as an outward sign with inward meaning, implies initiation and a new beginning. Thirdly, fellowship (koinonia), meaning spiritual and ministerial formation, has a corporate dimension. The discussion on "circumcision of the heart" and "baptism" underscores the importance of relying on God's grace in spiritual formation. The debate about the church as a body and its need to function as a corporate body underscores the importance of fellowship in spiritual formation as individuals and spiritual practice in ministry and ministerial formation.

Chapter 3 Notes

110 Romans 2:25-29

111 Genesis 17:10-13 and Leviticus 12:3

112 Romans 4:11

113 John Flavel, *Keeping the Heart,*Accessed May 8, 2018. www.christianitytoday.com/ct/2009/january/26.29

114 Rev Dr Benjamin Nzimbi, taught Religious Education in St Charles Lwanga School in Kitui. He is my distance cousin and went on to become the Archbishop of the Anglican Church of Kenya.

115 I trained and was certificated in couple counselling by Relate UK in 2006 basedin the city of York, England, UK

116 Bonaventure Ed. *The Soul's Journey Into God, in Classics of Western Spirituality*; (Ewert Cousins New Jersey; Paulist Press, 1978), 51.

117 This was published by Philip Jacob Spener, in 1675. The English translation was done by Peter C.Erb (Ed.) *Pietists: Selected Writings (Classics of Western Spirituality*), New York, Paulist Press, 2003. Also in Allen C. Deeter, *An Historical and Theological Introduction to Philip Jacob Spener's Dia Desideria: A Study in Early German Pietism*, PhD, Princeton University 1963

118 Bob Gass, The UCB Word for Today, Wednesday 29 March 2017

119 Galatians 2:20 (NKJV)

120 Colossians 1:27 (NKJV)

121 Ibid.

122 Ibid, Thursday 30, March 2017

123 Ibid Thursday 30, March 2017

124 More recent studies on the subject are summarized in A Gilmore (ed), *Christian Baptism: A Fresh Attempt to Understand the Rite in terms of Scripture, History and Theology*, London: Lutterworth Press, 1959 This is a collection of scholarly essays by thirteen clergy and scholars reflecting on different aspects of baptism ranging from: "Scripture, Tradition and Baptism"; "Jewish Antecedents"; "Baptism in the New Testament"; Baptism in the Early Christian Centuries" and "Theology of Baptism".

125 Encyclopaedia Britannica Vol 3, Chicago, 1911

126 Hornby, S A. and Deuter, M. *Advanced Learner's Dictionary of Current English*. Oxford: Oxford University, 2016

127 Webster's New World College Dictionary, 4th Edition. Copyright © 2010 by Houghton Mifflin Harcourt

128 Ray Pritchard, *What Does Baptism Mean?* Accessed November 15, 2017. http://www.jesus.org/following-jesus/baptism/what-does-baptism-mean.html

129 BBC- *Religion and Ethics – Converting into Judaism*, Accessed July 21, 2012 bbc.co.uk.

130 Merrill Tenney, in *Basic Christian Doctrines*, edited by Carl F. H. Henry, (Grand Rapids, Michigan: Baker Book House, 1962), 257

131 In Kenya, the country of my birth, there are 43 major tribes speaking over 70 dialects and early in life one is taught to identify not only with the main tribe but also with the various clans, my tribe is the Kamba and my clan is Mukitondo. Therefore learning to identify at baptism was next to nature.

132 Romans 6:3-4; Colossians 2:12

133 Ibid

134 John Bower, *The Oxford Dictionary of World Religions*, (Oxford: Oxford University Press, 1999).

135 See Frank Leslie Cross, Elizabeth A. Livingstone, "Baptism" in *The Oxford Dictionary of the Christian Church*, (Oxford: Oxford University Press, 2005), 151-154; See also *BBC –Religion and Ethics: Converting to Judaism*, bbc.co.uk Accessed July 21, 2012

136 See, James Alter, Why Baptists: The Significance of Baptist Principles in an Ecumenical Age, (Sidney OH: Anncient Baptist Press, 2008), 52-58

137 See "Luther's Large Catechism (1529)" in Martin Luther, Henry Wace, and C A. Bucheim, *Luther's Primary works, together with his Shorter and Larger Catechisms.* (London: Hodder and Stoughton, 1896)

138 Kenneth Cracknell, Susan J White, *An introduction to World Methodism*, (Cambridge: Cambridge University Press May 5, 2005), 193

139 A Gilmore, (ed.), *Christian Baptism: A Fresh Attempt to Understanding the Rite in terms of Scripture, History and Theology,*(London: Lutterworth Press, 1959), 16

140 Ibid

141 Ibid. p.17

142 Matthew 22:36-40

143 Kenneth Boa, *Conformed to His Image*, 415

144 Luke 9:46 and 22:24

145 The Fare well discourse is found in John chapters 13-17 and in chapter 17:20-23

146 Psalm 133

147 Acts 2:42. This fellowship continues in the first 8 chapters of the book of Acts until persecution started.

148 Koinonia, Accessed November 15, 2017 https://www.merriam-webster.com/dictionary/koinonia

149 Matthew 26:26-29; Mark 14:22-25; Luke 22:14-20

150 Romans 12:10

151 Romans 15:1

152 Romans 12:10

153 Ephesians 4:32

154 Romans 12:16 and 1Peter 3:8

155 Hebrews 10:24

156 Colossians 3:16

157 Galatians 5:13
158 Hebrews 3:13
159 1Peter 1:22; 1John 3:11; 3:23; 4:7; 4:11-12
160 1Thessalonians 5:11 and Hebrews 3:13
161 Proverbs 27:17
162 Ibid .416-417 cites " Let us make man in our image (Gen 1:26); Come let Us go down and there confuse heir language (Gen 11:7); Yahweh and Adonai Psalm 110:1; Ancient of Day and Son of Man" (Daniel 7:9-14)
163 Ibid, citing John 17:22-26 also 1 John 4:7, 11, 20-21 "if you love me you will love the people I love".
164 Ibid . Cites Zizioulas, John D. *Being as Communion*, Crestwood, (N.J.:St Vladimir's seminary Press, 1993)
165 Ibid
166 Ibid. p. 418 Cites, Bonhoeffer, Dietrich. *Life Together.* San Francisco: Harper an Row, 1954
167 Ibid. p. 419, 420
168 Google, Accessed May 8, 2018. http://www.azquotes.com/author/22359-Richard_Halverson
169 0nce in Matthew16:18& twice in 18:17.
170 Donald Guthrie, *New Testament Theology, IVP 1981 p.711*
171 Howard Marshall, "The Biblical Use of the word Ekklesia" in *Expository Times* 84 (1973), 359
172 As used in Jer 12:16; 18:9; 24:6; 31:4; 42:10; Amos 9:11.
173 Donald Guthrie, *New Testament Theology Vol.1, 167,*
174 P G S Hopwood,. *The Religious Experience of the Primitive Church,(*New York: C Scribner's Sons 1937), *233ff,*
175 Donald Guthrie, Ibid.,712; See also James Barr's discussion on Ekklesia in *Semantics of Biblical Language,* (London: Oxford University Press, 1961), 119
176 See, *Theologische Blatter 20, 1941, 265.* Also, W. Schrage, *"Ekklesia" und "Synaagogue" in Zeitschrift fur Theologiie und Kirche 60, 1963,.178*
177 See also J Y Campbell,. "The Christian Use of the Word Ekklesia" *in Three New Testament Studies, 1965, 41-54 Journal of Theological Studies 49, 1948*
178 M L Chapman, *"Church in the Gospels"* in M E Dieter, & D L Berg, (editors) *The Church: Wesleyan TheologicalPerspective.(*Prestonburg, KY: Reformation Publishers, 2008), 29
179 See Emil Brunner, *The Christian Doctrine of the Church, Faith and the Consummation,* D. Cairns trans. (Philadelphia: The Westminster Press, 1962), 22
180 Chapman, Ibid. p.30
181 See Deut 9:10; 18:16.
182 See, St Augustine, *The Anti-Pelagian Works of St Augustine Bishop of Hippo* (Classics Reprint), (London: FB & C Limited, 2015), Vol 3:304
183 Ibid

184 Ibid

185 Ibid

186 Acts 19:32, 39 & 41.

187 Jerusalem Acts 11:32, Antioch Acts 13:1, Ephesus Acts 20:17)

188 Acts14:23

189 Acts 15:41

190 Acts 1:15; 2:3-7;9:30-31

191 See R P C Hanson, *The Acts (The New Clarendon Bible),(*Oxford: The Clarendon Press, 1967), *46.*

192 See Alex Deasley, "The Church in the Acts of the Apostles", in Dieter, M E. & Berg, D L. (editors) *The Church: Wesleyan Perspective.(Prestonburg, KY: Reformation Publishers, 2008), 55*

193 Kenneth Boa, *Conformed to His Image,* 427. Some of the more salient metaphors are: Body of Christ (1 Cor. 12:27; Eph.5:29-30; Col. 1:18; temple of the Holy Spirit 1 Cor. 3:16-17; Eph 2:19-22; 1Pet 2:5; members of God's family Eph. 2:19; people of God's own possession 1 Pet 2:9

194 Ibid. citing Ephesians 4:16

195 Rachel Woods, *Into the Garden: Cultivation as a Tool for Spiritual Formation and Community Renewal,* (Cambridge: Grove Books, 2016), 3

196 ibid

197 Ibid. p.10

198 Ibid

199 Ibid.p.11 also citing T Horsfall, *Mentoring for Spiritual Growth*, (Abingdon: BRF, 2008) 57

200 Ibid p.11

201 Ibid. p. 12 here citing Dallas Willard, *Renovation of the heart: Putting on the character of Christ*, (Colorado Springs, Co.:Navpress, 2002), 22

202 Ibid

203 Ibid.p.13 also citing E. Allison Peers, (trans), *The Works of St Teresa*, Vol 1, (London: Sheed and Ward, 1946), 86-87

204 Psalm90 :12.

205 Rachel Woods,, *Into the Garden, 25*

206 Kenneth Boa, Conformed into His Image, 437

207 Google, Accessed April 4, 2017. https://www.loc.gov/rr/scitech/mysteries/geese.html, http://www.nature.com/nature/journal/v413/n6857/abs/413697a0.html

Four Chapter
Ministerial Formation

"Those who seek to lead others into the King's country should oft have traveled there and frequently gazed upon His face."
C.H. Spurgeon

The expectation in Christian ministry is that the minister or pastor officiates in divine matters. The hope in such a role is the minister or pastor knows God and tells other people about God. To fulfill such a position the minister needs to be able to transmit in 3D effect, to use photographic terms; these are: First, daily Christian experience in Bible Study, prayer and holy living; secondly, daily dealing with sin through confession and making amends and thirdly disciplined spiritual exercises. Ministers who have made a significant impact on others have done so by living contagious Christian lives that influence other people and compel them through love to want to follow them. Jesus' call to his first disciple and subsequent disciples is "follow me." Jesus had no earthly credentials to offer, like university degrees or seminary training to prove his competence in ministry; he offered his life, that is, who he was and how he lived. His earthly home town of Nazareth was not famous; on the contrary, it was a butt of jokes, and "can anything good come from Nazareth?"[208]When he tried to recruit his first disciples, and they asked him to identify himself by where he stayed or came from, his answer was "come, and you will see;"[209] and when his first disciples recruited others on his behalf when asked about him, they replied come and see. To have a personal relationship with God in Christ is paramount in Christian ministry and for anyone aspiring to be a minister.

The three callings

I was working as a simultaneous translator in 1998 for the Lambeth Conference at Canterbury in the UK, a role I had undertaken ten years before in Lambeth 1988. The dominant debates on these occasions were, in 1988, the dominant debate that characterized the conference was the ordination of women to the priesthood and in 1998 were Homosexuality and the consecration of gay priests as bishops. The 1998 Conference became the parting of the ways between bishops in the African part of the Anglican Communion and bishops in the West part of the Anglican Communion about the homosexuality debate. Speeches and debates were quite heated, with the majority of African bishops totally against homosexuality practices based on their understating and interpretation of the Bible in which they held a very firm belief that the Bible is the final authority in deciding matters of faith. They took the view that the Bible abhors and condemns homosexuality practices.[210] According to their understanding that is the end of the matter, there are no other nuances of interpretation. I detected clear cultural influences on the debate and societal shifts, especially in the exposure in the West of different views. Canterbury University hosted the conference, and translators used the university computer laboratories. I was quite acquainted with the then bishop of the diocese of Kitui in the Anglican Church of Kenya later the Archbishop of the Anglican Church of Kenya, Rt Revd Dr. Benjamin Nzimbi and his wife, Alice. The bishop is a distant cousin on my mother's side of the family and was my Religious Education teacher in secondary school, and I was one of the ushers at their wedding. We engaged in a conversation as I tried to help the bishop understand the context in which the bishops from the West based their arguments. In his response, he told me that in his understanding: There are three callings: First, he heard the call of God to be saved and become a child of God to which he responded at a young age assisted by his Christian parents. Then came the second call to offer for the ordained ministry, which he responded to, left teaching, and went to be trained and ordained as an Anglican priest. Then while serving as a priest, he went on to say he heard a third call from God to become a bishop, an overseer of the people and priests of God. He concluded by saying that those bishops who are practicing gay needed to heed the first call to be saved first, abandon their way of sinning (sic) according to him, homosexuality is a sin. Then they should follow the second step before they could even think of claiming the third calling to be bishops. In his understanding, anyone practicing homosexuality should repent of that sin first before they were accepted for ministerial training into the priesthood (sic)! With that entrenched finality of belief, I knew the Anglican Communion was engaged in a hard struggle that ended with most of the African bishops, including Nzimbi, as archbishop of Anglican Church of Kenya, boycotting the next Lambeth Conference, 2008. This illustration serves to distinguish personal spiritual formation and ministerial formation. In light of the illustration, both starts with the first call to respond to the good news of Jesus Christ's love to become children of God[211]followed by a subsequent response to the call to be set apart (ordained) for Christian ministry as a pastor, priest or minister, leading into ministerial training. One achieves this through rigorous training and ministerial vocational discipline. A Christian minister must adhere and adjust to the church and societal high spiritual demands and expectations to survive in Christian ministry. These expectations are right because he or she acts vicariously in a dual representative role, on the one hand, for God to the church as well as the community and on the other hand representing God to the people –the church and community. This dual representative role expected in a Christian minister has resonance in the OT in Leviticus -Aaron priesthood.[212] The primary role was to mediate between God and the people of Israel. As God's representatives, God provided the priests from the abundance of all of the other tribes[213] as they served in the Tabernacle as judges[214] and teachers of God's law.[215] Among the priesthood was the high priest who performed the atonement ritual on behalf of all the people.[216] He entered the Holy of Holies only once a year on the Day of Atonement to offer sacrifice for all people, including himself.[217] The behavior of the priests was expected to be stringently exemplary in holiness and ritual purity[218] such that God heavily punished any failure.[219] The Levitical priesthood was superseded after the Christ Event,[220] The minister in the New Testament thought seems to assume the representative role of Christ, in which the pastor, minister, or priest acts in the name of Christ. The ultimate meaning of acting vicariously in undertaking activities on behalf of others rather than self a role that is attributable to all believers in Christ through the Biblical concept of the priesthood of all believers. The concept of "Vicar of Christ" has been the dividing line in the age-long diatribe between Roman Catholicism and Protestantism. Roman Catholicism, confine the title "vicar of Christ to one person, the pope. In Protestantism, those who have spiritual, pastoral oversight over other Christians share the title reverend.

In English Protestantism, the title vicar is a designation of the priest in the Church of England who is in charge of parish/ parishes, church/churches and the religious needs of people in a particular area.

In this book, we adopt the meaning of minister as person, male or female who has responded to a call from God to preach the gospel of love in Jesus Christ to turn people to God, to represent and act vicariously, when faced by the religious needs of people before God. There are genuine and bogus self-styled-self-called ministers serving their interests and exploiting other people in the name of God. When I researched for my doctoral thesis in the latter half of the1980's, there were approximately six thousand New Religious Movements at that time. I recall a conversation on the airplane I had with Mr. Muli, the then-Attorney General, during one of my flights to Kenya, where I did fieldwork for my Ph.D. dissertation. I told him that I was researching the New Religious Movements. He told me that his policy was to say no to any request for registering a new religion; he said there were enough denominations in Kenya. After his tenure of office, the government liberalized, registration of new religious denominations, and the number of new churches and sects in Kenya increased exponentially not only in Kenya but across the continent of Africa, the epicenter being Nigeria.

The numbers are still growing, and some of the so-called churches are quite dubious doctrinally and in their practices in terms of what makes a church. There has been a proliferation of churches, since the turn of the second millennium. Most of these adopt business entrepreneurship, commonly known as prosperity gospel churches patterned after the American CEO Business approach. Most of these start as NGO's – Non-Government

Organizations - also known as Non-Profit Making Organizations. The majority of these are doing a tremendous work of preaching the gospel and helping the poor, but some are in the business of milking the poor, and one wonders whether the title churches fit them at all. It seems that numerous scandals follow the leaders of these so churches like a pied piper. The main problem is lack of accountability in which a leader gains a following, declares himself pastor or bishop, and then demands the followers to do what he tells them. The leader perceives dissent or challenge as insubordination and deals with it by expulsion or excommunication. The congregation lives in fear of the pastor, who assumes the rank of CEO. The autocracy and CEO model of church leadership are not discernible in the Bible or the early church; such autocracy in the church only finds resonance in the medieval ages in papacy before the rise of Protestantism. The parody is that such dictatorship is associated with some evangelical Protestantism!

In the Bible, the decisive test of a call to ministry is that such appeal is tested and affirmed by others and that it should entail some form of discernment and preparation by way of training and ultimately confirmed through ordination (being set apart) for ministry.[221] In the Old Testament, the priest Eli confirmed the call of Samuel,[222] and in the New Testament, others and the whole church confirmed the consecration of Paul and Barnabas by the laying on of hands after a period of prayer and fasting.[223]Most of the dubious so-called new churches start as pioneer ministries, of which the discernment is entirely in the hands of their founders and their perceived vision, which makes the adherents vulnerable to religious abuse and manipulation at the hands of the founders who develop an authoritarian style of leadership.

Ministerial formation starts at college or seminary for official training. Each denomination dictates most of the initial training, but some denominations would accept their candidates for ministry to be trained in international – interdenominational colleges. My wife and I trained in such colleges: Trinity College Bristol, London School of Theology, and Hartley Victoria – Luther King house in Manchester.

Some form of ongoing training known in most professions as CPD (Continuous Professional Development) follows the initial training. When I practiced as a counselor,[224] participating in CPD was and is still mandatory a sine qua non and remains so for most professions, including medical practice. In one of my congregations, there are several retired doctors. When I moved from Lincolnshire to Yorkshire, I approached several of them to see if they could be my GP (General Practitioner), but they all turned me down, saying they are no longer practicing; they no longer attend CPD, and so their licenses are no longer valid. Spiritual life is formative, requiring tools to help establish and sustain it. Formation of spiritual growth is both intellectual and practical; it requires specific knowledge developed through engagement with religious practices and disciplines acquired by the disposition of the attitude of a learner transformed continuously in the pursuit of spiritual life expressed in daily living.

Ministerial and spiritual formations are closely related, but there is a difference. In ministerial formation focuses more on training for ministry as one's sole occupation or to a full-time ministry. A ministerial formation-training program aims to prepare a person for mission and ministry in the contemporary world through taught courses, whose purpose is for the person to develop their understanding of the spiritual mission of God and the tasks of ministry. It involves courses on scripture, on theology, human development, pastoral practice, and on what it means to live and exercise ministry responsibly. There is no one size fits all in ministerial training. In the four institutions of official training that my wife and I attended, courses varied, and there were electives. The most excellent trainer for ministry is the director supreme of evangelism and Christian ministries, the Holy Spirit, but the Holy Spirit needs a conduit to channel His training, and this is where colleges of ministerial training headed by godly men and women come in. A balanced, comprehensive official training would cover at least the following areas:-

The evidence of call into the Christian ministry.

The call into Christian discipleship itself is not a leisurely walk into the park; it is a battlefield, it entails spiritual warfare, and unless a person has a clear call and conviction, they will not last. In my experience and observation, as soon as the call into full-time ministry is confirmed, it seems unexpected trials follow as if to taste the call of the person offering for ministerial training. Two years had barely ended after I responded to the call, and my brother died, leaving a family of six children without a proper carer. It felt as if I was being tempted to return to teaching to care for my brother's family. I resisted the temptation, and the Lord provided a way to care for the family while I continued with my ministerial training. Similarly, Margaret lost both her parents, shortly after she offered for the ordained ministry at Hartley Victoria in Manchester. There is also the trial of fighting within the church and fighting without the church. Fighting within refers to friction and at times, conflicts that ensue when Christians try to form working relationship within the body of Christ, the church. In a perfect world, one would expect these to be seamless and characterized by Concord. In normal circumstances, however, one finds the same difficult dynamics of human relationships in the church. I was once struggling with a conflict situation that arose in the course of my ministry. The greatest struggle in my faith was observing, intimidation, bullying, and injustice occurring in church context similar to the secular world and wondering how Christians could do such atrocities to fellow Christians in the same denomination even. My mentor, Rev Dr. Stuart Burgess, helped me a great deal by pointing out that the church is like a coin with two sides. The church operates as the body of Christ, sharing his love, care, and concern. When it functions this way, it is the greatest place to be and belong. It also operates as a human organization led by imperfect, fallen people, and as such, replicates the same ugly traits and weaknesses found in secular organizations. He normalized my situation by explaining that what I was experiencing was the later. I had heard a similar intervention from a Christian counseling therapist, but this time hearing it from my mentor with his many years of experience in ministry and secular organizations was a great help. In most cases in the church context, conflict manifests itself in the deployment of talents. We find this in Acts 6, where administrative wrangling surfaced among the first disciples of Jesus, the architects, and the founders of the church. In the later chapters of the book of Acts, we have a difference of opinion between Peter and Paul in terms of mission strategy, Paul preferring an extension of ministry to the Gentiles and Peter preferring to keep it in the house among Jews. We also find apparent conflict between Paul and Barnabas in their relationship with their young protégé John Mark. Paul felt that Mark's cowardice in the first missionary journey dismissed him from any further engagement in the second while Barnabas thought otherwise. Ministry is tough and contrary to the saying "when the going gets tough, the tough get going," I will say, as far as the ministry is concerned when the going gets tough in ministry, the conviction of the call keeps one going. Such a conviction has been my experience throughout my ministry. Prophet Amos evidenced this in the Old Testament when he met resistance as he proclaimed God's truth. He was entreated to compromise because his preaching was not palatable to the king. Amos testified that he was not engaged in a professional career as the son of a prophet or proselyte of a prophet, his inherited profession or career was that of a pastoralist or sheepherder, but God called him to prophesy. He was so convinced of it that he commanded the people to listen to what he had to say. Amos 7:10-17 (GW), "I am not a prophet, and I am not a disciple of the prophets. I am a rancher (farmer) and a grower of figs. But the Lord took me away from herding the flock and said to me, 'prophecy to my people Israel, and now listen to the word of the Lord." The Good News Translation, put is thus, "the LORD took me from my work as a shepherd and ordered me to come and prophesy to his people Israel." *Therefore listen!* (emphasis mine). Time and time again, ministers are tried and tempted to leave the ministry even before they finish training. The one thing that will make them stick with it is a conviction of a clear call by God into ministry. The teachers in colleges of ministerial training make sure the training cover the commitment, conviction of the call to ministerial training by offering comprehensive courses in the following areas:-

i. **Relationship with God /Spirituality**. Before candidates enter the ordained ministry, most established churches test and discern the call into the ordained ministry in various ways. Once they enter college relationship with God and their spirituality is fostered by designed courses in both practice and experience. Discipline in devotional life and worship form a central culture in colleges of ministerial training. The call to ministry is a call into intimacy, as covered in the chapter on grace. Experience of God is also developed corporately as the student minister learns to worship, listen, and work with others at times of planning acts of worship.

ii. **Worship**. It is through prayer and worship that Christian ministry brings people to encounter and develop their relationship with God, and this is widely covered and practiced in the initial training in the ministerial department.

iii. **Bible Study and Christian Theology**. One of the primary tools for a Christian minister is the Bible, and training in Biblical studies is paramount and knowledge of Christian theology to safeguard against secession into cults. In this, colleges teach some form of systematic theology and Biblical theology. Most colleges would include the philosophy of religion to give an understanding of the context of their ministry and prevalent secular thinking.

iv. **Evangelism/Missiology and Communication**. The central call in ministry is the Great Commission, making disciples of all nations. For the ministers to build the church, they need to be exposed to relevant methods of sharing the gospel with the outside world. This of necessity would require the student minister in their formation to learn how to communicate effectively both with those outside the church and those in the church. This would also involve helping the student minister to learn how to relate with people. Communication is a very vast subject, and it constitutes a basic lesson in ministerial formation.

v. **Church History**. Knowledge of the development of the Church from New Testament times to our day is vital in initial ministerial training. This is usually covered in various ways to help student ministers to discern their ministry in the context of the wider church. It is also crucial that the ministerial training should help the student to understand Christian tradition in its broader context. Knowledge of Church history provides a more comprehensive picture of ministry than one's denomination. It also pinpoints pitfalls one was to avoid making the same mistakes made in the past, as the saying goes, "Those who ignore history are bound to repeat it."

vi. **Community Engagement/Ecumenical relations**. Christian ministry is practiced formed in the arena of the broader world and collaboration with other churches. Learning how to engage with the world, the very context of ministry is essential to cover in the initial ministerial training. In this, the students would be encouraged to explore the ministry of the church in God's world. Also included in this would be the subject of the church's mission in social action or works of mercy. Some of the colleges deliver their courses ecumenically like the Luther King House Theological Training College in Manchester, which is a partnership between Anglicans, Baptists, Methodists, Unitarians, and United Reformed churches.

vii. **Practical Contextual Theology**. Through the theological reflection in learning and understanding, colleges teach contextual practical theology, including contemporary social issues like Black Theology, or feminist theologies, and other relevant matters in society.

viii. **Leadership and management**. The students are taught various aspects of leadership, in particular, collaborative leadership, which is vital in a modern egalitarian society. Transformational leadership, servant leadership, and learning how to motivate others would be crucial.

ix. **Ministerial practice/Pastoral Ministry.** This is a specialized calling and requires specific training on pastoral care, pastoral practice, and management of the pastorate. It would also require knowledge of how to visit the sick and conduct various services that lie within the ministry, like baptisms, weddings, and funerals.

The above list is by no means exhaustive; different colleges devise various curricula to accommodate the needs of their ministerial students. The above list, however, would form the kernel of the training courses' lowest common denominator. When I trained at the London School of theology, which started as an affiliated college of London University, it coined its original name as London Bible College. I recall an address by Dr. Michael Griffiths, the then principal of the college reminding students to note that the word Bible is at the center of the name of the college. He was implying Biblical studies were the emphasis of the college. Such was true, for it is at the London School of Theology where I studied Biblical Hebrew and Greek, also Hermeneutics. It does not mean that all the college taught was Biblical studies; as an academic international, interdenominational institution, it taught other subjects as well. I remember taking a course on Islam, and the rationale given by the college was that student ministers need to understand other faiths among which they were going to discharge their ministry. Spirituality was emphasized by regular attendance at chapel services and Fellowship groups. Although the college did not offer Practical theology as a subject at that time, students participated in leading worship in the surrounding churches. In order to earn my Advanced Diploma in Pastoral Studies, it was mandatory to participate in evaluated preaching in local churches with feedback to the college from the churches one preached. In addition to these basic courses, colleges devise other courses to meet the specific needs of ministerial students according to their perceived needs and contexts of ministry. In my ministerial training experience, I found this to be the case in two other colleges of ministerial training that I have attended, Scott Theological College, now Scott Christian University in Kenya and Trinity College, Bristol, in the UK. Scott Theological College taught such courses in my initial ministerial training, administration, and management, bookkeeping, and touch - typing. I recall my class demonstrated against these subjects, in particular, because I felt they were a waste of my time, for I attended the college to learn how to be an evangelist or pastor. The college painstakingly explained that in the African context of ministry at that time, these were practical courses that would help us as ministers in case we were appointed to churches that could not afford a person with knowledge of bookkeeping forcing us to train one. About these extracurricular subjects, the rationale was that as ministers we could be appointed o churches where they could not afford a secretary to do typing. We so disliked the course on administration and management, which was taught in the afternoon during the scorching heat that sent most of us to sleep, we nicknamed the course "judgment"! Looking back over forty years, these were the most helpful practical courses I ever received; they were never repeated in any other college, although they have been invaluable. Another such subject offered at Trinity College, as a mandatory extra elective, was leading and participating in leading worship. Those of us who had joined the college only to take academic courses leading to the award of the Bachelor of Divinity from London University, we found a course in leading worship unnecessary, but the college explained that Trinity College was primarily a college for training ordinands for the Anglican church and as such leading worship was mandatory. Trinity College, Bristol, was international, taking students from all over the world. It was the first college I attended outside my country of birth, Kenya, and it helped form my ministry by learning to appreciate worshipping and interacting with other denominations. It was my first time also to interact with Christian students from other nations and formed strong friendships with students from Canada, Holland, Nigeria, Singapore, Uganda, USA, and the UK. As I look back on my ministry, it was from my time at Trinity College Bristol, and at the London School of Theology that my ministerial ecumenical appreciation of other denominations developed. While ministerial formation may focus on vocational training, it also focuses on the spiritual development of the minister as a Christian person. One of the most challenging aspects of ministerial formation is transition from being a "personal" Christian, whose faith is known to the believer and by those closest to them, to being a "public" Christian with a role, recognition and responsibility to a community and the rest of the world in exercising holiness, wisdom, worship, prayer and compassion. The role of a church minister has both a public and a private persona. It has both positive and negative presentations. The positive presentation is when the minister lives a life for all to see as an example. Some Biblical passages suggest such a way of life is required of a minister and even commends it as follows: 1Timoth 3:1(CEB). "This saying is reliable: if anyone has a goal to be a supervisor in the church, they want a good thing." The Bible then goes on to give stipulations as follows: 1Timohy 3:1-7 (TLB), "a pastor must be a good man whose life cannot be spoken against…he must be hardworking and thoughtful, orderly and full of good deeds, etc." The Message translation of the Bible puts it bluntly as follows: 1Timothy 3:1 (MSG), "If anyone wants to provide leadership in the church, good! But there are preconditions."The writer to the Hebrews talks about lives laid bare for nothing is hidden from God."[225]What this means is living transparent lives, in which the Apostle Paul refers to Acts 24:6 (NLB), "as having a clear conscience before God and all people."

The negative impact occurs when this extends to its extreme, and the minister and his family feel as if they are living in "gold-fish-bowl" or glasshouses in the public eye of their congregation lacking private space. This extreme occurs when the perception turns the minister and his family as "the holy family" in which the children feel as if they have lost their identity to be themselves rather than meet societal expectations and demands of public protracted holiness and perfectionism. According to The World Council of Churches, a global conference on Ecumenical Theological Education in Oslo in 1996, ministerial formation is "grounded in worship and combines and inter-relates spirituality, academic excellence, mission and evangelism, justice and peace, pastoral sensitivity and competence, and the formation of character.

> For it brings together education of: "the ear to hear God's word and the cry of God's people; the heart to heed and respond to the suffering; the tongue to speak to both the weary and the arrogant; the hands to work with the lowly; the mind to reflect on the good news of the gospel; the will to respond to God's call; the spirit to wait on God in prayer, to struggle and wrestle with God, to be silent in penitence and humility and to intercede for the church and the world; the body to be the temple of the Holy Spirit."[226]

Given the intensive and comprehensive nature of ministerial training, it must be followed by CPD – Continuous Professional Development. I recall some words from late Jack Philips, one of my tutors in my initial vocational training in Africa, when he said, "we are not here to educate you but provide you with tools for your education," implying that ministerial training and formation is a continuous exercise. If a minister graduates from the college with a learner's mind and inquisitiveness, that minister will survive the rigors of ministry, which is a long haul. However, if a minister graduates and leaves ministerial training college with the attitude: "I have learned all there is to learn I am now a fully trained and ordained minister," such a person is unlikely to last long in ministry. Worse still are those who look down on formal training for ministry and claim that the Holy Spirit is their teacher as if the Holy Spirit was against formal institutions of training. The apostle Paul more than any other writer in the New Testament, emphasizes the importance of being taught and guided by the Holy Spirit in ministry. He also emphasizes the importance of formal training, taking pride in his training under the feet of the famous Rabbi, Gamaliel. Paul says Acts 22:3 (NLT), "I am a Jew, born in Tarsus, a city in Cilicia, and I was brought up and educated here in Jerusalem under Gamaliel. As his student, I was carefully trained in our Jewish laws and customs. I became very zealous to honor God in everything I did, just like all of you today." I almost fell into this trap in the mid-1970s when my call into the ministry surfaced. I had been preaching for seven years after committing my life to Christ. I was gaining some popularity as a preacher, and I had quite a good number of people that I had led to the Lord. I was teaching in a secondary school, and that earned me more preaching opportunities. The first person to share with me openly that they had discerned a call of God in my life for the ordained ministry was Dr. Gehman, then a teacher at Scott Theological College. My work among students at Kabaa High School, where I did my A level studies, moved him to approach me to consider the ordained ministry. The second person was Lenah Kithyululu, later the wife of my best friend, the late Timothy Munywoki. I resisted the call preferring to be a freelance, evangelist, and preacher of the gospel.

I continued battling the discernment of the call, and then I decided to share it with my closest friends. Most of them discouraged me, saying that I was doing well and feared that if I join a theological college, my fire for the Lord would be dampened or extinguished. One such friend was the late Edwin, who thought that I was destined to take over as pastor of the Deliverance Church that met at the City Hall in Nairobi at that time; and implored me not to go to a theological college. Edwin Mbiti Ndonga was a very close friend; I led him to the Lord following a youth rally message I had preached at Musengo in Mutonguni. He resisted the altar call, but when he got home, he was convicted by the sermon and sent for me from my other friend Hasting Banda where I was staying for the night. I went to him, and he surrendered his life to the Lord in tears. I later was the best man at his wedding. It was tough for me to resist the advice of such a friend against attending theological training for ministry.

It was the apostle Paul in his advice to Timothy that persuaded me, 2Timothy 2:15 (KJV), "Study to shew thyself approved unto God, a workman that needeth not to be ashamed, rightly dividing the word of truth."I felt the voice of God telling me, Daniel, I want to use you in the future, and I want you to prepare by going to study my word. God proved it by providing me with an anonymous scholarship for four years for my initial vocational ministerial training. To this day, I do not know who paid for my fees at the theological training college. Looking back, forty years later, I am glad I did. Religious and theological landscape in Kenya and most parts of Africa have so much changed with self-appointed pastors, apostles, and bishops. The phenomenon of the self-proclaimed and self-declared pastors has escalated to the point that the issue of accountability and integrity is not relevant anymore. This phenomenon is not common in the Bible.

For example, prophet Elisha rather than declare himself a man of God and make demands, it was the Shunamite woman who recognized him as such and told her husband. "then the woman said to her husband, "Behold, now I know that the one who often comes our way is a holy man of God. Please let us make a small room upstairs and put in it a bed, a table, a chair, and a lamp for him. Then when he comes to us, he can stay there." (2 Kings 4:10 Berean Study Bible)

When I arrived in the UK in September of 1979, I was interviewed and asked why I had chosen to go for further studies. My reply, as cited in the Africa Inland Mission Magazine, London 1980, was, "I am studying because everything that has been tried elsewhere and failed is exported to Africa." What I was referring to was everything religious, implying that the aim of my further studies was apologetic. What amazes me is how prophetic my words were looking back to the current religious milieux in Kenya and indeed across Africa with the excesses of the prosperity gospel, self-appointed bishops, CEO type church government that exploit church members with lack of accountability and false teaching and doctrines to undiscerning membership. I am concerned about false teaching and pastoral charlatans and exploitation of undiscerning church members but not dismayed. I rejoice that the church in Africa is growing, and like the apostle, Paul says, Philippians 1:15, 17-18 (NIV) "it is true that some preach Christ out of envy and rivalry, but others out of goodwill....The former preach Christ out of selfish ambition.... But what does it matter? The important thing is that in every way, whether from false motives or true, Christ is preached. And because of this, I rejoice. Yes, and I will continue to rejoice."

A second factor why training is essential is that it helps curb spiritual pride. In one of my appointments as superintendent minister, I sadly observed a very gifted minister lose their pastoral charge for that reason. In my attempt to intervene to try and assist, my efforts met an arrogant rebuttal stating that when the minister worked as a teacher before they offered for the ministry, they said they run the classes assigned without the headmaster's interference. The implied message was that as a trained teacher, that minister had learned all that there is to learn to run the class; her training is all that is required, and the certificate as a teacher proves it! It was not long before their pastoral ministry came to an end, and transferred to another department in the church. A few years later, the said minister left the denomination and joined another. Ministerial training helps a great deal in developing humility, *a sine quo non* in pastoral ministry. The correct attitude is to leave college saying, I have attained some tools to keep growing in my ministerial spiritual formation.

Image illustration by Douglas Barrett Wilkinson

Are you tired? Worn out? Burned out on religion? Come to me. Getaway with me, and you'll recover your life. I'll show you how to take a real rest. Walk with me and work with me—watch how I do it. Learn the unforced rhythms of grace. I won't lay anything heavy or ill-fitting on you. Keep Company with me, and you'll learn to live freely and lightly." Matthew 11:28-30 (MSG)

Ministerial burnout

I took a post in 2010 for my second stint as a superintendent minister. My appointment coincided at the same time as that of a minister from another denomination, that had an interregnum for some time. This newly inducted colleague was quite gifted as a preacher and musician; he played the piano in the ministerial singing group while I played my guitar during ecumenical services, and we got on very well and lived on the same street. Five years later, when I was due to move on from my appointment, this ministerial colleague had experienced burnout, left the ministry, and started a landscaping business to support his young family. He cut himself off from colleagues, and on several occasions, I met him, and he avoided a conversation, which was understandable. I found this quite a sad thing to witness. The church in the denomination he served went back on interregnum, and life went on as usual. At the fraternal meetings, colleagues would try to find out information about him and the church he served reported that they did not know. The only whisper one would gather was that the minister had had a breakdown before insinuating that was his nature. I was somewhat shell - shocked that such a thing could happen in a Christian community where caring for one another is preached as a Biblical requirement. Around that same time, my wife had cruel curtailment of her appointment and was on the brink of a breakdown following a sadly shameful and unfair episode in her ministry. She was a minister in the pastoral charge of several congregations, and I was working hard using all my counseling skills to make sure she did not quit the ministry. Thank God she did not, for she is a very gifted minister. Ministerial burn –out simply stated stated occurs when ministers lose their enthusiasm and excitement for their ministry, they become bored and decide to quit the ministry.

They do so when the work that once excited them no longer does so, and they start to feel that doing ministry is like performing thankless chores. H. Newton and Donald Falkenberg observe that "ministerial burn - out is a common hazard that need not destroy its victims...burn - out does not have to happen."[227] The fact of the matter is that it does happen and seems to have become more of a problem in the last few decades, as the church in the West, in general, grapples with decline. Some of the causal factors include working long hours, being on call 24/7, not keeping the Sabbath – taking a weekly day off, not having enough holidays, adverse effects on the family feeling as if living in a glass house with too high societal expectations. According to recent newly revised statistics,

> 72% of the pastors report working between 55 to 75 hours per week. 84% of pastors feel they are on call 24/7; 80% believe pastoral ministry has negatively affected their families. Many pastor's children do not attend church now because of what the church has done to their parents. 65% of pastors feel their family lives in a "glass house" and fear they are no good enough to meet expectations.[228]

The subject of ministerial burnout is quite extensive. Suffice it to say that the article "Soul Shepherding" aptly summarises it thus:

> Pastors and other ministerial leaders are often under so much stress that they find themselves just hanging on by a thread, about to burn out from exhaustion or blow out emotionally. Pastoral/ministerial stress today is enormous. The expectations that people put on their pastors/ministers today and that pastors/ministers put on themselves are debilitating.[229]

Ministerial burn - out sometimes is equal to parading a facial façade on the outside but feeling inwardly fatigued, emotionally drained, always fighting bursts of anger, inward fear or, panic attacks, morbid tears and depressed or what C.H. Spurgeon once termed "the ministerial fainting fits" in his *Lectures to My Students.* One does not have to experience all these factors to have a burnout, but any combination of most of these is a good warning sign. In his article Ministerial Meltdown and Burnout,[230] Alan Palmer identifies six causal factors for ministerial burnout.

First, is what is known as the Sisyphus Complex represented in the picture above.

This complex is drawn from a figure in Greek mythology trying to push a heavy stone uphill only for it to fall back before it reaches the summit. It refers to the endless ministerial, "To-do list," of which for most ministers is nebulous with work expanding to fill the time available. The bulk of my ministry as a minister has been in England besides my foundational ministerial training and pastoral ministry in Africa and some short spells of ministry in America. In the UK, most ministers work at home in the manse or the vicarage, with few exceptions that may have an office in the church. Because of this, there is a fusion between personal time, family time, and work (church) time. When this situation is not adequately worked out, the ministers find themselves having a continuum of working hours or being on call 24/7. The solution, which is very hard for most ministers, is to have a boundary between work and personal time. When this boundary fails, burn - out may ensue because of the lack of measurement to establish achievements of the day. The answer lies in planning each day, each week, each month and year, and trying to detach personal space from work. In the UK, the stipulated working hours per week for full-time staff in the secular field of work is 37.5 hours. If each week the minister looks at what needs to be done for that week and allocates these weekly hours to the tasks and leave the rest for personal space and time with the family, it will minimize burn - out. Most ministers are out of shape physically because of lack of exercise, and the excuse is always that they do not have the time! It is common knowledge that a healthy soul proceeds out of a healthy mind and a healthy mind out of a healthy body. Some ministers even allow themselves to become obese, thus setting a bad example in spite of the Biblical injunction to take care of our bodies because it is the temple of the Holy Spirit.[231] Time management in ministry is easier said than done because, in my experience, most ministers experience bullying and taunting from church members, telling them that they only work one day a week. I had often fallen into this trap when our two boys were growing up to whom I profusely apologize. The question one might ask is this: Is this clinical way of working possible? For a long time, I thought it was idealistic and not achievable and believed the lie that it is not at all possible to regulate ministerial hours until circumstances forced me.

In 2008-2009, I was in an appointment that entailed commuting from Manchester to Blackpool. I lived with my wife in the Manse at Manchester, and it was a comfortable journey by motorways all the way (M60, M62, M61, M6, and M55), which I could do within the hour. In reality, because of the motorways, the fifty-mile journey was more comfortable to commute than driving across Manchester city itself. The arrangement was that I would travel three days a week, but three months into the appointment, my wife fell ill and needed my daily attention, resulting in me having to commute daily. In my entire ministry, this proved to be the most efficient appointment in terms of my time management ever. I was forced to develop a daily "to-do list" before I left my home in Manchester, I will plan my day, and on hitting Blackpool, I started with my first item on the "to-do list" and go through it in the day. I would do what I had to do, visiting, attending meetings, taking services before I started my journey back to Manchester. The efficiency occurred because I put down on paper what I needed to do on that day allocated time, went to Blackpool, did it, and returned to Manchester feeling mission accomplished. By the end of that year, my time management, and the boundary between family time and work had improved one hundred percent. My ministry in Blackpool remains one of the high points in my Christian service in the UK; it was brief but quite sweet. The following year I had an appointment on secondment to another denomination that involved commuting between Manchester and Rochdale, and I repeated the same work pattern, and my discipline on time management felt imposed on me. My experience in these two appointments taught me that the Sisyphus complex and the feeling of endless "to-do list" could be avoided by stringent disciplined personal time management on a daily and weekly basis. For those ministers who may feel overwhelmed by work and somewhat experiencing the Sisyphus complex, they should try daily scheduling of the hours and stick to it; it works.

The second causal factor for burn out is unrealistic expectations by both the minister and the congregation about what the minister is supposed to do. Some denominations try to narrow down the role in compliance with employment law, but most circumvent the law by saying that they do not employ ministers, but they are in covenant with the church, God employs them, yet make demands on the minister as if they hired them. When I started work with the British Conference of the Methodist

Church, they defined the terms of the appointment in rather general loose terms and the ministers; also described their ministry and what they had to offer in general terms too. I recall reading in what was known as the yellow book in which the churches and the ministers seeking appointments advertised. Some ministers seeking assignments described themselves as GP, meaning general practitioners indicating their ministries offered nothing specific but general practice of ministry. In the last few years, however, ministers have been encouraged to define their gifts and talents in more specific detail. The expected role in the advertised appointment is specified in what is now known as "Letter of Understanding" in which the church defines the assignment concerning specific tasks. Such specificity has enhanced and facilitated the matching process of ministers to the available appointments. It goes without saying that when clergy and congregation alike express unrealistic expectations for the minister's role, ministers are set up for burnout.

Thirdly, Carping criticisms whereby ministers get a constant barrage of criticism until they lose their confidence and switch to maintenance and survival mode, serving without enthusiasm or excitement. Fear of criticism turns some ministers into congregation pleasers and instead of developing Billy Graham mantra, "The Bible says" or "thus says the Lord," the minister's focus turns into what the congregation wants them to do instead of what the Lord wants them to do in a given specific appointment. The result is that the tail wags the dog. Also, because of misplaced unrealistic expectations, both the church and the congregation lose vision and focus, leading to the minister to experience burnout. It also has the negative result of enormous turnover, the church changing ministers more frequently than is necessary, and worst of all is the terminating of the minister's appointment in what in the Methodist Church is known as curtailment. I said worst of all because it ends in hurts and pains, and some cases, if not properly handled, could do irreparable damage to both the church and the minister. Although the national church guideline legislation provides for curtailment by mutual agreement when curtailments occur except in cases of discipline, in practice, they are rarely bilateral. Burnout and low ministerial morale tend to be more prominent in the denominations where laity has assumed a leading role in the deployment of ministers. In these denominations, the congregation assumes the role of the employer, and the minister lives under constant fear of doing what the congregation wants or suffers the dismissal. Where such ministers have family constraints like having children in local schools, compromise of one's ministry under pressure with an eye to the needs of the family feels like the only option. When that happens, lack of work fulfillment sets in, and soon it's Siamese twin, burn - out follows.

In South Africa, in one of these denominations where laity hold the upper hand in deployment of ministers, there is a saying in Xhosa: "Abantu becawa abamfuni umfundisa ukhoyo ngoku, bancoma lo umkileyo, banjonge lo uzayo - "The present minister is not treated well by the congregation, they praise the minister who has left, and they are looking for the one who is to come." There is no easy solution to enduring a barrage of negative criticism; it is the worst interaction in human relationships and saps the energy of the soul and is perniciously destructive. Human beings thrive on encouragement and not criticism. When faced with a barrage of criticism, the minister has two unhealthy secure options: the first is to buckle up and turn into a crowd-pleaser that most chooses for the sake of a comfortable life. The second is to adopt a saying I used to see when I was growing up as a teenager along

Kitui Mombasa highway in Kenya written on some long-distance lorries in the Swahili language-"Kibambayee – waache waseme ndiyo kazi yao- let them speak that is their work." The problem is that neither of these two options is healthy. Developing a rhinoceros skin, toughing things out and ignoring what people are saying are not reasonable solutions at all; because they could adversely affect the minister; or if the criticisms are valid, damage the church. The healthier response is a synthesis in which one develops resilience, listening to and constructively engaging with what is said fearlessly without being aggressive. In that way, the criticism is exposed, evaluated, and dealt with rather than allowing it to fester until it erupts like Mount Vesuvius. Incessant criticism is crippling and would burn out the best of ministers.

Fourthly, clinging vines by which Malony and Falkenberg mean working with difficult people constantly criticizing and sapping one's energy. I would characterize these as *strangling ivy*. Some many uncertainties and imponderables face student ministers as they enter the ministry. One certainty, though, is that they will encounter working with difficult people. Two ministers were having a conversation in a ministers' fraternal and started talking about their encounter with difficult people; they both discovered they had them. One of them reminded the other of a saying that "God in his wisdom never allows difficult people to congregate in one church but scatters them all over." Another discouraged minister said, "The trouble makers never seem to leave, and the helpful, cooperative people never seem to stay." In my experience of such people, I would refer to them as strangling ivy because of their disruptive, destructive nuisance and sapping of energy. In some churches are people who feel that their primary mission is to straighten out their ministers rather than love them, and their chosen straightening tool is criticism. They decide to cling to ministers with their criticism like climbing ivy, and they do similar damage that ivy does to brickwork or the tree it climbs on, sapping all the moisture and making the brickwork or the tree brittle and fragile or causing it to wither. A minister explained to me why she felt the need to curtail her ministry, and one of the reasons was that a woman in her congregation who was continually criticizing and writing unpleasant letters to the superintendent minister about her and when the minister was preaching the woman would attend another church where the superintendent minister was preaching.

When I was superintendent, I came across such a person, and she took on criticizing nearly everything I did. I can recall her vividly; she had red eyes, which was somewhat unusual. I remember once receiving a phone call from her, complaining about two words, "paradigm shift" I had used in the Circuit monthly magazine article. She said she could not find it in the dictionary, and hand rang around, and most people had never heard of it; they are not academic. After the conversation, I rang the senior circuit steward and related to the incident. His advice was not to worry about her because she was like that. He said that when he was chief steward in that church; he would receive a phone call from this woman as soon as the service ended, usually at a very inconvenient time when he was having lunch with his family, complaining about trivia such as wrong hymn or tune used by the minister, or some similar mundane thing. I felt relieved that her criticism was not personal and learned to ignore her, and because I was as high as she could go, she mellowed down and stopped ringing me with complaints. My experience of such people is that they are seasoned champions of criticism; they have the staying power, for they have seen so many ministers wilt and wither at their criticism, and there is no easy way of dealing with them. One way is for the superintendent, who would be aware of such champions to protect the minister through wise interventions, but if the issue is left to fester, it will drain the energy of the minister and end up in a burnout. Typical of such champions was an older man who was having a chat with a visiting minister, who asked him how long he had been in that church, he said over forty years. The minister remarked, you must have seen a lot changes in this church to which he replied: "Yes, I have witnessed a lot of changes, and I have opposed every one of them."

Fifthly, toxic confidences when the minister becomes a recipient of grueling painful and hurtful information from members of the congregation and having to bottle it up. In the time it will start to adversely affect the minister if there is no safety net or scaffolding to support the minister, such information could lead to burning - out. Structured supervision, such as is practiced in most professions, would go a long way to alleviate such pressure and possibly prevent possible burnout. The principle in counseling is that you cannot receive without offloading and function normally. We would argue this point forcefully in the section on mentoring and in particular, the purpose of peer mentoring. In the case where there is no supervision, ministers should seek out spiritual directors for the sake of their well-being and survival in ministry.

Sixthly, living in a "goldfish- bowl" in the public glare of their congregations. Akin to unrealistic expectations discussed earlier in which the minister and his family are perceived as "the holy family" with the undue expectation of perfection. Given current affairs, societal demands for ministers to be perfect are waning, but practical measures could be made to make sure the minister and his family are given private space to alleviate stress. Earlier I mentioned a secondment appointment to another denomination. That appointment was created by a curtailment of the previous minister who found the living arrangement stressful, and the church failed to address the issue. The church was an old grade two listed building built in the days when the minister's residence was attached to the church such that the minister's study in the house opened and led into the pulpit! The minister I replaced had expressed the stress the arrangement was causing to the family, in particular, the husband who did not attend church felt compelled to move out and live with their son because of lack of privacy. When I took the appointment, they found me a different office outside the manse; they even bought me my first Smartphone, iPhone 3GS, while they rented the parsonage. I commuted from my wife's manse to this appointment. Lack of privacy could cause stress and lead to burn - out. This list is not exhaustive but identifies the kernel of ministerial burn - out. These six stress causal factors leading to ministerial burnout highlighted by Malony and Falkenberg are by no means exhaustive. Many others could be cited as expressed by the following text that I received from a friend entitled: "A Pastor" posted on social media and forwarded to me by a senior minister.[232] It read as follows:-

A PASTOR: No one knows: What a pastor hears, What he sees, The secrets he must keep, The temptations he encounters, The tears he sheds, the sorrow he endures, the loneliness he manages, The bitterness he experiences, the lies leveled against him by some of the people he serves! How he accommodates those, who pretend they love him, but behind him, they destroy him. How he tries to live superhuman life. The lack he suffers, the discrimination he must not react to, the accusations he has to be mute at, The expectations he strives to cope with, Even a fellow does not know what the other goes through. He is alive for God, and yet he lives for a man! A pastor & the priesthood is what no one can fully understand or comprehend! The priesthood is. A mystery! The pastor is a mystery too! A mystery is something incomprehensible! So ALL you can do for him is to pray for him. A day must not pass without standing in the gap for him/her! Wish him well, & endeavor to understand him! Make him happy, at least, for an unhappy pastor is dangerous and a disaster to the Church of God! May our Saints intercede for all our pastors and their families, & bless their apostolate!

There are no secure solutions to ministerial burnout, but as the Greek saying goes, "The bow that is always kept bent will lose its power." A variant of the saying goes, "The bow that is always kept bent will break."Staying in a stressful situation makes ministers ineffective; however, much rhinoceros skin and resilience they may develop. The worst thing of all is for the minister to seek therapy through such wrong things as alcohol to mask the feelings of hurt, smoking, or even sex fantasy like pornography or entertaining wrong dalliances or relationships. Some of these could lead to the minister being disciplined and bowing out in disgrace. The number one antidote to burn - out that I have found in ministry is striking the right balance between work and personal time.

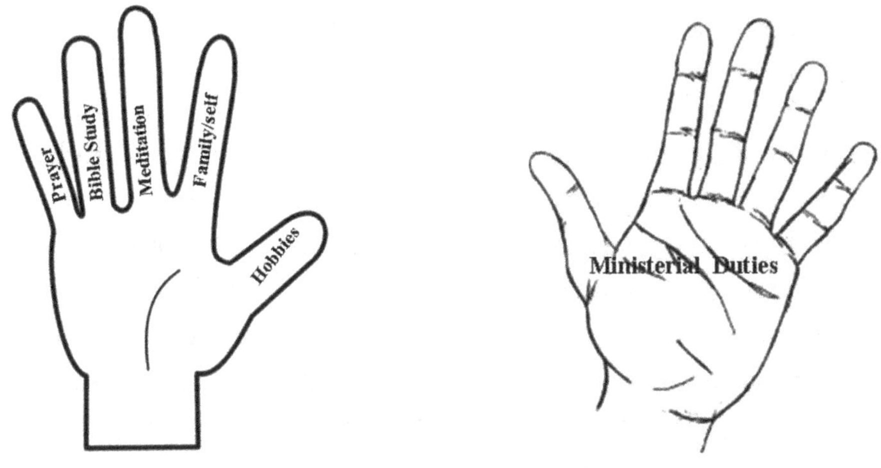

"You must make time to come apart before you fall apart." (Paul Chappell)

ACTIVE HAND = Personal time (items 1-5) SECOND HAND = Ministry/Pastoral duties

1. Prayer
2. Bible Study
3. Meditation
4. Family/self
5. Hobbies

Let me illustrate with our two hands, if you are left or right-handed, imagine your most active hand to be your time for self. You must make yourself a priority because once you are not well yourself, you are of no use to anybody, including yourself. Jesus said, "love your neighbor as you love yourself."[233]Hold onto your active hand these five things: On the smallest finger hold on to Daily Prayer life. On the second finger, Daily Bible reading. On the middle finger meditation, on the pointing finger time with family, spouse, or self if you are single and on your thumb hold onto recreational hobbies like sport, reading good books, listening to music, watching relaxing videos, or going to the movies. On your second handhold on to whatever your vocation or work throws at you or requires of you. Whatever happens, however busy you are at work, pledge never to drop any of the five vital things or disciplines on your active hand. Some spiritual aspects of your self-care overlap with your ministerial duties; if so, that is a bonus; the tragedy is neglecting any of the five disciplines on your active hand. Anyone who could manage to keep this balance would keep burn - out at the bay. Jesus, our prime example in life, kept prayer life and intimacy with God by keeping regular quiet time with God paramount in his earthly ministry. He consequently founded the most significant enterprise on planet earth, the church, and he also ended his earthly ministry in ultimate triumph and victory. Recreation was paramount to Jesus during His earthly ministry. Jesus told his disciples, "come apart and rest a while"[234] when the pressures of ministry intensified. What Jesus said in effect was, *come apart and rest or you will fall apart* (emphasis mine), and this is an antidote to vocational burnout The Bible does not give us a portrait of Jesus' recreational life, but we can glean some snippets that indicate he had some social and recreational lifestyle. The scriptures present Jesus in John, chapter two, attending a wedding. Also, as one who socialized, Luke 7:34 (NLT), "The Son of Man, on the other hand, feasts, and drinks, and you say, 'He's a glutton and a drunkard, and a friend of tax collectors and other sinners!" In terms of physical exercise, it is illustrated in the international joke which tells the story of a boy who wanted a car for his sixteenth birthday. The father made a bargain with the boy that the boy should improve his grades in school, read his Bible, start attending church, and cut his long shaggy hair. As the sixteenth birthday approached, the boy went to his dad presented his grades; which had all improved to A's, his dad also observed that the boy had been reading his Bible and attending church.

The boy, however, had not cut his long hair, and when his dad pointed that out, the boy replied, "but dad Jesus had long hair!" to which his dad replied, "yeah, and Jesus walked everywhere he went." We may chuckle at this story, but it is right in Jesus' time walking was the most available means of transport that must have kept Jesus physically fit and healthy. Time spent recharging one's battery and doing physical exercise is not time wasted, but time invested in making one more effective and efficient. Physical training is commendable in scriptures in 1Timthy 4:18. It is a fact that we achieve more when we are rested and refreshed than if we plod on when we are exhausted. Jesus' call to his ministry is to a life of rest. William Barclay translated Matthew 11:28-30 as follows: "Come to me all you who are exhausted...come to me all you who are weighed down by your heavy burdens, and I will give you rest. Take my yoke...exchange your pressure for my peace." If ministers live balanced lives, holding on their vocational work appointments on the one hand and balancing it on the other hand with their concern for self and family, they will keep burnout at bay and enjoy the ministry of peace and rest that Jesus has called them.

Chapter 4 Notes

208 John 1:46
209 John 1:39
210 Usually by referring to Romans 1:18-32
211 John 1:11-12
212 Leviticus 28:1-3
213 Numbers 18:8-14
214 Deuteronomy 17:8-13
215 Deuteronomy 33:10
216 Numbers 27:21; 1 Chronicles 6:49 and Leviticus 24:9
217 Hebrews 9:7
218 Leviticus 21
219 Abihu and Nadab (Leviticus 21) and sons of Eli (Leviticus 10:1-2)
220 Hebrews 7:11
221 This pattern finds precedence in the OT in the Call of young Samuel and the confirmation by the priest Eli and in the New Testament, the setting apart of Barnabas and Paul for their ministry of teaching and evangelism in Acts 13:1-2
222 1Samuel chapter 3
223 Acts 13:1-2
224 I was trained and certified as a counsellor by Relate UK, in York England and worked for the organization from 1998-2010 when I took long leave of absence due to commitment as Superintendent Minister.
225 Hebrews 4:13 see also Hebrews 13:18
226 *World Council of Churches, Ecumenical Theological Education Conference,* Oslo, 1996 See also J S Pobee, & World Council of Churches. *Towards Viable Theological Education: Ecumenical Imperative, Catalyst of Renewal.* (Geneva: WCC Publication.1997)
227 "Pastors." Accessed May 17, 2018. https://www.christianitytoday.com/pastors/1980/fall/80l4057.html
228 Statistics in the ministry", Accessed May 17, 2018. http://www.pastoralcareinc.com/statistics/
229 https://www.soulshepherding.org/2009/11/pastors-under-stress/
230 http://www.livingleadership.org/pastoral/ministerial-meltdown-and-burnout.html
231 1 Corinthians 6:19
232 Social media SMS forwarded to me by Dr Johhanes Makau, 24 May 2018
233 Mark 12:31
234 Mark 6:31

Five Chapter

Pillars necessary for personal and ministerial formation.

Introduction

It is a known fact that strong pillars support every magnificent architectural building. Today tourists travel to Athens, Corinth, Greece, Palestine, or Rome to see columns that supported vast famous amphitheaters, coliseums, and temples. The scripture in 1Corinthians 6:19-20 says that the bodies of Christians are the temple of the Holy Spirit. This spiritual temple also needs strong pillars to support it to grow into Christlikeness.

There is a massive amount of literature on spiritual formation. In this chapter, I am going to appraise seven disciplines that I perceive as seven vital pillars or tenets that are necessary and should be a minimum for any Christian who wants to develop the character of Christ. Spiritual and ministerial formation are closely linked like the helix of DNA. What the minister is in his or her private life affects and determines their behavior and ministry. The individual Christian wishing to grow into Christlikeness and the minister wishing to emulate Christ's ministry must heed the words of Jesus John 15:5 (NIV), "I am the vine you are the branches, apart from me you can do nothing." When Jesus said,

"I am the vine, you are the branches,"; He was referring to that vital relationship between the followers of Jesus and God that is necessary for the disciples to be fruitful both in their Christian lives and in Christian Ministry. Jesus emphasized it in saying that apart from him, his followers could accomplish nothing. What this teaching means in broader terms is that certain practices can help us attend to the work of grace in our lives and in our times. These practices are often called spiritual disciplines. What are the nature of the disciplines and their place in spiritual growth? In this book, we have come to refer to these as "pillars," disciplines and practices that help us consciously develop the spiritual dimension of our lives. A person of faith freely chooses to adopt individual lifestyles, habits, and commitments to grow spiritually. There is nothing externally imposed about spiritual disciplines. In adopting them, one recognizes that one's innate spiritual aptitude cannot develop fully without practice or exercise. People choose spiritual disciplines only if they have a strong desire to grow. If one's desire to develop spiritually is not deep enough to overcome one's resistance, one will find oneself unable to maintain any discipline; however, good one's intentions are. It may help to understand that spiritual disciplines are not ends in themselves. Instead, they are simply means of grace. They are how we put ourselves to the place where God can bless us. Disciplines like prayer, spiritual reflection, and hospitality have the character of garden tools. They keep the soil of our love for God clear of obstruction. They keep us open to the mysterious work of grace in our hearts and our world. They enable us not only to receive but to respond to God's love, which in turn yields the fruits of the spirit in our lives. Every spiritual discipline tutors us in our relationship with God and affects our relationship with other people.

Spiritual disciplines, like all good things, can be pursued for the wrong reasons. If the motives are distorted, the practice will not yield the desired results. Discipline helps us live our Christian lives with a bright and joyful purpose to know and glorify God in our lives. It would be convenient if we could practice the presence of God in all of life, without expending energy on particular exercises. But the capacity to remember and abide in God's presence comes only through regular training. If we wish to experience the love of Christ "in the flesh" in our daily existence, we will eventually need some intentional practices of spiritual disciplines that strengthen our faith like pillars to support a building structure or food vitamins to support our bodies. These pillars are Scripture, Prayer, Fasting, Meditation, Journaling, Mentoring, and learning to apply means of Grace.

Scriptures

The use of scripture is a sine qua non for any person wanting to develop in their spiritual formation and ministerial development. Trying to lead a Christian life without a disciplined dependence on scripture is like trying to navigate through a foreign place, country, town, or city without a map or modern SatNav (Satellite Navigation). It is like trying to operate a modern gadget without the user's manual. It may sound naïve to compare our lives with a modern gadget, but the complexities of life could justifiably be compared to it and in particular, knowing how to operate it. It is easy to feel that we are in control of our lives, but the constant dilemmas that we face too often prove us wrong, calling for the need for a guidance manual. Scriptures are God's guidance manual. Indeed they are His Love Letter telling His children how to navigate through life and enjoy it. Unlike other religions,

Christianity is not burdensome; Jesus calls His followers to a life of rest, Matthew 11:28-30 (NIRV), "Come to me, all of you who are tired and carrying heavy loads. I will give you rest. Become my servants and learn from me. I am gentle and free of pride. You will find rest for your souls. Serving me is easy, and my load is light." Matthew 11:28-30, (LBT) "Come to me and I will give you rest – all of you who work so hard beneath a heavy yoke. Wear my yoke for it fits perfectly – and let me teach you, for I am gentle and humble, and you shall find rest for your souls, for I give you only light burdens." Matthew 11:28-30, (MSG) bluntly, "Are you tired? Worn out? Burned out on religion? Come to me. Getaway with me, and you'll recover your life. I'll show you how to take a real rest. Walk with me and work with me – watch how I do it. Learn the unforced rhythms of grace. I won't lay anything heavy or ill-fitting on you. Keep company with me, and you'll learn to live freely and lightly.[235] From these four modern translations of Matthew 11:28-30, we deduce that Christianity, compared to other religions, is easier and less burdensome. It is refreshing; working with Jesus and in tandem with His Spirit, is compared in the original Greek language with a young ox yoked together with an experienced ox, plowing together, being trained on the job as it made it easier. Christian discipleship entails keeping company with Jesus and learning from Him, learning from scripture how He led His life on earth and allowing His Holy Spirit to dwell within us for ongoing instructions, guidance, and comfort. When viewed from this vantage point, scripture takes a completely new meaning. Scriptures take new meaning from being burdensome religious laws, rules, and regulations to the dulcet tones of SatNav telling us which route to take and which route to avoid for an easy drive to our destination, the heavenly Jerusalem. From these verses, it suggests that Jesus is making comparisons with other religions portrayed as burdensome in their imposition of rules and regulations as humans strive to meet God's standards. Christian discipleship, however, guided by scriptures becomes one of delight, joy, and rest. It becomes a journey marshaled and mastered by grace. Jesus declared, John 10:10 (MSG), "I came so they (His followers) can have real and eternal life, more and better life than they ever dreamed of." When understood in this sense. Christian scholars perceive Christianity as a relationship rather than a religion. In his book, *Life with God: Reading the Bible for spiritual transformation,* Richard Foster makes the point that too often our study of the Bible focuses on searching for specific information or some formula that will solve our pressing needs of the moment. He suggests that if we approached the Bible differently, and instead of transforming the text to meet our needs, allowed it to transform us, it will turn our reading of the Bible into a spiritually transforming experience.[236] Kenneth Boa puts it this way, "the study of Scripture is the primary vehicle for laying hold of a divine perspective on the world and our purpose in it. This discipline is pivotal to our spiritual nourishment and growth. Consistent study of the Word cultivates eternal values and priorities, provides guidance for decision making, assists us in overcoming temptation, and enhances our knowledge of God and ourselves."[237] There is the famous saying by Thomas Dewar: "Minds are like parachutes - they only function when open."[238] Using that imagery, I would suggest that a closed Bible is of no use; the Bible works best when it is opened and read. We need open minds and hearts that are honest to gain new insights and ready to change our thinking once challenged by scripture. We need to approach scripture with a positive attitude of reverence and receptivity willing to apply and obey what we learn from it. We need an attitude that perceives the Bible not simply as a textbook but an oracle to be obeyed.[239] Transformative Bible study needs to adopt the 4A principle: Ask-Answer-Accumulate and Apply. Boa sums it up thus, "Ask key questions that when answered, will provide insight into the meaning of the passage. Use the text (immediate and broad context) as well as standard tools (a concordance, Bible dictionary, or encyclopedia or a Bible dictionary) to answer your questions. Accumulate practical principles such as promises to claim, commands to obey, or sins to confess. Apply these principles to your life and relationships."[240]

There are three major approaches to the reading of scripture. Firstly, reading for information an effort to master the text and the content. Secondly, reading for transformation and letting the text master the reader. Thirdly, there is developmental reading as devotional reading for spiritual growth whose goal is to permit the image of Christ to be formed in us through study and meditation of Holy Scriptures. These three approaches are so intricately intertwined that it is hard purely to engage in one without the other. Tremper Longman has suggested the following as the major distinctions of the two main approaches, informational and transformational.[241]

There are several ways of reading the Bible.

Firstly, reading to find out the information:

1. Looking for the biblical author's intended meaning. The meaning of the text doesn't change, and this should be determined before one starts making applications to one's own life.
2. Reading the Bible passage in context. Is the text you are studying a transition, introduction, summary, or is it the second point of three that the author is taking on a broader theme?

3. Identifying the type of passage you are reading. Philippians 2:6-11 is a hymn. Micah 3:9-12 is a doomsaying. The type of literature makes a difference.
4. Considering the historical and cultural setting.
5. Studying the grammar and structure within the passage. Remember the axiom "if you run into a, therefore, see what it is there.
6. Interpreting experience in the light of Scripture, not Scripture in the light of experience. Otherwise, you are likely to be reading your ideas into the Bible.
7. Always seek the full counsel of Scripture. If a passage you are considering seems obscure or unclear, check out what the rest of the Bible has to say on this theme. Bible concordances, dictionaries, and commentaries are helpful in this and many other ways. Objective as it is, however, the Bible is not a "paper pope" from which we can extract infallible judgments every time we need to win an argument or a doctrinal debate. Early Protestants, who had just excommunicated the real pope, were tempted to make of the Bible, a paper pope with which to hit each other over the head. Such an approach amount to trivializing the divine revelation. Informational reading is linear and tends to lead the reader to cover as much material as possible, sometimes driven by such efforts as reading the Bible in One-year schemes. It also seems to adopt a problem-solving approach that risks being judgmental and analytical.[242]

Secondly, Transformational reading for Spiritual formation: Formative Bible study, embraces **both informational and transformational** concerns and practices. Formational reading is reading in-depth to capture the dynamic of the message. Speed is not nearly as important as openness to the mystery of God in the Word. The approach is humble, detached, willing, and loving. It is a relational rather than a functional approach. As in transformational reading, the reader invites the text to master him/her rather than trying to grasp the text, win a debate, or get a sermon. The informational and formational aspects work to keep us from imbalance. The devotional life is subjective by nature. In reading scripture today, we need to be aware of the influence, and the grip of relative morality that could be put as "the truth for you is not the truth for me." Also, we need to be aware of societal, cultural intoxication with the individualism that says that truth is different for each of us, and you have a lot of private and improper interpretation of Scripture. Bible study that begins with me and my felt needs is not legitimate. We must first establish what the text says and what it means in its original context (Sitz im Leben) to apply correctly it to us today. The meaning does not change just because we have a new temptation, our child has rebelled, or we lost our job. First, we need to get the meaning of the passage. How it applies to us will change as we do.[243] Correct use of scripture demands that we are not free to make the Bible say whatever we need to hear. Though our felt needs are urgent—and the Bible does often speak to them—the Bible does not exist primarily to help you feel better, reduce stress, and find joy, peace, or self-actualization. The Bible is the revelation of God in Christ, and the Gospel Jesus came to demonstrate. To reduce Bible study to self-motivation, mental hygiene, or psychological "up-cheering" is to trivialize both the Bible and the spiritual life.

Formative Bible Study involves the following:-

> **Step 1. Observation**: Notice every word. Use the shifting emphasis method. Notice what happens as you emphasize different words as you read it aloud.

Step 2. Interpretation: What does the Bible text mean? What does the context contribute to the meaning? Step into the shoes of the Bible characters in the text and view the issues from their point of view.

Step 3. Correlation: What have others said about this text? Compare what you have gotten out of the passage with the interpretation of others. Check your study Bible or a concordance to see what other Bible passages speak to this same issue. Check a reputable Bible commentary.

Step 4. Evaluation: Ask questions like these: "What part of this passage is particularly valuable to me right now? Why am I glad I read this passage today?

Step 5. Application: "Lord, what do you want me to do with what I have read?" Ask the Text Questions an old and simple favorite is to ask questions of the passage you are studying only. Here are some often used ones:-

i. What does this passage tell me about God?
ii. What does this passage tell me about Jesus Christ?
iii. What does this passage tell me about the Holy Spirit?
iv. Is there a sin to avoid?
v. Is there a command to be obeyed?
vi. Is there a prayer to make m own?
vii. Is there a promise to claim?
viii. What does this passage teach me about myself?
ix. What does the passage say about Christsian service?
x. Is there something here I should memorize?
xi. Is there something here I should share?
xii. Is there an example to follow or avoid?[244]

In trying to clarify the text, there is also what is known as **Stepping into the Scene Method.** The "Step into the Scene" methodology is ancient. It got into the Wesleyan heritage through Richard Baxter and his 17th-century book *The Saint's Everlasting Rest.* John Wesley reprinted this book in the 18th century. It is not some New Age concept—it has been in the Christian tradition a long time.[245] A typical example of this method is in Luke 12:13-21.

For example, trying to visualize the scene in one's mind as follows**:** Imagine that it is early in the day, and Jesus has called His disciples together for a staff meeting. It is going to be a long day. Already Jesus' fame has spread, and a vast crowd is spreading out before them in a valley. But before the preaching, teaching, and miracles are to begin, Jesus called the staff meeting. Try to visualize that they are on the crest of the hill partially hidden by cedars and boulders. It is still fresh where the shaded staff meeting is taking place. Jesus is lecturing to His dozen disciples about: the *hypocrisy* of the Pharisees (vv. 12:1-2), *comforting* them with God's providence (vv. 12:4-7) and encouraging them about *faithful witnessing* for Christ (vv. 12:8-12).

Imagine a self-absorbed joker who demands that Jesus settle a financial fight then interrupts this staff meeting. By the time Jesus gets around to answering, the crowd has surged forward. The staff meeting is over for now, and Jesus addresses the crowd. Reread verses 13-21 in light of this scene-setting. The following nine steps explain how it works in real life. You read the passage first and then go through these steps:-

1. Imagine the Bible scene before you.
2. What are the temperature, the weather, and the time of day? What sounds do you hear? What is the scenery like? What smells are present? What animals are there?

3. Then step into the scene yourself. Try to imagine and identify the person standing on your left and your right.
4. How is the person next to you dressed? How is Jesus dressed? How are the disciples dressed?
5. Listen to the dialogue, the parable, try and catch every word. Do not miss anything.
6. Notice the characters in the story: The Multitude; The Disciples
7. The Questioner: The Rich Fool, Jesus and God
8. With what character did you identify most? Which did you resist most?
9. What did you perceive Jesus' mood and attitude to be?
10. Did you get any new insights into the meaning of this Bible passage? Jot down your feelings, insights, and ideas.

Then try to step out of the scene and then write a letter about the incidence. You can always step back into it. But step out of the scene and think it over. Then write a letter (or e-mail message) to one of the characters. Tell the person whatever is on your heart. Write only three or four paragraphs.

Here is a sample letter to a person who interrupted Jesus with a financial problem. Let us call the person, "Mike." Dear Mike, Count on you to mess up. Did you ever miss the point? You have not one clue as to what the gospel is about, not an inkling of what the Carpenter has been teaching all along—that it is better to make a life than to make a living. He showed you how trivial your "problem" really was. As kind and tender as Jesus is, He would not give your problem the time of day. Now, if you had been confessing your sins, you would have had His undivided attention, but no, you wanted to grab an inheritance. Talk about selfish.

Moreover, speaking of sins, I imagine that you have plenty of them. You strike me as the sort of person who runs a pawnshop and charges widows and homeless people 200 percent interest, is that not right? Do you read the Wall Street Journal more than the Bible, do you? You did achieve one thing. You became famous. Centuries of Christians now know you as the dunce who interrupted Jesus with a question so selfish that it provoked the parable of the rich fool. Could you see yourself in that parable? Probably not, but I sure did. I saw you, and you looked a lot like me."

Sincerely yours,

Prayer

> *"Minutes invested in Prayer will give you a greater return than hours spent in ceaseless activity."*[246]

Prayer to a Christian is as vital as air to a living person, and just as air provides life and vitality to the physical body, prayer does similarly to the spiritual life. Mike DeVries observes that "just as breathing is pretty essential to our physical well-being, so is a prayer to our soul."[247] In the analogy of prayer as breathing, the Christian exhales bad emotions of anxiety, anger, brokenness, disappointment, doubt, fear, frustration and sorrow and inhales from God words of affirmation as a child of God, assurance, faith, hope, joy and peace found in the scriptures. In this sense, a life of prayer and meditation on scripture go together. There is a galore of quotations on prayer. For this book and in relation to spiritual formation, we have identified the following seven: God's command to "pray without ceasing" is founded on the necessity we have of His grace to preserve the life of God in the soul, which can no more subsist one moment without it than the body can without air. *(John Wesley).*

"A prayer-less soul is a Christ-less soul. Prayer is lisping of the believing infant, the shout of the fighting believer, the requiem of the dying saint falling asleep in Jesus. It is the breath, the watchword, the comfort, the strength, the honor of a Christian. *(Charles H. Spurgeon).*

"You may as soon find a living man that does not breathe, as a living Christian that does not pray." *(Matthew Henry).*

"Prayer does not change God, but it changes him who prays." *Soren Kierkegaard*

"Prayer makes a godly man and puts within him the mind of Christ, the mind of humility, of self-surrender, of service, of pity, and prayer. If we pray, we will become more like God, or else we will quit praying." *(E.M.Bounds)*

If we want to see mighty wonders of divine power and grace wrought in the place of weakness, failure, and disappointment, let us answer God's standing challenge, "Call unto me, and I will answer, thee, and show thee great and mighty things which thou knowest not." *(J. Hudson Taylor)*

"No learning can make up for the failure to pray. No earnestness, no diligence, no study, no gifts will supply its lack." *(E. M. Bounds).*

Someone said a life of prayer takes us *inward* to the *transformation* we need. Prayer changes the person who prays. If one is not prepared to change and be changed, one should not attempt to pray. Otherwise, it makes prayer a meaningless "form of godliness" or something we do not have time for. "When prayer is overlooked or appended as an afterthought to service, the power of God is often absent. It is dangerously easy to move away from dependence upon God and to slip into the trap of self-reliance. Christian service is most effective when prayer not only precedes it but also flows together with it."[248] "Prayer is God's delight because it shows the reaches of our poverty and the riches of His grace."[249]A life of prayer moves the Christian upward into intimacy and friendship with God. As one lingers daily with God in adoration, rest in Him, and listens to Him, one moves from thinking and feeling that God is a part of one's life to the realization that the Christian is a small part of his life. "A life of prayer moves us outward into the ministry and service we need. Interceding takes our minds off ourselves as we make of our hearts an arena in which God and the prayed-for ones can meet. A life of prayer develops the practice of faith that we need as we learn that God can be trusted. After Calvary, God has a right to be trusted. And that includes all the requests and petitions that we bring so anxiously to Him."[250]

John Wesley, like the Apostle Paul, has two phases to his life. First, as an Anglican clergyman who tried to serve God in the power of the flesh following religious ritual, even attempting to be a missionary in the USA. After his abysmal failure, he had the "warmed heart experience," his conversion that ushered the second phase to his life, serving God in the power of the Spirit guided by scripture. This change brought John Wesley an intensity in his prayer life that characterized his ministry ever since. In his prayer life, he used a series of questions prayerfully each day to let the Holy Spirit sort him out with God. John Wesley always repented whatever the Holy Spirit pointed out to him and regularly asked God to fill him afresh with His Holy Spirit. His prayer life went through the following questions:

Am I consciously or unconsciously creating the impression that I am a better man than I am, in other words, am I a hypocrite?

Am I honest in all my acts or words, or do I exaggerate?

Do I confidentially pass on to another what I was told in confidence?

Can I be trusted?

Am I a slave to dress, friends, work, or habits?

Am I self-conscious, self-pitying, or self-justifying?

Did the Bible come alive to me today?

Do I give it time to speak to me every day?

Am I enjoying prayer?

When did I last speak to somebody else to trying to win that person for Christ?

Am I making contact with other people and using them for the Master's glory?

Do I pray about the money I spend?

Do I get to bed in time and get up on time?

Do I disobey God in anything?

Do I insist upon doing something about which my conscience is uneasy?

Am I defeated in any part of my life, jealous, impure, critical, irritable, touchy, or distrustful?

How do I spend my spare time?

Am I proud?

Do I thank God that I am not as other people, for example, the Pharisee who despised the publican?

Is there anybody whom I fear, dislike, disown, criticize, hold resentment toward, or disregard? If so, what am I doing about it?

Do I grumble or complain about always?

Is Christ real to me?

These are intense heart-searching questions, and anyone going through them in prayer will, without a doubt, find himself or herself transformed from one degree of glory to another. When we pray we need to:-

a. **Be purposeful and ask what the motivation of prayer is?** As someone once said, our prayers must mean something to us if they are to mean anything to God. The ultimate test for any invocation of the petition is whether we can say directly to Jesus, "Give me this for your sake and the glory of your name."
b. **Be specific and ready for an answer.** Note the specificity from the prayer in 1Sam chaps. 1:12-30 "if you give me a child, I shall give him unto you" 1:11; 27,28 & 2:11

c. **Record or journal our prayers,** otherwise how will we know when the Lord has answered them? Journal what we are praying for if we cannot remember what we asked God for, why should He?
d. God answers prayers in three ways (YES, NO, WAIT): *i.* **Yes,** I thought you would never ask. Or **Yes,** and here is more. ii. **Not yet**. *iii.* **No,** I love you too much. No, but my grace is sufficient. "Getting all you want would bring incalculable damage and grief to you.
e. Be thankful for unanswered prayer. It may be a sign of God's favor"[251] *"Delayed answer is not denied."*

Why should we pray? My shortest answer to this question is simply this: We pray for IT: Intimacy and Transformation. There are many books on prayer, and also many reasons why we should pray. There are also many memorable quotes on prayer, two of the most famous are by Archbishop William Temple when he said, "When I pray coincidences to happen; when I don't, they don't." The context of this statement was when leaders of the Clapham Sect of British social reformers such as William Wilberforce, daily gave themselves to three hours of prayer and organized Christians throughout the country to unite in special prayer before critical debates in Parliament. Cynics and religious skeptics jeered at William Temple regarding prayer. It is then that he replied to his critics who regarded answered prayer as no more than coincidence, "When I pray, coincidences happen; when I don't, they don't." [252]The second is by the Philosopher Søren Kierkegaard: "Prayer does not change God, but it changes him who prays."[253] Kenneth Boa gives ten reasons why we should pray. (Fellowship with God, It is a command, follow the example of Christ, for power, for help, for change, understanding, and knowledge; for joy and peace, to accomplish God's purposes and for change of our attitudes and desires.)[254]For our purpose in this book, I would condense these into only two with the mnemonic **IT** standing for **Intimacy** and **Transformation**. As noted in the earlier chapters, the spiritual formation has to do with the continuous process of change into the image of Christ. Prayer helps us accomplish this by developing intimacy with God and allowing Him to transform us.

INTIMACY

In the New Testament, the word, Abba appears three times. It is Aramaic that translates Abba Father, Jesus at Gethsemane used it[255] and is also found in the Pauline corpus[256] in each case addresses God in a relation of personal intimacy. In today's English, its dynamic equivalent would be "daddy." Ultimately, prayer develops our intimacy with God by enhancing our fellowship with Him[257]as we follow the example of our brother Jesus Christ and other biblical characters[258]that developed intimacy with God through prayer, and consequently, it is a biblical injunction.[259] This intimacy ensues because of our more in-depth understanding and knowledge of God that develops through prayer.[260] This intimacy is further enhanced in the joy and peace of answered prayer or patience and peace through unanswered prayer that give us new perspectives of our petitions and circumstances[261]and also our attitudes and desires as we learn to pray in accordance with God's will.[262]There are many commentaries and expositions on the Lord's Transfiguration (Matthew 17:1-8; Mark 9:2-8); Matthew 9:28-36); and they all emphasize different lessons, but the experience that I find most appealing in the transfiguration is that of intimacy and the words "this is my beloved son, listen to him."

TRANSFORMATION

It may sound trite but true that prayer is powerful; it makes those who pray to experience God's power and transforms those who pray.[263] Prayer changes our understanding of God's purpose in our lives and leads us to say, "Not my will, but His will be done."[264]It also helps us transform our petitions in prayer into worship, emulating the Lord's Prayer, where the emphasis is more on worship than a petition. Prayer changes us to see God's will in heaven and on earth as paramount. The transfiguration of Jesus recorded in the gospels makes this point poignantly. The three synoptic gospels[265] record the story to underscore its importance. Luke's account makes this point brilliantly: "As he (Jesus) was praying, the appearance of his face changed, and his clothes became as bright as a flash of lightning."[266] The modern translation puts it thus: "While he was in prayer, the appearance of his face changed, and his clothes became blindingly white."[267] There is a saying that prayer changes things; it is also true that prayer changes the one who prays. There is a modern analogy in photography whereby the clarity of the image is defined by the exposure of the "shutter speed" on a camera to the image in that how fast it opens and closes, and how much light is let in defines the clarity of the picture taken. The longer the exposure, the more detailed the image will be on the photographic film or sensor.

Similarly, the more we expose ourselves in prayer in the presence of God, the more our character is transformed into the image of Christ. The longer we fix our eyes at Him, the more the 'image' of Jesus is formed in us. For those who want spiritual formation in their lives, a life of prayer is imperative. The transformative power of prayer is illustrated in the rise of the Holiness Movement in the early Wesleyan Methodism. Recently Brian Hoare, former British Methodist president, composed the hymn *"Born in song God's people have always been singing,"*[268] possibly referring to Methodist people who are renowned for their singing and the Wesley hymns. In reality, Methodism was born in prayer. Although the founding of Wesleyan Methodism is credited to John Wesley, it is his brother Charles Wesley who started the movement when his brother John was away.

Along with two fellow students, Charles formed a small club for the study and the pursuit of a devout Christian life. On John Wesley's return, he became the leader of the group. The group met daily from six until nine for prayer, psalms, and reading of the Greek New Testament. They prayed and fasted on Wednesdays and Fridays until three o'clock. In 1730, as a result of their prayer life, the group began the practice of visiting prisoners in jail and caring for the sick. Spirituality was at a low ebb in Oxford at that time, and the Weasleys' group provoked an adverse reaction. They were referred to as "religious enthusiasts," which in the context of the time meant religious fanatics. They were nicknamed the "Holy Club," as a matter of ridicule. Opposition increased when a member of the club, William Morgan, died, and his death was attributed to their life of rigorous fasting in prayer. In response, Wesley explained that Morgan had stopped fasting eighteen months before he died. It is in that letter, which was widely circulated that Wesley referred to the name "Methodist," stating that "some of our neighbors are pleased to compliment us." The name "Methodist" was used by an anonymous author in a published pamphlet (1733) describing Wesley and his group, "The Oxford Methodists." In response to the question of how he drew a crowd, John Wesley replied: "I set myself on fire in prayer, and people come out to watch me burn." It is safe to conclude that a life of prayer inevitably transforms into a life of self-sacrificial service. Prayer life is the powerhouse in a life of witness for Christ. Prayer makes things happen as William Temple (1881-1944), Archbishop of Canterbury (1942-44), who has been described as the spiritual father of the Welfare State once observed, "When I pray, coincidences happen, when I don't, they don't."[269] This popular quote has been turned into numerous plaques and is a popular quotation in encouraging prayer life.

Fasting

Fasting as a concept has two significant usages, as a political tool to make a political statement and as a religious tool for spiritual benefit. Fasting can also be imposed for medical reasons before a major operation. Fasting as a discipline for spiritual formation is different from fasting to make a political statement or protest. It is also different from a hunger strike used as a method of non – violent resistance like that of Mahatma Gandhi, which led to a significant impact on the British and the Indian political establishments. It remains the most effective and most renowned fasting for political reasons. Fasting as a religious discipline is practiced in most faiths in world religions. The Bahai observe fasting in March. The Buddhists fast during their spiritual retreats. In Hinduism, fasting forms an integral part of their religious practice. In Islam, fasting is mandatory in the month of Ramadan. In Christianity, most denominations observe fasting during the season of Lent, leading to Easter. For the Eastern, Orthodox fasting is taken seriously and can occupy large portions in a calendar year. The Roman Catholic and Anglican churches have the strong traditional discipline of fasting during Lent that starts on Shrove Tuesday and Ash Wednesday. In Methodism, John Wesley stipulated that,

> "It is expected of all who desire to continue in these societies that they should continue to evidence their desire of salvation by attending upon all of God, such are: the public worship of God; the ministry of the Word, either read or expounded; the supper of the Lord; family and private prayer; searching the scriptures and fasting or abstinence."[270]

Also, in the directions given to band societies on 25th December 1744 mandated fasting on all Fridays of the year.[271]John Wesley himself fasted before receiving Holy Communion to focus his attention on God and asked other Methodist Christians to do the same.[272]As the Methodist church developed worldwide, various strands develope, but they all seem to be united by the desire to observe fasting during Lent. The discipline of the Wesleyan Methodist church requires Methodists to fast on the first Friday after New Year's Day and after Michaelmas day. The United Methodist Church of America states that: "There is a strong Biblical base for fasting during the forty days of Lent leading to the celebration of Easter. Jesus, as part of his spiritual preparation, went into the wilderness and fasted forty days and forty nights according to the gospels."[273] In the Gospels, Jesus talked about the discipline of fasting in his Sermon on the Mount.[274] He delivered the teaching in the context of "how to pray," implying that it is part of praying. In fasting, one goes an octave higher in prayer in pursuit of God's guidance and wisdom. It is advisable to use fasting when there are particular difficulties in seeking wisdom and God's breakthrough. "Jesus not only endorses fasting but stresses it is to be done in secret...we do this to get the leadership of the Holy Spirit, ...the purpose is to get God's attention; fasting is undoubtedly a way of showing your desperation."[275] When Jesus gave instructions in the Bible regarding fasting, he assumed that his disciples fasted hence the words "when you fast," not if you fast. Jesus' disciples were Jews, and in Judaism, fasting meant complete abstinence from food and drink, including water for six days of the year. Yom Kippur – the Day of Atonement in Judaism is the holiest day, and fasting is expected of every man or woman above the age of puberty (bar mitzvah and bat mitzvah), as legislated in the Torah."[276] In the early church, fasting was an established practice, "while they were worshipping the Lord and fasting, Holy Spirit said, "set apart for me Barnabas and Saul…so after they had fasted and prayed, they placed their hands on them and sent them off ." [277] In appointing elders, Paul and Barnabas prayed and fasted.[278] In the Old Testament, Moses fasted for forty days.[279] On the Day of Atonement, fasting was mandatory.[280] Although fasting was a well-established discipline in Judaism, by the time Jesus taught about fasting, it had become a platform for ostentatious piety [281] for which Jesus' teaching was corrective measure. In spiritual formation, there will come times when one feels like they are at crossroads in discernment, by fasting one goes that one octave higher seeking clarification of God's will. Principally there are five reasons for fasting:-

i. Fasting for *food* for the body to provide a feast for the soul
ii. Fasting for *indulgence* in favor of chastity discipline of sexual urges
iii. Fasting for the *social company* to make room for solitude.
iv. Fasting for *noise* and entertainments in order to make time for silence.
v. Fasting for *acquisitiveness* in order to live in frugality or Christian simplicity.

According to Kenneth Boa, "The practice of fasting is abstention from physical nourishment for the purpose of spiritual sustenance."[282]Adele Ahlberg Calhoun cautions against using fasting to manipulate God. She says, "Fasting is not a magical way to manipulate God into doing our will; it's not a way to get God to be an accomplice to our plans. Neither is fasting a spiritual way to lose weight or control others. Fasting clears us out and opens us up to intentionally seeking God's will and grace in a way that goes beyond normal habits of worship and prayer. While fasting, we are one on one with God, offering him the time and attentiveness."[283]For any Christian wanting to deepen their spiritual formation and ministry, fasting is one of the disciplines that have to be embraced and practiced. I hope that the little that I have said on fasting so far would whet your appetite to incorporate fasting as one the pillars of your spiritual formation. For those who may want to explore the subject of fasting further, there are resources available[284] to take you deeper into the matter.

Meditation, Solitude, and Lectio Divina.

Meditation, solitude, and Lectio-Divina belong together. They represent a time in spiritual formation when one withdraws oneself for a "one to one" or face to face with God. A time set apart to be in the presence of God ready to commune and hear from Him. This discipline is much more required in the digital age we live in, whereby we are always engaged by one form of gadget or another. Indoors we are always engaged by the TV, the computer or Play Station. Outdoors whether walking or jogging, we have our ears plugged into iPods or mobile phones. Our modern lives have been taken over by a cacophony of noise. Having a quiet time these days has become like a competition; it is now a matter of making the time for it. Otherwise, it does not occur. Naturally, it is as if the world of gadgetry has invaded our lives, especially in the last decade. I have watched it over my two sons, the eldest, Jonathan in his thirties, and the youngest Andrew in his twenties. Jonathan grew up in the age of reading stories. He knew *Thomas the Tank Engine* and *Postman Pat*, inside out as well as some Nursery Rhymes. He developed into an avid reader. Andrew grew up in a world of IT gadgets. I promised Andrew on his sixteenth birthday, a present of his choice. I recall him leading me to Argos Store in Oldham, Manchester where I almost fainted when he pointed at the iPod and when I asked how much it was expecting to be a few pounds, it was in hundreds of pounds, the most expensive toy I had ever bought for our children. To this day, Andrew could hardly sit down and read a book! For this matter, for a Christian who intends to have spiritual formation, meditation, solitude, and Lectio Divina are imperative. "In our society, we increasingly tend to be human doings rather than human beings."[285]The discipline of meditation provides a corrective measure.

Meditation

In his devotional material, Bob Gass tells the following story: "Butterflies cover more ground, but bees gather more honey. That's because the butterfly flies over the flowers, whereas the bee lands on each one and stays there long enough to extract the nectar. That's the difference between merely reading your Bible for a few hurried minutes, and taking time to meditate on what you're reading. Meditation isn't something difficult and mysterious that only scholars and 'spiritual' people do. It's just thinking profoundly and continuously about a passage of Scripture, memorizing it, letting it take root, and 'owning it' until it becomes a life force operating within you each day. The point isn't how much Scripture you memorize; it's what happens to you in the process. Meditating on God's Word clarifies your understanding and corrects your conduct. It enriches your thinking and equips you by making you think different thoughts than if you were watching TV, for example, or texting, or talking on your mobile phone, or shopping. The psalmist writes Psalm 1: 2-3 (CEV) 'The Law of the LORD makes them happy, and they think about it day and night. They are like trees growing beside a stream, trees that produce fruit in season, and always have leaves. Those people succeed in everything they do' Meditating on God's Word is the cure for moral and spiritual weakness; for a life with no focus; for lack of intimacy with God; for chronically weak faith that causes you to fail and keep missing God's best. So open your Bible, read it, and pray, 'Lord, what are you saying to me?' Then meditate on His answer."[286] Meditation is a vital discipline found in nearly all major religions. It involves both solitude and silence. It is observable in the life of Jesus Christ. At the start of His ministry, Jesus spent forty days alone in the wilderness, an event recorded in all the synoptic gospels to mark its importance.[287]Mark portrays Jesus' habit of starting the day in solitude and silence in prayer: "in the morning, long before sunrise, Jesus went to a place where he could be alone to pray."[288]In John's account of Jesus' feeding the five thousand, "Jesus realized that the people intended to take him by force and make him king. So he returned to the mountain by himself."[289] Matthew makes it explicit thus: "After sending the people away, he went up a mountain to pray by himself, when evening came, he was there alone."[290] Luke's account portrays the use of solitude as Jesus' habit: "He would go away to places where he could be alone for prayer."[291]Jesus spent time by himself in solitude meditation before significant events in his life. "In the solitude of the wilderness Jesus prepared to inaugurate his public ministry;[292] in the solitude of the mountain he prepared to select his disciples,[293] and in the solitude of the garden, he prepared to sacrifice his life for the sins of the world.[294]

> Silence is a catalyst of solitude; it prepares the way for inner seclusion and enables us to listen to the quiet voice of the Spirit….In solitude, we remove ourselves from the influence of our peers and society and find the solace of anonymity. In this cloister, we discover a place of strength, dependence, reflection, and renewal, and we confront inner patterns and forces that are alien to the life of Christ within us.[295]

Meditation has been described as a close relative of the disciplines of prayer and study, and it is thought to be dependent on the disciplines of solitude and silence,[296]and these two are couples that go together in a symbiotic relationship: "silence gives depth to solitude and solitude creates a place for silence."[297]Meditation is pivotal to human existence, "it is an integral component of Christian spirituality."[298]It directs the conscious mind during the day and is an excellent way to practice the presence of God."[299]The mind is continuously active and cannot switch off thoughts. Our actions, habits, character and eventual destiny start from thought as the adage goes: "Sow a thought, reap an act; Sow an act, reap a habit; Sow a habit, reap a character; Sow a character, reap a destiny."[300] Our conscious brain is such a powerful machine that we either instruct it on what to meditate on, or it will pick on an aspect in our lives to mull over. "It is impossible to think about nothing. The mind does not shut off; the issue is not whether we will think or even meditate; it is what we will think about and where we will direct our thoughts."[301]Meditation is frequent in other ancient religions like Buddhism, Hinduism, and even in the New Age Movement. The significant difference is that in these other religions, the emphasis is to empty the mind and our conscience. In Christianity, however, the attention is on focusing (meditating) on something valuable. The Bible exhorts Christians to meditate on the Word of God."[302]Failure to choose a topic for meditation leaves room for the brain to determine what is natural to our fallen nature, negative thoughts. It is natural to human instincts to focus on what we lack than what we have. We find it easier to make prayers of petition rather than prayers of thanksgiving. "Gossip and criticism are often more appealing in conversation about others than commendation and praise... The heart will make room for that upon which it dwells"[303]In her book *Battle of the Mind*, Joyce Meyer based on the verse "As a man thinketh so he is.[304] Also, Mark 4:24 shows what our thoughts measure our thoughts for knowledge. Her basic thesis is that you can change your life by changing your thought patterns as negative thinking leads to destructive negative living, while positive thinking leads to positive living. One of the famous quotes from her book is that "You cannot have a positive life and a negative mind."

What are the mechanics and art of Meditation?

The easiest way to get started in the art of meditation is to adopt the Nike policy "just do it," or as Kenneth Boa puts it, "the only way you will develop skill in meditation is by doing it, even when it does not seem to be effective."[305] One of the technics that develop meditation is to read a Psalm before going to bed and try to focus our thoughts on it rather than letting our mind wander all over the experiences of that day. The second thing to do is to choose a passage and try to put it in the first person and praying it back to God. There are two such passages in scripture that render themselves for such, Psalm 23 and the Lord's Prayer in Matthew 6:9-13. Let me illustrate when I am going through a difficult patch in my Christian life, and I personalize Psalm 23 it comes out so powerfully it dispels or eases off my worries. Psalm 23:1-6 (TEV) "The Lord is *Daniel's* shepherd; *Daniel* has everything he needs. He leads *Daniel* in fields of green grass and leads *Daniel* to quiet pools of freshwater. He gives *Daniel* a new strength. He guides *Daniel* in the right paths, as he has promised. Even if he goes through the deepest darkness, *Daniel* will not be afraid, Lord, because you are with him. Your shepherd's rod and staff protect *Daniel.* You prepare a banquet for *Daniel,* where all his enemies can see *Daniel.* You welcome *Daniel* as an honored guest and fill *Daniel's* cup to the brim. I know that your goodness and love will be with *Daniel* all of *Daniel's* life, and your house will be *Daniel's* home as long as he lives." I find using that portion of scripture meditatively like that quite powerful. May I suggest that you try it for yourself.

Similarly, when I pray for my wife, *Margare*t and replace her name through the Lord's Prayer, it comes out quite powerfully as follows: *Margaret's* Father Lives in heaven,

Hallowed be thy name in *Margaret.* May your kingdom come in, *Margaret.* Your will be done in *Margaret* on earth just as if she were with you in heaven. Give Margaret this day her daily bread, and forgive *Margare*t her trespasses as she forgives those who trespass against her. Lead Margaret, not into temptation, but deliver her from the evil one. Let Margaret's joy be your Kingdom, your power, and your glory forever. Amen.

The third thing is to commit to pursuing and applying the truths of that passage into one's life. Jim Downing, in his book *Meditation,* talks about (H.W.L.W – His Word Last Word) before retiring to bed and argues that this program the subconscious mind during the night in light of scripture."[306] Kenneth Boa sums it up this way: "meditation directs the conscious mind during the day and is an excellent way to practice the presence of God."[307]

What is Lectio Divina?

Related to scripture is the discipline known as Lectio Divina. It comes from Latin that translates as "Divine reading,"; also sometimes referred to as "spiritual" or "Holy reading." It originates from the 6th Century and is attributed to St Benedict.[308] It was adopted by the Catholic Church and developed in the Protestant Church by the Puritans. It represents a method of prayer and scriptural reading intended to promote communion with God and to provide spiritual insights. The principles of Lectio-Divina were expressed around the year A.D. 220 and practiced by Catholic monks, especially the monastic rules of Saints: Pachomius, Augustine, Basil, and Benedict.[309] It could also be defined as an ancient prayer practice that helps cultivate the ability to listen to God in the whole of life, a contemplative awakening and awareness of the divine. It is divided into four parts:-*Lectio* ("reading"); *Meditatio* ("meditating"); *Oratio* ("pray"); *Contemplatio* ("contemplating").The practice of prayer contemplation - Lectio Divina is popular among Catholics and is gaining acceptance as an integral part of the devotional practices of other religions. Pope Benedict XVI said in his 2005 speech,

> I would like in particular to recall, and recommend the ancient tradition of Lectio Divina: the diligent reading of Sacred Scripture, accompanied by prayer brings about that intimate dialogue in which the person reading hears God who is speaking, and in praying, responds to him with trusting openness of heart (cf. Dei Verbum, n.25) If it is effectively promoted, this practice will bring

> to the Church – I am convinced of it – a new spiritual springtime.[310]

Lectio - Reading

Lectio involves reading a Bible passage gently and slowly several times. The Bible passage itself is not as important as the savoring of each portion of the reading, always listening for the "still, small voice" of a word or phrase that somehow speaks to the reader. Jean Leclercq's study [311] has established that in the Middle Ages, while the universities prepared the clerics for parish life, rural monasteries focused on spiritual formation within a liturgical framework to equip monks for contemplative life. During the middle ages, two approaches to scripture developed in the universities, also known as scholastics, majored on objective, theological cognitive reflection, while monasticism focused on the subjective, devotional, and practical meditation. The monastic approach deals more with the formation of the person while the scholastic majored on the acquisition of information. The two extremes led to intellectualism and personal enthusiasm. Lectio Divina produces the balance of the two, calling both for intellectual information and spiritual response. Lectio is adaptable for people of other faiths in reading their scripture—whether that is the Bhagavad Gita, the Torah, or the Koran. Non-Christians make suitable modifications of the method to accommodate religious traditions.

Further, the four principles of Lectio Divina can also be adapted to the four Jungian psychological principles of sensing, thinking, intuiting, and feeling. The actual practice of Lectio Divina begins with a time of relaxation, comfort, and clearing the mind of mundane thoughts and cares. Some lectio - practitioners find it helpful to concentrate by beginning with deep, cleansing breaths and reciting a chosen phrase or word over and over to help free the mind. Then they start with the four steps starting with Lectio. Good discipline would require a choice of place, time, and consistency. Also outstanding is a systematic selection of the passages of scripture to meditate. There are set programs like Reading the Bible in One year that could help in engaging with Lectio. It is advisable to start Lectio with prayer, a simple prayer like "open my eyes, that I may behold wonderful things from Your law"[312] or the most familiar used by preachers before they start their sermons: "Let the words of my mouth and the meditation of my heart be acceptable in your sight. O Lord, my rock and my Redeemer."[313]

Meditatio–If we liken Lectio to chewing and swallowing food, meditio will equate to digestions. It entails reflecting on the text of the passage and thinking about how it applies to one's own life. It is at this stage that the scripture is applied to our circumstances. Like a sponge, we allow our mental will to absorb the message of scripture and saturate our emotions and feelings. At this stage, we align our strong wills, which are usually in opposition to God as a result of the fall to be informed and aligned to the sovereign divine will. We gain new insights and perspectives into God's will. "Meditation attunes the inward self to the Holy Spirit so that our hearts harmonize and resonate with his voice…in such a way that our whole being is transformed into greater conformity with Jesus Christ."[314] Once the sponge of our lives is fully saturated with the word of God, in times of difficulties, reminiscences of scripture flood in our lives, giving new perspectives to the trials, we may be facing. The fruit of formal meditation, develop the mind of Christ in us."[315]Meditatio could be compared with progressive revelation. God's ultimate revelation is indeed in Christ the living word, but there is a sense in which God continually reveals himself to believers through scripture addressing the mind, emotions, and the will. Meditatio provides such moments for God to reveal himself in his written word. The psalms offer a fertile ground for meditation, for, in the Psalms, we encounter the psalmists grappling with their encounter with God in varying circumstances.

Oratio –Earlier, we discussed the discipline of prayer. In this section, as part of Lectio-Divina, it is responding to the passage by opening the heart to God. In so doing, it is not primarily an intellectual exercise but is thought to be more of the beginning of a conversation with God. Prayer is a two-way conversation; here, it is the second part where we allow God to speak back to us. In oratio, confession and repentance ensue as the word of God opens our live, and God reveals the dark hidden parts of our lives.[316]In Oratio, we respond to God in the prayer of praise and thanksgiving as a result of exhortation or encouragement received in Lectio and meditatio, or adoration and confession for a rebuke received either in Lectio or meditation.

Contemplatio–The principal concept in this stage of Lectio –Divina is listening to God and allowing Him to confront our imaginations. This has been described as a freeing of oneself from one's thoughts, both mundane and holy, and hearing God talk to us. This entails opening the mind, heart, and soul to the influence of God. It has also been described as "a theological grace that cannot be reduced to logical, psychological, or aesthetic categories."[317]In contemplation, we come closest to the experience described by Rudolf Otto, in terms of the numinous in his analysis of the experience that, in his view, underlies all religion. His views became the foundation of the Phenomenology of Religion and the study of comparative religions. He calls this experience "numinous," and says it has three components (*mysterium*-"wholly other"; *tremendum*-"unapproachability, overwhelming, might, majesty" *fascinans*-"attractiveness in spite of fear, merciful and gracious").[318]Contemplation "is a discipline of silence, of loss of control, of abandoning the attempt to analyze and intellectualize, and of developing the intuitive faculties."[319]The connection between Bible reading and prayer is one to be encouraged; they should always go together. However, the dangers inherent in contemplation per se are its similarity to transcendental meditation and other dangerous cultic rituals. It has the potential to become, and often does become a pursuit of mystical experience where the goal is to empty and free the mind and empower oneself. The Christian, on the other hand, uses the contemplation of Scriptures to pursue the knowledge of God, wisdom, and holiness through the objective meaning of the text to transform the mind according to the truth. The Bible says people are destroyed for lack of knowledge, not for lack of mystical, personal encounters with Him.[320]

Those who take this supernatural approach to the text can disconnect it from its context and natural meaning and use it in a subjective, individualistic, experiential, even "name-it-and-claim-it" way for which it was never intended. In this sense, lectio and Gnosticism dovetail into one. Christian Gnosticism is the belief that one must have a "gnosis" (from Greek γνωση- gnosis, "to know") or mystical, inner knowledge obtained only after one has been properly initiated. Only a few can possess this mystical knowledge, limiting the number of those "in the know." The idea of having inside information is very appealing and makes the "knower" feel consequential, special, and unique in that he/she has an exceptional experience with God that no one else has. The "knower" believes that the masses do not have spiritual knowledge, and only the truly "enlightened" can experience God. Thus, the reintroduction of contemplative, or centering, prayer—a meditative practice where the focus is on having a mystical experience with God—into the Church. Contemplative prayer is similar to the meditative exercises used in Eastern religions and New Age cults and has no basis whatsoever in the Bible, although those who pray contemplatively do use the Bible as a starting point.

Further, the dangers inherent in opening our minds and listening for voices should be obvious. Those who pray contemplatively are so eager to hear something—anything—that they can lose the objectivity needed to discern between God's voice, their thoughts, and suggestive demonic infiltration into their minds. Satan and his minions are always eager for inroads into the minds of the unsuspecting, and to open our minds in such ways is to invite disaster. We must never forget that Satan is ever on the prowl, seeking to devour our souls[321] and can appear as an angel of light,[322] whispering his deceptive lies into our open and willing minds. The devil knows where the Bible claims to be all we need to live the Christian life.[323] Those who practice "conversational" prayers, seeking a special revelation from God, are asking Him to bypass what He has already revealed to humanity, as though God would now renege on all His promises embodied in His eternal Word.[324]That contains the definitive statement about the sufficiency of Scripture. It is "perfect, reviving the soul"; it is "right, rejoicing the heart"; it is "pure, enlightening the eyes"; it is "true" and "righteous altogether,"; and it is "more desirable than gold." If God meant all that He said in this psalm, there is no need for additional revelation, and to ask Him for one is to deny what He has already revealed.

The Old and New Testaments are words from God to be studied, meditated upon, prayed over, and memorized for the knowledge and objective meaning they contain and the authority from God they carry, and not for the mystical experience or feeling of personal power and inner peace they may stimulate. Sound knowledge comes first; then, the lasting kind of experience and peace comes as a byproduct of knowing and communing with God rightly. As long as a person takes this view of the Bible and prayer, he/she is engaging in the same kind of meditation and prayer that Bible-believing followers of Christ have always commended. Lectio Divina is commendable in that it strikes a balance between intellectualism and sheer emotionalism. "It is a personal process that cultivates a spiritual outlook of trust, receptivity, expectation, worship, and intimacy with God."[325]

Journaling

Journaling is a term coined for the practice of keeping a diary or journal that helps explore one's thoughts and feelings surrounding the events on one's life. It is also described as a personal record of occurrences, experiences, and reflections regularly kept, a diary, an official record of daily proceedings of a legislative body. A journal is also defined as a book in which a daily record of happenings is kept.[326] The term journal or diary is used interchangeably for a daybook to record daily happenings.[327]A spiritual journal is a "focused journal" that centers on one's devotional and spiritual life. There are many kinds of journals written every day either in diaries or in individual books dedicated to journaling. In diaries and general journals, people record everything that goes on in their lives. Some keep work or professional journals, recording critical developments in their workplace. Teachers often keep professional journals about their work with individual students. Some persons keep journals of their dreams. Some people meticulously keep family journals with cute sayings the kids say at every birthday and Christmas and still more adorable photos of it all. What is meant by spiritual journal, however, is that it focuses on one's spiritual journey as one interacts in their lives and in the happenings of life and particular in pursuing and practicing what some have referred to as Wesleyan-scriptural holiness and spiritual formation of one's inner self, and with the Lord. One's work, family, and events of everyday life may be included in one's responses when they bring spiritual joys, problems, and issues. In the spiritual journal, however, is not the place to record mundane chores like family occasions, unless one is homing in on a spiritual lesson learned in the day. It entails setting a time each day to sit oneself down and reflect on one's spiritual journey. It provides an opportunity to acknowledge one's spiritual blessings but also sets up new spiritual goals for the days ahead. It may involve writing specific prayers that help galvanize inspiration. It is recommended that one review journal entries at least once a month, each time focusing on one's spiritual journey. Once developed as a discipline, it is a source of daily inspiration and motivation, giving occasion to note down one's thoughts as they flow through one's mind. Journaling is an antidote to negative thoughts that lead to depression as it provides an occasion to count one's blessings, helping develop feelings of gratitude by which research has shown that people who make a point of feeling gratitude are happier and healthier. Journalism develops as a discipline as one gets into the habit of writing down prayers as they form and flow in one's mind and heart. The best practice is to apportion about 20 minutes daily to one's journal. The cumulative effect of this discipline is that it leads to spiritual growth that does not just happen; it has to be desired and planned for and requires an apportioned time to accomplish it. The act of reviewing the journal helps in establishing a sense of spiritual goals and direction in one's life. The spiritual journal deals with personal private thoughts; therefore, it helps one release one's thoughts, positive or negative, without fear of judgment. In this sense, it acts as a safety valve for one to ventilate and at times, validate one's thoughts. Once developed, journaling becomes one's all-accepting non-judgmental friend. It becomes an aid to personal spiritual growth and development. Journaling as a discipline dates back to around 10th Centurthe y in Japan. Successful people throughout history have kept journals. It is from their journal that presidents compose their memoirs. Oscar Wilde, the 19th Century playwright, said: "I never travel without my diary: one should always have something sensational to read on the train." Through the centuries, believers have found good reasons to write a spiritual journal. In this book, we explore the values and techniques of this spiritual discipline briefly.

What is the purpose of the Spiritual Life Journal?

There are five benefits of having a spiritual life journal.

i. It acts as a means of deepening one's relationship with God.
ii. It enhances spiritual growth by cataloging what God is doing
iii. It increases self-knowledge
iv. It integrates one's life and puts it in tune with what God is doing
v. It gives purpose and focuses on our spiritual lives.

What are the benefits of a Spiritual Journal?

1. **One learns** a lot of what one needs to know about one's inner being, what Loren Eiseley called that "ghost

continent within." One's journal will become a sort of mirror of self and soul. 2Cor 3:18, (NRSV), "And all of us . . . seeing the glory of the Lord as though reflected in a mirror, are being transformed into the same image." We are, as Thomas Aquinas said, to "gaze with love on God and share what has been seen with others." The first one the mirror reveals is we in all our needs. A journal is a mirror that helps keep us honest with ourselves. As Huck Finn discovered, "You can't pray a lie. I found that out."[328]

2. **Life patterns** emerge, revealing that one's life has not been haphazard. One starts to see the footprints of seeking God marching through one's life. C. S. Lewis puts it this way,

    a. "We think we have chosen our friends. In reality, a different birth date . . . A different college, taking the 'other job'—any of these changes might have kept us apart from our current set of friends. . . . As you look back, you discover that a Secret Master of Ceremonies has been at work. And . . . He is still on the job."[329]

3. **Journaling helps us trace back the footprints of God's grace in our lives**, as illustrated in the *Footprints in the Sand Poem,* 1939 by Mary Fishback Powers. In the poem, Mary traces two sets of footprints hers and God's. When the footprints reduced to one set, hers only she enquired from God why, and God replied, "when you saw only one set of footprints, it was then I carried you."[330]God is at work in every believer's life, and the discipline of journaling is one way of tracing God's companionship in Christians' lives.

4. **One's capacities and skills in Bible study**, meditation, confession, and prayer will increase. Evil forces and even neutral ones make it hard for the Christian to stay close to God. We need to develop the skills of devotional life. If some believers were given an hour to pray, they would not know what to do or how to proceed. Journaling sharpens your spiritual tools. "Pausing . . . To jot down our thoughts has a way of quieting and de-cluttering our overactive, decentred lives . . . to find [again] our lost center in Christ."[331] Jones aptly put it thus, "I know that a faith that does not hold my intellect will soon not hold my heart."[332] "Keeping God's love and forgiveness uppermost.. .prevents . . . Becoming merely self-analytical. Journal writers know that they must guard against excessive introspection . . . looking at themselves under a microscope, trying to analyze every fault and failing, every small success or consolation."[333]
5. **A regular time** to reflect and write can help bring integration to the flashing forces that fragment thought, befuddle hearts, clutter agendas, and reduce you and me to flustered ineffectiveness. The journaling time stops the frenzied flow of experience and helps you look at it again, make sense of it all, and set priorities.
6. **It helps to clarify unexamined assumptions**, presumptions, and opinions inherited or adopted from the culture by measuring them against Christian standards. We live too much of our lives out untested and in sub-Christian traditions, what Muto calls "pre-focal vagueness." In an intriguing new book called *Can Asians Think?* The author, an Asian himself, has no doubts about the intelligence of Asians. He makes the point that: Asians are not required to think because powerful

cultural traditions make the decisions for them. Whom they will marry, their status in the family, their conduct, their vocation, and what they will do with their money—all this and more will be dictated by the culture.

7. **Journaling is one way that one explores the uniqueness of one's spiritual journey.** It helps one stop going through life, imitating the religious experiences of others. God has a faith journey plotted to meet each individual's unique needs, vulnerabilities, gifts, and strengths. One's journal helps one learn one's own story. "It is a book in which one carries out the greatest of life's adventures— the discovery of yourself."
8. **One's spiritual journal helps one discover and act upon the "aha" moments**—those times when two or three ideas connect, and a life-changing insight is born. Perhaps no greater insight comes than the one in which one discovers that God is not a part of one's life, but that one is a little part of His life. Stevenson observes that in journaling as a Spiritual Discipline, *"to miss the joy is to miss all."*[334]
9. **One's journal becomes a friend and coach as one faces those "crossroad"** or "hinge" moments when one must filter powerful emotions and weigh decisions, opportunities, and alternatives about family, vocation, and life.
10. **Journaling helps many people develop a confident lifestyle** marked by joy, playfulness, and hope. E. Dee Freeborn says that journaling adds a "serendipitous dimension of hilarities, of cheerfulness into the holy lifestyle." Secure in Christ; these journalers do not take themselves too seriously. Your joys are great gifts from God. These moments deserve to be treasured, pondered,

relived, and cherished," writes Ronald Klug. Journaling about them serves as "a good antidote to self-pity and depression."[335]

11. **Journaling can help break the power of painful memories of the past.** Richard Peace writes about a man whose father repeatedly brutalized him. Journaling helped him escape the awful prison of those memories. "Often, the act of making memories concrete by putting them and our responses to them in writing robs them of their power over us. We bring them from the darkness into the light." "A journal helps you to see if you are still on the Way or sidetracked . . . in some pleasant spot that has you deceived."[336]
12. **One's journal can sometimes serve as a safety valve** for emotions that threaten to get out of control. For example, in the experience therapy of writing a stern letter and then have the good sense not to mail it. Writing in one's journal can be like that sometimes. Susan Muto says,

    > "Writing releases pent-up, potentially volcanic emotions. I can let go of a lot that disturbs me when I write. Immense mountains are relativized into normal molehills; once I see them sketched on a paper. If I don't write out these hurts and anger, they have a way of festering inside."[337]

Journaling is about growth in grace, that is, Christ-likeness. As we gaze upon the face of the Saviour, we come to reflect the Lord's image more and more according to 2Cor 3:18. Journaling helps keep the disciple's attention on the things that matter most as they reflect on the person of Jesus Christ, whom they follow and seek to imitate.

What Goes into a Spiritual Journal?

1. Significant events and happenings in your work or study.
2. Family matters.
3. Key relationships and conversations at home, school, and work.
4. Important ideas encountered in reading, thinking, writing, or discussion.
5. Achievement or failures that occurred this day.
6. Feelings: the most substantial feelings of contentment, joy, happiness, hope. The emotional lows, depression, discouragement, fear, guilt, worry, etc.
7. Internal happenings: intuitions, new appreciations, inner convictions, and insights about your character or self.
8. Major news stories: floods, war, strikes, peace, treaties, etc.
9. Notable physical experiences: exercise, work, illness, exhaustion, etc.
10. Spiritual events: prayer, Bible study, worship, etc.
11. Affirmations, conclusions, decisions, commitments made, or beliefs clarified or confirmed.
12. Spiritual failure, besetting sins, repentance, etc. Acts of ministry or Christian service.

The following are examples of people who used journaling and through their journals, influenced not only their lives but left legacies that have helped many people for centuries. The two best known are John Wesley and St Augustine.

John Wesley's Journals

The following are samples of John Wesley's journals. "I returned to London, and on **Sunday 22** buried the remains of Elizabeth Duchesne, a person eminently upright of heart, yet for many years a child of labor and sorrow. For near forty years she was zealous of good works, and . . . Shortened her days by laboring for the poor beyond her strength. But her end is peace. She now rests from her labors, and her works follow her."

Tues. 31—We concluded the year with solemn praise to God [the New Year's Eve watch night service]. . . . It has never been intermitted for one year. .since the year 1738; in which my brother and I began to preach that strange doctrine of salvation by faith.

Wed. January 1—We met, as usual, to renew our covenant with God [The Wesley Covenant Service]. It was a solemn season; wherein many found his power present to heal.

Thurs. 2—I began expounding, in order, the book of Ecclesiastes. I never before had so clear a sight either of the meaning or the beauties of it. Neither did I imagine that the several parts of it were in so exquisite a manner connected, all tending to prove the grand truth—that there is no happiness out of [outside of] God.

Wed. 8—I looked over the manuscripts of that great and good man, Charles Perronet. I did not think he had such deep communion with God. I know exceeding few that equal him, and had he had a University education, there would have been few more exceptional writers in England. [338]

Mon. 13—I took the opportunity of spending an hour every morning with the Preachers, as I did with my pupils at Oxford.

Wed. 15—I began visiting those of our society who lived in Bethnal-Green hamlet. Many of them I found in such poverty that few could conceive of. . . . O, why do not all the rich that fear God constantly visit the poor? Can they spend part of their spare time better? Certainly not. So they will find in that day when "every man shall receive his own reward according to his own labor." Such another scene I saw the next day. . . . I have not found any such distress, no, not in the prison of Newgate. One poor man was creeping out of his sick-bed, to his ragged wife and three little children; who were more than half-naked, and the very picture of famine; when one bringing in a loaf of bread, they all ran, seized upon it, and tore it to pieces in an instant."

St. Augustine's confessions.

At age 31, Augustine was trying to break away from a sensual life of wine, women, and song—particularly women. From his journals, known as St Augustine's Confessions, we get details of his conversion in which Augustine wrote: "The very toy of toys, and vanities of vanities, my ancient mistresses, still held me; they plucked my fleshly garment, and whispered softly, "Dost thou cast us off?" He expressed his musings whether he could live without these passions in these words: "Thinkest thou, thou canst live without them? He described his internal turmoil, as "controversy in my heart was self against self." He goes on to describe, "a deep consideration had from the secret bottom of my soul drawn together and heaped up all my misery in the sight of my heart, there arose a mighty storm, bringing a shower of tears." He ascribes his conversion to a voice he heard asking him to read the Bible as follows:

I heard . . . a voice . . . chanting . . . "Take up and read; Take up and read. I arose; interpreting it to be no other than the command from God. . . . Eagerly . . . I seized, opened [the volume of the Apostle] and in silence read the section, on which my eyes first fell: "Not in rioting and drunkenness, not in chambering and wantonness, not in strife and envying: but put ye on the Lord Jesus Christ, and make not provision for the flesh," in concupiscence. . . . Instantly . . . light as it were of serenity infused into my heart, all the darkness of doubt vanished away.[339]

From Augustine's journals, they lead us into his most intimate moments with God, similar to John Wesley's journals in which he gives an account of his conversion with the words, "I heard my heart strangely warmed," of which the Methodists celebrate on 24th May as Aldersgate day. From both these great Christian giants, we learn the importance of journaling as a spiritual discipline and pillar for spiritual formation and growth.

The significance of journaling.

To summarize, the discipline of journaling is significant not only in the spiritual realm but also in the secular world. Prominent people end their careers by publishing their memoirs, which simply put are a collection of their lives' journals. The recovery of journaling as a spiritual discipline has brought back an essential part of the Christian heritage. Some of the most celebrated literature in the world is the journals of pilgrims whose recorded journey still lights our way to spiritual formation. At the top of the list is Augustine's Confessions. The journal is not about confessing dark, wicked sins (though some are included); it is more about confessions of faith, that is, affirmations of belief and devotion. Blaise Pascal's journal, *Pense'es,* is a "must-read."

John Wesley's journal has been reprinted many times. Wesley almost required his preachers and lay leaders to keep daily journals. Because of that, we probably know more about the Methodist revival in 18th-century England than any other Christian era. The journal of John Woolman, the Quaker who led the fight against slavery in America, is included in the Harvard Classics. Other notable journals are those of Teresa of Avila, Julian of Norwich, Hildegarde of Bingen, Evelyn Underhill, and Henri Nouwen. Dag Hammarskjöld's journal, *Markings*, has gone through 20 printings. The Journal of Danish theologian Søren Kierkegaard ranks as great literature. Journaling is a term coined for the practice of keeping a diary or journal that explores thoughts and feelings surrounding the events of one's life. Journaling is one of the easiest and most powerful ways to accelerate your personal development. By getting your thoughts out of your head and putting them down in writing, you gain insights you would otherwise never see. I highly recommend journaling for spiritual formation.

Questions for reflection

1. To what extent has spiritual journaling been part of your experience of spiritual formation?
2. Do you feel more strongly than ever that spiritual journaling can nourish your own spiritual life?
3. Do you feel you could make an affirmation or pledge to do spiritual journaling as a result of reading this section in this book?

Mentoring

Introduction

When Jesus called his first disciples, he said: "follow me, and I will make you fishers of men."[340] In saying this, Jesus was inviting his disciples to a life of discipleship that entailed mentoring. They were to become by being made. Jesus spent three years teaching and demonstrating to his disciples what it meant to follow him.

In the course of his teaching, he spelled out what this meant by giving the imagery of oxen yoked together, the young oxen learning from the experienced oxen. He said, "Take my yoke upon you and learn from me, ...and you will find rest for your souls for my yoke is easy, and my burden is light."[341]Without getting into all the technical exegetical ramifications involved in this text, suffice it to say that the key thought when Jesus said this was contrasting the life of discipleship compared with the burdensome Pharisaic legalism of his day in which Pharisees had proliferated the ten commandments into over six hundred for the ordinary people to bear. Jesus was contrasting the call to follow him as rest in light of existing Judaism legalism of his day. It was a call to rest made easy by the fact that just as a yoke eases the load with animals, making it less burdensome, so it is with the life of following him, in which he shares the burden with his followers. The yoke or burden of following Jesus as the Christian's mentor makes it easier; otherwise, the challenge of a Christian life without being coupled with Jesus would be too hard to bear alone. Yoke as a verb means pairing, coupling, harness, hitch up, team up, attach or fasten together. As a noun, it means a wooden crosspiece fastened over the necks of two animals and attached to the plough or cart that they pull together. A yoke symbolizes slavery, servitude, and suffering. It also has overtones of the bearing of a cross. What makes it easy is that the Christian is coupled with Jesus Christ and bear the cross and suffering with him. Christian formation becomes more comfortable once the followers of Jesus are connected to Christ and learn to walk in His Spirit, with the Holy Spirit as a mentor. The Message translation of the Bible elucidate the meaning of this text as follows:

> "Are you tired? Worn out? Burned out on religion? Come to me. Get away with me, and you will recover your life.

> I will show you how to take a real rest. Walk with me and work with me-watch how I do it. Learn the unforced rhythms of grace. I would not lay anything heavy or ill-fitting on you. Keep company with me, and you'll learn to live freely and lightly."[342]

The teaching Jesus intended through the imagery of the yoke is elucidated in the saying: *a joy shared is doubled and a burden shared is halved*. The call to follow Christ entails Christian service, which in turn requires learned skills from the master on how to serve. Mentoring is at the very heart of Christian discipleship, but the tragedy in Christianity as someone recently said: "We have become quite happy to call ourselves Christians with little or no thought of following."[343] Or, as another added, "we have drifted away from being fishers of men to being keepers of the aquarium."[344] From Jesus' teaching and example, Christian discipleship entails mentorship. "The men who are making the greatest impact for God in this generation are men who have placed themselves under the tutelage of other godly men."[345]Jesus called his disciples that they might be with him (accompany him) and that He might send them out to preach."[346] It is crucial to notice the order of the verbs in this sentence: to be and to send. Jesus called the disciples first to be with him before he sent them out to make other disciples. The verb translated "to be with him, accompany him" implies having communion with him, learning of him before he commissioned them. To be with him first also involves knowing him first before they could carry out his mission. In other words, Jesus mentored his apostles first before he ordained them to the office of discipleship. Having an intimate relationship with Jesus comes before serving him. He invited the disciples to learn from him and follow his example in making other disciples. This relationship was aptly summed up by Barclay as follows:

> Here we see what might be called the rhythm of the Christian life. For the Christian life is a continuous going into the presence of God from the presence of men, and coming into the presence of men from the presence of God. It is like the rhythms of work and sleep...The rhythm of the Christian life is the alternate meeting with God in the secret place and serving God in the market place.[347]

Paul, the author of nearly half of the New Testament, says this: "Imitate me as I imitate Christ."[348]The word translated imitates from the Greek imply following. It has three shades of meaning: First, "an artificial likeness unfeigned" implying concreteness and genuineness; Second, "an artificial likeness feigned"-indicating concerted effort to deceive, appearing genuine like counterfeit money, jewelry or watches; Third, following after a pattern, model, an example with intent to copy or strive to replicate. It is this third meaning that we find implied and applied in Christian discipleship. Christians are called to be imitators of God as beloved children.[349]Christians are exhorted in imitating God to strive to live a holy life because "He who called you is holy, you also be holy in all your conduct, because the Bible says, 'Be holy, for I am holy.'[350]Jesus, during His earthly ministry, taught that He lived a life of imitation of God his Father, in his long diatribe with Jewish leaders.[351]The evidence for this type of following or imitation shows forth in loving others. "We have known and believed the love that God has for us. God is love, and he who abides in love abides in God and God in him. For God so loved the world."[352] The kind of followership or imitation envisaged in Christian discipleship could be illustrated by two stories. The first is about a school that had a "Hero/Heroine Day" in which students were encouraged to dress up as their favorite hero/heroine. One of the pastors who had a son in that school thought his son would dress up in some football or rugby club uniform showing one of the sports stars. The boy, however, amazed his father when he dressed up with a coat and tie. The father wondered and asked why the boy did not dress like any hero. The boy replied, "Yes, I am; I am dressed the way you dress." The second illustration is from a discussion among preachers expressing the merits of the various translations of the Bible; one liked the King James Version, another American Revised Version, yet another the Contemporary English Version, and they all gave their reasons for their choice. The fourth said, "I like my mother's translation best." In amazement, the other three exclaimed, "We did not know your mother had translated the Bible"! "Yes, she did," the fourth replied, "She translated it into life, and it was the most convincing translation I ever saw."

There are several books on the market on mentoring,[353]covering various aspects of the subject. For this book, we will look into mentoring from the perspectives of spiritual formation and will steer clear of the other valid details of mentoring as a subject. We do this in keeping with our authorial intention for the book, elucidating the dynamics in spiritual formation.

What is mentoring?

A survey of existing literature on mentoring indicates that mostly, a mentor would be older or more experienced than the person mentored. It has a closer affinity in meaning to shepherding, and the relationship implied in scripture between the shepherd and the sheep in which the shepherd as the mentor, cares (shepherds), pulls alongside, protects the person mentored. Most literature tends to address mentors and person mentored or protégés in masculine terms. We acknowledge that there are feminine mentor-person mentored relationships of this kind. In this book, however, instead of attempting to change the convention for gender and political correctness, since the subject is only tangential to the main subject of this book, we would keep with the convention. In-group dynamics, the mentors tend to be the stronger members of the group to whom the younger, more vulnerable members of the group look towards to find their identity. The difference in the analogy of the sheep-shepherd is that the persons mentored have the responsibility of choosing their mentor, while the shepherd chooses the sheep. The second difference is that for a good mentor-person mentored relationship when the person mentored needs food, and the mentors should assist them in finding food themselves rather than feeding them, whereas the shepherd feeds the sheep. The mentor-person mentored relationship should adopt the adage: "Give a man a fish, and you feed him for a day. Teach a man to fish, and you feed him for a lifetime."[354]The person mentored seeks and establishes a relationship with a mentor and should keep that responsibility. The purpose of mentoring is not for the mentor to carry the protégé (person mentored), but for the mentor to help the protégé learn to walk on his own."[355]A Mentor-person mentored relationship seems to be an innate psychological impulse in primates intricately built-in within human DNA. Mentoring exists in the psyche of all human beings depicting a longing to imitate somebody, for example, a lawyer, doctor or Christian leader would grow up with longings to be like an older faithful person whom they trusted and admired in their profession during the formative years. The Christian life is an imparted life of faith that grows and develops through Christian nurture and imitation firstly of older faithful Christians but ultimately the imitation of Christ on whom every Christian should fix this/her eyes, the source and goal of the Christian faith.[356]Every growing Christian needs a relationship with another Christian who is living closer to

Jesus to keep the boomerang of the Christian faith and character developing. Jesus spent three years teaching and training his disciples, not only through teaching but also in watching him, learning his attitudes and deep-seated character traits that could only be learned and imparted through observation. The first disciples looked up to Jesus as a mentor; the term disciple is a literal translation of the Greek μαθητής-"mathetes," one who sits at the feet of the master. There is an intentionality in this type of relationship. Jesus called his disciples and said, "Follow me," and they intentionally left their fishing equipment and followed him. In the Pauline epistles, the Paul-Timothy relationship was intentional. Similarly, the literature review shows that mentor-person mentored relationship is intentional and mutual. The person mentored has a choice of the mentor they choose to follow and must have the freedom to change the mentor if they do not feel that the mentor is leading them in the right direction. The sting in the tail in the mentoring relationship is that someone is watching us, and there is a need constantly to keep asking whether we are worth following or attract followers. When Peter decided to go back to his old profession, he never thought of the impact his decision would have on the others, surprise, surprise they all said, we will go with you.[357]When the Apostle Paul urged the Philippians to work out their salvation with fear and trembling,[358]the Greek word translated "fear" in this context principally means reverence and respect.[359]The trembling principally refers to a holy and healthy fear of offending God through disobedience and an awe and respect for His holy majesty. Also, I conjecture that it also could mean Christians should live their lives vigilantly, for they do not know who is watching. It urges Christians to live their lives as if on constant CCTV observation 24/7 and especially about children and young people who are constantly watching mature Christians. On

Fridays on our day off, Margaret and I look after our three - year - old grandson, a perfect mimic of all we do and say. He makes us constantly alert on what we do or say in front of him because, without a doubt, he would mimic it. Therefore, on Fridays, when our grandson is around our house, we live on tiptoe alert for fear of him imitating something wrong. There should also be fear and trembling on the part of the mentor, realizing how easy it is to lead a person mentored astray. The words "imitate me as I imitate Christ" should be inscribed on the mantelpiece of every Christian and recited in their daily prayers as a reminder that someone is watching them. This sting in the tail calls for every practicing Christian to take seriously the words of Jesus, Matthew 18:6 (ESV) "whoever causes one of these little ones who believe in me to sin, it would be better for him to have a great millstone fastened around his neck and to be drowned in the depth of the sea." We may not fully grasp the first-century Biblical world imagery used in this text, but the severity of the punishment for misleading a young person either in age or in faith is not in doubt. Before we could fully grasp what is mentoring, perhaps we should ask another question.

What is a mentor?

A mentor is that individual outside your family who "at a critical moment, redirected your path so that today you look back and say 'I would never have become who I am if not for that person's influence.' These persons invited you into their lives in a way that has indelibly marked your own life...a person who was used by God strategically to change the course of your life. A mentor is a person who fundamentally affects and influences the development of another, usually younger man."[360] The Hendricks draws the title of their book from Proverbs[361] and says that "it is the process of being sharpened against the whetstone of another man's wisdom and character."[362]The theology of mentoring pervades all scripture and is illustrated in the way Jesus lived and conducted his ministry on earth, claiming that he followed what His heavenly father told him. According to Hendricks, "The principle of modeling is underscored by the doctrine of the incarnation, the truth God became flesh. God always wraps His truth in a person. That's the value of a godly mentor. He shows what biblical truth looks like with skin on it."[363] There are many examples in scripture on modeling and mentoring; the most noteworthy are young Samuel struggling to understand God's call and the intervention and wise guidance of priest Eli.[364]In the New Testament, we have the mighty Apostle Paul struggling to fit in the fellowship of the early church. Then steps in Barnabas mentored him in launching Paul's new spiritual formation by introducing him to the Christian fellowship in Jerusalem that was afraid of Paul because of his past antagonism to the Christian faith known at the time as the Jesus' Movement. Before Barnabas, the Lord had used Ananias to mentor Paul on Straight Street in Damascus in the house of Judas.[365] The author of the letter to the Hebrew Christians mandates modeling and mentoring as normative in the Christian community.[366]The ministry of mentoring opens a chain of blessings whereby those who are blessed through it go on to bless others, and that way, the spiritual formation becomes a conduit and upward spiral of spiritual reproduction. In one sense, mentors are like seasoned guides who help novice explorers or tourists in a new area navigate the terrain of spiritual territory in the journey of faith. When I worked as a Relate counselor, one of the guiding principles that became my mantra was the axiom that many marriages could be rescued from breaking up by early intervention. Mentoring provides early intervention in the journey of faith and helps avert loneliness, isolation, and despair that face young Christians. Mature Christians need mentors, too, because of the innate nature of self-praise and self-aggrandizement that prevent people from seeing their weaknesses. Jesus alluded to this in his teaching on the Sermon on the Mount when he talked about the easiness to spot the speck of sawdust in a brother's eye while paying no attention to a plank in one's eye[367]. Working with a mentor makes one aware of one's blind spots and enhances accountability. Mentoring enhances objectivity and enables one to differentiate between reality and one's perceptions. Mentoring defends one from the tunnel vision that might lead to delusion and catastrophic decisions. It also enhances self-knowledge that tends to be elusive for most people. Mentoring helps in developing fundamental, long term personal growth and development by addressing long term objectives and core values. Spiritual mentoring is a developmental process that entails a learning curve and requires the person mentored willingness to learn and take the initiative. According to Scripture, spiritual formation and personal development defy settling for the status quo, comfort zone, or complacency.[368] For that matter, mentoring in terms of getting someone to help one push to the next level in spiritual development is both crucial and critical. A mentor assists one to recognize when one's spiritual life stagnates because most mentors will work with set objectives and set goals, which is why most mentors would like self-starters and self-motivated people pursuing specific goals in their lives. A mentor would spot gifts and talents in person mentored and seek to encourage them to develop these talents to fruition for the greater benefit of the Christian body ofbelievers. Most mentors would like to work with winners; they prefer people willing to go somewhere or achieve something in their lives. The life of faith is pictured as a life of champions because Christians fight from victory, not for victory, for Christ has won the victory. To the despondent –despairing Hebrew Christians, the writer of the letter to the Hebrews gives the imagery of the Christian life as a race, a life of champions in an arena and not spectators[369]. The only spectators in the arena are champions themselves spurring the competitors as if saying, "we have done it; you can do it too." It refers to these spectators as witnesses cheering out that it is doable. Mentoring is a "life-on-life relationship, is about one life influencing another life"[370] for the better. Where influence is involved, power follows, and danger lurks around the corner because of the nature of human frailty in misuse of power. Influence and power are like Siamese twins; they travel together. Influence by its very nature is rooted in the issue of power, and by choosing a mentor, one inevitably empowers that person, granting that person "the power to affect one's life."[371]To guard against misuse of that power, checks, and balances should be put in place. In the case of such a relationship, the first check is that the person mentored should retain the choice and the responsibility to end the relationship if the person mentored feels the relationship is not beneficial. A good mentor will respect this option of the person mentored and accept servant leadership in the relationship. If the mentor oversteps proper boundaries and becomes authoritarian or manipulative, the person mentored must assert the right to end the relationship before it becomes toxic and destructive to its intended objectives of spiritual formation. "There is one Lord, Jesus Christ; He is the only one person to whom we should ever cede total control of our lives. To hand over that authority to anyone else is spiritual adultery."[372]By definition, "a mentor is someone committed to helping another grow and realize their life goals."[373] A mentor is a person who is "a vibrant Christian who can challenge you from a biblical foundation."[374]For that matter, the agenda of the person mentored remain paramount, leaving no room for authoritarianism, manipulation, or power control. The term mentor might give the false notion that one needs to have only one person as a mentor. Hendricks, whose writings might earn him the title of a guru on the subject, suggests that one needs ideally three types of mentors: a Paul, a Barnabas, and Timothy. "Everyman here should seek to have three individuals in his life, you need a Paul, and you need a Barnabas and a Timothy. A Paul, an older man who can build into his life, a Barnabas, a peer, a soul brother to whom he can be accountable, and a Timothy, a younger man into whose life he is building."[375] To sum up, a mentor "is someone committed to helping you grow and realize your life goals."[376]

What are the primary qualities of a mentor?

Hendricks[377]gives a list of marks or characteristics that define a good mentor in great detail. For this book, let me suggest three primary qualities of a mentor that influence spiritual growth.

a. **Spirituality.** Jesus, in the Sermon on the Mount,[378] said: "A good tree cannot bear bad fruit, and a bad tree cannot bear good fruit."[379]If one is looking for spiritual growth, one of the primary qualities one should be looking for should be someone who has developed spiritual maturity. The convention in mentoring is "do as I do, not do as I say." If a person mentored is looking for spiritual formation and development, the depth of spirituality, congruence, and personal development should attract them to the mentor. Going for a person void of these qualities is like looking for good fruit from a bad tree, to use Jesus' imagery. Therefore "it is a basic principle of spiritual maturity; you cannot impart what you do not possess."[380]Spiritual formation is a process, and those who have formed spirituality have done so over a period. They would have done so through severe discipline, which is what it takes to develop and be formed spiritually. Lack of a disciplined life is the number one hindrance to spiritual formation. People who have established deep spirituality have the discipline required to help others develop in their spiritual formation.

b. **Ability to Relate:**
When I worked as a counselor, the agency I worked for Relate UK had a saying "it takes two to relate." That statement had two meanings. First, as an agency dealing with relationships, it meant it takes two people to be in a relationship. I used this often to help clients when involved in what we called "split agenda," where one partner wanted to be out of the relationship, and the other was desperate to maintain it. I used this to help the client who was desperate for the relationship to continue to realize that, however much they wanted the relationship; it takes two people to be in a relationship. For the relationship to work, both must be willing to work on it. The second, as a slogan advertising the type of work we did, it aimed to encourage clients who were in a relationship to see the importance of involving their partners, rather than trying to solve the problem on their own. We achieved more working with couples together than dealing with them separately. When we transpose this saying into the mentoring relationship, for it to work, both the mentor and the person mentored must be able to relate and build relationships. The mentor must take an interest in the interests of the person mentored, and the person mentored must know what they want, show willing to work at it, and develop the right kind of relationship with the mentor that will make it happen. It would be almost impossible for

two reserved introverts to form a mentoring relationship. In this regard, Jesus Christ is the primary example of a mentor par excellence. He has the interests of every individual Christian at his heart and longs to relate, Jesus says, "Look! I stand at the door and knock. If you hear my voice and open the door, I will come in, and we will share a meal as friends."[381]Christ offered His life for building a relationship with humankind. What we mean by the ability to relate is having,

> "Ability to initiate and sustain a productive give-and-take relationship with another human being. An effective mentor has to be willing to give of himself to another human being. He must be capable of establishing and maintaining a relationship with another human being."[382]

The Apostle Paul talking of his relationship to the Thessalonians Christians put it thus, "We loved you so much that we were delighted to share with you not only the Gospel of God but our lives as well because you had become so dear to us."[383]

c. **Ability to Communicate**.

Communication is the key to human relationships; one could have many talents, but unless those with gifts can communicate, their abilities will be less beneficial to others. Communication is a two-way process, speaking and listening should take place in keeping to the axiom, "God gave us one mouth, two ears and two eyes God intended us to use them in the same proportion." We should listen twice to speak once; as a counselor, I would say we should listen four times as much as we speak once. We should listen twice, (using our two ears), observe twice (using our two eyes) before we open our mouth once. Listening is an art, of which the most crucial aspect is paying close attention to active listening. Active listening entails listening not to reply or speak but listening to understand. Active listening involves reflecting to check and make sure one has understood what is said. Communication splits three ways - by mouth, ears, and eyes. Let me explain, one of the most important lessons I learned in training, as a counselor, was that we communicate 8% verbally, 37% by tone of voice, and the rest 55% by body language or non-verbal communication. We read body language through observation with our eyes, also by our ears, hearing sounds like sighing and groans and finding out what our clients' sighs and groans mean. In this sense, we listen with our ears and eyes. An effective communicator must de facto be an active listener. "One of the keys to good mentoring is good listening."[384] Communication is always a two-way process. In a mentor-person mentored relationship, while a good mentor is always a good listener, the cororary is also true; a good person mentored should always be a good listener. "Mentoring is not about your mentor displaying his/her brilliance; it is also about the client or protégé learning to step up to the next level so that you develop your competencies."[385]

Mentoring in other professions

When I trained as a counselor, I discovered that in professional counseling, it is required of counselors to have a supervisor to whom they could "off-load" regularly. In current legislation in the UK, it is a requirement for each counselor to have supervision in place before setting up counseling practice. It is also required to see the supervisor regularly, usually once a month or after so many sessions, for mutual support to be effective in counseling. In some organizations like Relate UK, counselors are also encouraged to attend supervision groups regularly, where counselors share their experiences, check what is happening with them in their practice, offload and receive professional support from colleagues. During my practice, it was mandatory to see a supervisor after thirty hours of counseling with clients. During initial training, a new counselor was required to attend a session for observation of an experienced counselor and also to be observed in counseling before being allowed to see clients unsupervised. The initial period of monitoring is a form of mentoring to facilitate healthy formation as a counselor. In Christian Spiritual formation, mentoring is about caring for one's soul by attaching oneself to another for mutual support. It could start as spiritual friendship in prayer partnerships or couplets and develop into spiritual guidance or formal mentoring. Spiritual mentoring takes various forms, ranging from shepherding, spiritual equipping, encouragement, exhortation, and nurturing of spirituality. In any of these forms, it entails a response from the person mentored to the mentoring process. "People who are serious about spiritual growth and ministry need to be part of a rational network that includes vertical mentors and horizontal (peers or co-mentors) relationships." Mentoring involves spiritual direction. The word direction is somewhat a misnomer because it might imply authority, but it has nothing to do with authoritarianism, it has to do with helping people discern with guidance the spiritual pathways in the life of the person mentored. A good spiritual director is, at best, an accompanist observing the outworking of grace in another person's life and finding ways to help them overcome the barriers that may hinder them from hearing God's voice or in implementing spiritual disciplines.

Mentoring and ministerial burn out:

Serving as a minister is a lonely business. It is draining spiritually, emotionally, and physically. Its rigors are such that it is wise to have a spiritual mentor and attend fraternal meetings for mutual support. When I reflect on my ministry over the last thirty years in the British Conference of the Methodist Church, I have four people that I credit for my success, support, sustenance, and formation in ministry in the British Methodist Conference: Rev Dr. Stuart Burgess, David Woodward, Geoffrey Pratt, and Rev Dr. Keith Garner. Each one of these people acted as my mentors in ministry. Although there was no formal designation for them to act as mentors in any official capacity, they each played a pivotal role in my formation as a Methodist Minister in the UK. Primarily, I owe my ministry in the Methodist Church in Britain to Rev Dr. Stuart Burgess, former chair of district and president of the conference. I met him first at Birmingham University in 1987 as our chaplain when my wife did her undergraduate studies while I pursued my doctorate studies at the university. He took great interest in my wife and me as students from overseas. He went on to accept me as an associate non-stipendiary minister and made me his assistant chaplain at St Francis Hall Ecumenical University Chaplaincy. He mentored me as a Methodist minister from other churches and planned me to preach in the South Birmingham Circuit. He encouraged me to join the British Methodist Conference and after resisting for seven years, agreeing only to serve the Methodist church as a non-stipendiary minister while I worked at the Embassy in London to finance my studies and later as a salesman after graduation. When the Lord made it clear that he wanted me to serve in the British Methodist Conference, I was accepted into full connexion in 1995 and served under Stuart as chair of the district when his role as mentor became more formally pronounced. He went on to encourage and mentor my wife, who worked for him voluntarily as district chair office administrator, and through his influence and support, he later laid hands on her as former president of conference during her ordination at St Mary's in Scarborough in 2008. Dr. Burgess is a mentor par excellence and has a knack of knowing how to walk alongside people in their Christian journey. The second person was David Woodward, who was my superintendent in my first one -year full-time appointment as a circuit minister when I started in the Otley and Aireborough circuit. I had requested for a one -year appointment through Stuart Burgess, to taste the waters and see if God was calling me to serve in the British Methodist ministry. My appointed was to pastor three churches - Menston, Huby, and North Rigton in the Otley and Airborough Circuit. I was raw and rooky in British Methodism. David took me under his wings and mentored me with friendship and constant encouragement so much so that I became convinced that God was calling me to minister in the British Methodist Conference. To become a member of the British Conference, I needed to attend an interview for an assessment. I showed some resistance because I did not fully understand what it meant, but David encouraged me, I recall running to catch a train to Victoria Hall in Sheffield with David almost dragging me by the hand not to miss the train and consequently the interview which would have meant missing out from being received into full connexion that year. At that time, I did not know how exact Methodism is with its procedures, schedules, and meetings. David's mentorship helped me so much that this appointment went so well that it forms the hub of my success in the British Methodist ministry.

The impact of that one-year ministry has lasted to this day, such that when Menston Chapel celebrated its 130th chapel anniversary, I was its guest speaker, all thanks to David Woodward, not only as my superintendent but also as my mentor. The third person was the late Rev Geoffrey Pratt, my second superintendent in my first full-time five-year appointment. The appointment was challenging because I had the largest section in the circuit with over 300 members and the largest church in the circuit, Poppleton and possibly largest in the district at that time. I needed a lay worker, Denis Wilson, to assist with the pastoral overload. The challenges in this appointment were immense, not least ministering to an upper-middle-class congregation filled with elite professionals in an exclusively white-only area. I discovered in Geoffrey Pratt mentorship that developed into a caring friendship and one whose help was only a phone call away. The mentorship developed into deep mutual respect. I recall a conversation after completing a third refurbishment project in my section, asking him to organize a rededication of the Hessay Chapel in which Stuart Burgess, the chair of the district, was to preach and dedicate the chapel. I recall him encouraging me with these words, "Daniel you have pastoral oversight of this section; Hessay is one of your churches, it is your honor to organize the service and invite me as superintendent and the chair as your guests, not for me to take over as superintendent and organize it. I had asked him to do so as an honor and observance of the protocol. I felt deeply honored when he encouraged me to lead the show, as it were. I also recall facing a tricky situation at Lidgett Grove Methodist Church, and I asked him to chair the church council and deal with the situation himself. He declined, I reminded him as superintendent according to Constitution, Practice, and Disciplines (CPD) of the Methodist church that he was the chair of all church councils in the circuit, he said that he was aware of that, but insisted that I was the right person to chair the meeting, and he would be in attendance as a member. I chaired the meeting, and he attended in support. The meeting effectively dealt with presenting difficulties in the situation. After the meeting, he called me aside and told me this, "Daniel if I had agreed to chair that church council I would have undermined your authority as a minister in pastoral charge and every time a minor issue arose, the members of that church would be on the phone to me. By being in the meeting, however, and supporting you as I did, they now know who their minister is and where they should channel their problems and listen to your advice and guidance". As a mentor, Geoffrey was a great encourager and believed in teaching on the job. I also recall his training me on how to make the circuit plan as he indeed did with all the other ministers. As a result, three ministers moved from his circuit to be superintendents: Rev Ian Souter in Cornwall, Roger Dunlop in London and I in Lancashire. He was so approachable that I found it easy to consult him with any matter, however mundane. Our conversations started something like this, "Geoffrey, it is Daniel again, what is the matter this time, Daniel?" I would then go on and relate to the problem. I could sense the warmth and interest he took talking to me through his freedom in the way he spoke to me as a colleague and how he guided me. Two such occasions come to mind. I recall phoning him when two congregations, the largest congregation, Poppleton, and one of the smallest, Rafforth, wanted me to lead their services at the same time, creating a dilemma for me. I phoned Geoffrey, and after I related the problem to him he giggled on the phone as usual and said, "Daniel, there is no problem here, whenever such a dilemma occurs, your decision is easy and simple, you always go with the larger congregation"! Another occasion, after guiding me, he concluded with these memorable words, "Daniel, you will learn soon, to accept all resignations and to say no to all offers of second-hand pianos." Geoffrey was a great motivator and mentor; the Lord rest his soul in eternal peace. The fourth person was Rev Dr. Keith Garner; he was my chair of the district in my first appointment as superintendent. Keith went beyond his call of duty as chair of the district in exercising the unwritten rule "that chairs exist to strengthen the arm of the superintendent." He became a real mentor. He helped me get out of very tricky situations through his able mentorship, always with a smile and a giggle. He did not only wait for me to go to him, but he also anticipated situations and alerted me of dangers; without his help, I could have ended in disaster, there is a sense in which through his wisdom and kindness he saved my ministry. I felt like a young eaglet learning to fly under the mentorship of mother eagle! Keith showed me how to handle a difficulty colleague without resorting to the use of the superintendent's power; he mentored me in assessing wisely my re-invitation. The situation was that I felt a dilemma torn between moving on and asking for an extension of my appointment as superintendent of the Littleborough circuit in Lancashire. By asking for an extension, it was going to enable my wife to finish her ministerial training at Luther King House in Manchester and for my son to finish his secondary education in one of the most prestigious high schools, Crompton House, a church school. After carefully listening, Keith said these words which have remained with me since, with his usual grin and smile, he said: "Daniel, your family circumstances are part of God's will in evaluating whether to ask for an extension or to move on." Those words clarified it for me. Keith's mentorship was second nature to him. I recall in 2003 presenting a candidate for the ministry from my circuit to the district panel and went with the candidate as the supporting superintendent. The candidate was a very able preacher, an academic university lecturer. He, however, interviewed so badly, he was going to be rejected by the panel or referred, but Keith intervened in, and through his wisdom and through careful intervention he saved the day without forcing the panel in any way, the candidate went through and is now a very successful minister. All credit to Keith for the way he mentored the situation. In mentioning these four persons as mentors, I am appealing to the reader to reflect with me and thank God for those people God puts on our path to help us as mentors and at times unawares and to remember that we are who we are today largely because of those who invested in us yesterday.[386]'The thought of mentoring others unawares reminds me of the story I recently read on the internet, entitled: "I wish I could be a brother like that."[387] It relates how, in the Philippines, a man parked his car in his office complex in downtown Manila. There was a street boy nearby and to earn some money; the boy asked if he could watch (guard) the man's car while he was in the office. Several hours later, when the man came back to get his nice Mercedes, he paid the boy some loose change and, as he was getting in his car, the little street boy said, "Mister, you sure have a nice car." The man was quite surprised that this boy had even spoken to him and said, "Well, thank you." Then the little boy said, "Where did you get your car? Did somebody give it to you?" The man replied, "Well, yes, somebody did give it to me. My brother gave it to me." As he continued to get in the car, he expected the boy to say something like, "Oh, I wish I had a brother who would give me a nice car." Instead, he heard the little boy say, "Your brother gave it to you? I wish I could be a brother like that". The story goes on to relate how the man enquired from the boy whether he had siblings, and the boy said yes. Then the man offered to drive to the boy's, shady slam home to see the boy's sibling. On arrival, the boys rushed home and brought his brother, who was in a wheelchair, due to a debilitating illness. It turned out that the man's brother was a surgeon. He invited the boy to bring his sibling to his brother, who diagnosed the problem and cured the boy so that he did not need a wheelchair anymore. What a successful conclusion for the story! My wish and prayer, having received all this mentorship, is to emulate the words of the street boy from Manila: "I wish I could be a mentor like that." My comments on each of the four people are not to eulogize them because none of them need my eulogy, for their integrity and influence speaks for itself. My objective was to highlight how God used each one of them as a conduit for my ministerial formation. Each one of them became my role model for ministry at the British Conference. The lasting memory of each of them is how they each treated me like a colleague with a commitment to come alongside me as mentors whenever I needed help. Throughout our interaction, although they were my line managers or in secular terms, my bosses, I never felt it that way. I perceived and experienced them first and foremost as friends for whom I could consult on anything. Friendliness and approachability are a sine qua non in any mentoring relationship. They became my role models because I do not respond well to authoritarianism, perhaps because I experience bullying in my childhood in primary school. I also lost my father when I was nine years old, and all my recollection of him is that he was a gentle, soft-spoken man, contrary to my mother, who was the family disciplinarian. It is possible in my formative years I grew to like gentleness in leadership rather than authoritarianism. I recall when I was appointed a superintendent for the first time, I initially resisted being a superintendent because I associated it with authoritarianism and administrative red tape. Nevertheless, I was persuaded to take the appointment still with misgiving. I recall during training one thing which won me over to accept it, and it was this: the trainer told us that there are two models of superintending, either as the outdated old model, Mr or Mrs. Big Foot who exercises bigfoot everywhere sometimes holding progress and making his or her weight and presence felt. The alternative is Mr. or Mrs. Facilitator/Encourager, who comes alongside his people to facilitate/encourage their ministries. It is the latter, which won me over as it resonated with the mentorship I had received from my first two superintendents and with my first two chairs of the district. I resolved never to bully or boss my colleagues and endeavored during my thirteen years as superintendent minister to model my ministry upon my mentors. Mentoring is critical both for personal spiritual formation and also for formation in Christian ministry. Luciano De Crescenzo said, "We are each of us, angels, with only one wing, and we can only fly by embracing each other." Colleagueship mentoring or peer mentoring is a good example for Christian leaders in the quest for spiritual formation and development in ministry skills; Paul talks about taking the whole armor of God in Ephesians chapter 6. In this text we find that, all the parts of the body are covered, the front part of the body by the shield, the feet, the head, the chest and the loins except the back which needed no cover because the Roman army formed a phalanx interlocking their shields as they moved forward in attack. Due to this battle formation, other soldiers covered the back of fellow soldiers. The flying formation of gees illustrates the importance of peer mentoring and small group fellowship and cultivating the culture of responsibility, accountability, and mutual support in small groups.

The Lost Art of Mentoring:

I grew up in an African primal society where boys were expected to be modeled in hunting by the father or other male figures and girls by their mothers and other female characters. That village background left an indelible mark on my societal formation. To this day, I am a very poor cook; to be dead honest, I loathe cooking. My wife has trained our two boys to be such good cooks that they put me to shame, and I wish I had their cooking skills. One day I did my best in cooking an Indian curry dish only for the youngest, Andrew, to remark, "You have tried dad"! I was expecting a well done! The reason why I am so unskilled in cooking is that in the family household where I grew up, the kitchen was out of bounds for boys. Their place was outside the house in the compound known as "Thome" in vernacular, which was the male fireplace – made up like campfire made of logs of wood, where boys congregated around the fire with the male figures: fathers, uncles, brothers, and other village elders to impart wisdom to the younger generation. From this gathering, wise sayings, clan traditions and values, riddles, bravery, hunting skills, and bravery in battles defending one's clan and tribe were imparted. Girls had similar mentoring from their mothers, grandmothers, and aunties usually done in the kitchen, and other women regularly gathering when they went to draw water. Grandmothers played a significant role in modeling girls. Boys and other men were served their food at "thome" around the fireplace and usually ate with other men. Boys were also taken on hunting coaching. I recall my last such trip was when I was just between sixteen and seventeen years of age. It is as vivid in my mind as if it happened yesterday.

To start with, boys would accompany adults into the bushes and forests, and the expert shooters (skilled sharpshooters) would take their places with their bows and arrows in an ambush while boys chased the animals towards them. The hunting was for food, usually deer, waterbucks, and antelopes. There was no village butcher or supermarket. The only way to get meat for food was through hunting or fishing. When it was my turn to become a sharpshooter, I took my place in ambush behind a large tree, and to my surprise and shock, the biggest heard of waterbucks come past my spot. I froze, and I could not shoot. The group so heavily I criticized me for chickening out; in fact, one of my uncles was so furious he almost hit me! I never went back hunting to this day. In African primal societies, mentoring was imparted verbally and on the job.

When we turn to Western societies, it seems similar forms of mentoring took place in the distant past. "In the past, mentoring happened everywhere. On the farm, boys or girls were mentored alongside mothers, fathers, and extended family members. From the earliest years, these mentors gave children a sense of "maleness" and "femaleness" and taught them what work was all about and how it was done, what character meant, and what were the duties and obligations of each member of the community."[388]Modern society, however, seems to have replaced such mentoring with formal education and certification from institutions. Such has resulted in shifting the stamp of approval from an overseer, a mentor, and placing the criteria for judgment of people upon knowledge rather than wisdom, an achievement rather than character, profit rather than creativity."[389] In the second part of their book[390], Hendricks elucidates in detail the dangers and pitfalls in a lack of mentoring in society. The discussion starts with Hendricks, reflecting on a question once asked by his young daughter, "Daddy, why do big people stop growing?"[391]The loss of the art of mentoring accounts for lack of personal, spiritual, and professional growth in modern society. It also accounts for family breakdown and youth delinquency. In the West, "by the age of six, the average American child will have spent more time watching television, videotapes, and motion pictures than that child spent in an entire lifetime talking to his father. Holywood is raising the next generation!"[392]Lack of mentoring is also responsible for church decline in the West for the simple reasons that older Christians are not able to make new disciples. In most traditional churches in the main denominations, the job for making new Christians; instead, the congregation leaves it to the professional ministers. My ministry over the last three decades has been in the three largest counties in the North of England: Yorkshire, Lancashire, and Lincolnshire. Let alone making new disciples, I have been amazed to find Christians, church stewards even, also known as deacons or elders in other church denominations who cannot string a prayer together talking to God using their own words without having a written prayer! I must put a caveat to this statement. Not all church stewards have been like that. I recall in one of my smallest churches, Thorner being lead in vestry prayer by Mabel Oram, a ninety-five-year-old woman, who is, of course, hard of hearing at that age. She "shouted" a vestry prayer once for me speaking to God so intimately as if he was in the next room. I felt tears of joy, and that prayer uplifted me as I went to the pulpit. As I reflect on my ministry in the last few decades, the Methodist Church, by and large, in most cases with few exceptions, has been involved in endless vicious cycles. The pattern has been, whenever a congregation faces decline, they go for a change of minister to come and fill their empty pews, instead of attending courses to be taught how they can bring new people to faith or even make their faith grow towards maturity in the likeness of Christ. In one congregation, I was invited as their minister because the church was in decline and was going through a review concerning the future. I then asked one of the lay leaders, how much prayer is accompanying these plans? She stunned me with the answer, "we do not do prayer in this church." I thought it was a joke or hyperbole, but two years into the appointment, I found out that she was right. I then suggested that we run an Alpha course, on two occasions, senior members in the lay-leadership of the church told me we do not like the Alpha Course! My profile over the same period has remained the same: I perceive my role as a church minister as one of "equipping the saints for the work of ministry."[393]By holding on to this conviction and style of ministry, I have faced criticism in some churches and even accused of laziness. In a few places where the sense of what I was trying to do, empower the congregation to reach out, it has borne much fruit. One of the churches I served in Lancashire, their membership plateaued, or was starting to decline when I arrived. I suggested beginning an Alpha Course as a discipleship resource in mentoring new Christians and strengthening the existing ones. After much debate in the church council, it was agreed to give it a go. The congregation was in an upmarket area, in Lancashire and finding finances was not a big issue. However, there still was a question of how they would fund the Alpha resource materials. A decision was taken to ask for free-will contributions rather than ask the local church council to authorize that expenditure. I felt the Lord impressing on my heart to do something to encourage them, so I used part of my tithe and paid for the alpha material as an anonymous gift.

One person who was very keen to see some spiritual form of outreach rather than relying on the annual social event the Pantomime offered to coordinate the Alpha initiative. Six years later, I received a note from the person who took on the leadership of running Alpha. She told me that Alpha was still going on; it had run six times. The person added that although attendance was quite low, soul by soul and silently, deep commitments were being made, and lives were being transformed, and the Holy Spirit was moving at that church. The Alpha Course is a relatively new outreach initiative. I recall attending a conference in Mid -1990's during its infancy at Holy Trinity Brompton in London. Holy Trinity Brompton church organized conferences to explain to people planning to use Alpha and make it work for them as a tool for outreach and making disciples. I was privileged with a few others to have lunch with its founder, Right Reverend Sandy Miller, now a bishop. He explained more in detail about how he was moved by the Lord to start Alpha Courses. I suggested Alpha to the Lancashire upmarket congregation because I had a similar experience in York. In York, Alpha Course made a difference, in a rather stagnating, upper-middle-class congregation not only in spurring the growth of the church but also in changing the mindset of the church members who took part in terms of their spiritual growth in affecting their lives and those of other people. My spiritual formation took place in Africa, where I was nurtured spiritually by the Kenya Students Christian Fellowship in which reaching out to other students with the message of the gospel was second nature. Its motto came from Acts 2:32 -This Jesus whom you crucified, we are his witnesses. Leading other people to Christ and mentoring them into discipleship came naturally from the time I committed my life to Christ. It was a big shock when I went to Britain in 1979 and found this not to be the case and even a greater shock when I found Christians who have been attending church for donkey's years and could not pray extempore, let alone leading another person to Christ. When I started as a full-time minister in Yorkshire, my main church had 218 members. The circuit decided to host a seminar for all churches in the circuit on church growth run by the Bible Society. As I tried to encourage my churches to get involved, I ran across stiff resistance. I can recall a conversation from one of the most experienced lay preachers in that church who was also the senior circuit steward at that time. He told me, "Daniel, what do we need this course for we are the largest church in the circuit/ district, we have over two hundred members?" I remember telling him tongue in cheek that was the size of the Sunday school in my church in Africa, which had over three thousand members. I shared this conversation with my first superintendent, David Woodward, expressing my surprise and exasperation. David told me, "Daniel you have a culture shock, you have lived in Africa where the church has been growing fast for decades, here in the West we have lived with church decline for the last thirty years that is your difficulty." David believed in church growth and attended Easter People, the Methodist equivalent of the Spring Harvest, a weeklong conference of spiritual renewal in the week after Easter. The art of mentoring new Christians by older Christians has become the lost art of some of the churches in the West. This loss makes it difficult for the church to renew and revive itself. If this art were rediscovered, it could become a catalyst to counter church decline in the West. The call to follow Christ, however, is a call to the perpetual growth process. It is also a call to a perpetual life of mentoring new Christians. Christians who are themselves involved in personal growth and spiritual formation will find it second nature to mentor other Christians. Christians who are stunted or stagnated in their spiritual growth will find it hard to mentor new Christians. Christian faith is a growth process, daily longing to be like Christ in his love, patience, holiness, and forgiveness. Mentoring is also a Biblical mandate – "teach and admonish one another with all wisdom - grow in the grace and knowledge of our Lord Jesus Christ"[394]A Christian mentor is a person who is committed to helping another person grow and keep growing and helping that person realize their life goals in following Christ. In general, terms, a mentor provides wisdom, as practical skills for living, a source of Christian information, a sounding board for a younger growing Christian, nurtures Christian curiosity, and is a couch in holy living. "The object of mentoring is to build a relationship that impacts another person's life."[395]The mandate to make disciples, also known as the great commission[396]is a commission to "a ministry of multiplication."[397]Most Christians show reticence to engage with the mentoring ministry for all sorts of reasons: apathy, feelings of inadequacy, lack of time. These fears or excuses arise when mentoring is thought of as something done to the person mentored, but the mentoring relationship helps both the mentor and the person mentored, "we grow most in the process of helping others grow."[398]As I look back on my Christian formation, the period I felt I grew most was when I was in my sixth form in a Catholic High School, where the Lord used me to start a Christian union and became its first chairperson. The Lord used me to get other boys to come to Christ in such a way that I could not believe what was happening, the only Bible verse that kept coming to my mind was "this is the Lord's doing, it is marvelous in our eyes."[399]When I arrived at that staunch Catholic High school, the protestant prayer - a group comprised of about five students. By the time I left the school in two years, we had grown to over thirty. I recall organizing what was known as Weekend Emphasis - a series of teaching, exuberant worship accompanied by testimonies, prayer, and praise that started on Friday and went on through Saturday, with the climax on Sunday afternoon, consisting of a Christian Rally attended by students from other Christian Unions in the surrounding secondary schools. The rally that weekend was so big that there was no one classroom big enough to accommodate the numbers, such that we were allowed to use the Roman Catholic Chapel! I invited the local theological college, now Scott Christian University, to sent representatives to come and lead the weekend teaching. They sent two of their senior students, Jones and Julius. It felt like revival had broken in that school. I was only twenty-one, I had no theological training, I had only been a Christian for four years, I came from a non-Christian home, and yet other boys were so touched by my preaching and witnessing that they committed their lives to Christ, through God's grace. I honestly cannot remember how I nurtured them, and some went on following Christ, some becoming prominent Christians, one in particular Anthony, founded a church and went on to be deputy provincial director of education in the country, he usually referred to me as his father in the faith because I mentored him as a young Christian. Anthony was in the second year in that high school when I joined as a fifth former. I recall his sharing how the Lord touched him as he observed my life unashamedly proclaiming Christ publically as a sixth former. One memory I took out of that school is that it earned me my first guitar. I learned to play the guitar in my previous secondary school, St Charles Lwanga, where the Lord used me to start the Christian union, and I became its first chairman. I used it to form singing groups for praise in worship, but I could not afford school fees. I mainly relied on bursaries and philanthropy, let alone afford a guitar. At my sixth form schools, in Mangu and Kabaa high school, I took Maths, Physics, Chemistry, and Biology. It is Chemistry that fascinated me most in line with my chosen career at that time, to be a pharmacist. I formed a friendship with the chemistry teacher, Mr. Griffin, who came from the US under the Overseas Volunteer Service. I spent extra time with him in the chemistry laboratory until late in the night observing experiments. One time, we made acetylsalicylic acid (Aspirin), and I was quite proud of it. But my spending time with Mr. Griffin had a hidden motive, I wanted to convert him to be a Christian, so I took every opportunity to witness to him, and I used borrowing his guitar as a good excuse to start the conversation. After some time, I went to borrow his guitar, chancing an opportunity to witness to him. Then unexpectedly, he gave me this shock, he said, "Daniel, you know I do not use this guitar a lot, and you seem to be putting it to good use, you can keep it, it is now yours!" Although I cannot remember the exact time when I led Anthony to Christ, perhaps he could be one of the boys who responded after an altar call following one of my preaching services, or perhaps my lifestyle and witness touched him. In either case, his testimony was that I influenced him to become a Christian. Mentoring is not a profession; it is a duty of every Christian who wants to make a difference for Christ. "The most compelling question that every Christian must ask is this: What am I doing today that will be an influence for Jesus Christ in the next generation. We cannot hold onto the world; we can only hand it to others."[400]Reflecting on David's prayer in Psalm 71:17-18, Hendricks underscores the importance of doing something for the next generation and observes that:

> "Somehow, David was not impressed by his crown, his kingdom, his wealth, his wives, or even his incredible talents as a ruler, warrior, a builder, a musician, a poet. The only thing that mattered to David was, 'what does God think of me?'"[401]

That determined his purpose. David was not a perfect man but a purposive man. Today we live in a society driven by the question of what is in it there for me? Modern society is driven by self-gain, and since mentoring is not like counseling, where we charge a fee for helping someone, we tend to put it aside. Mentoring, however, is within the DNA of our psychosocial makeup. Eric Erikson, a German psychoanalyst who was a protégé of Sigmund Freud, developed in 1950 his eight stages theory of identity and psychological development that all human beings go through. He calls the seventh stage, the middle-aged adults between the ages of 46-65, and defined generativity as "making your mark on the world through caring for others as well as creating and accomplishing things that make the world a better place."[402]Getting involved in other people's lives and helping them make a difference is one of the most fulfilling things one could ever do to boost their self-worth. The converse is true; self-absorption is the least fulfilling life there is. Perhaps this is what Jesus was alluding to when he said, "For whoever wants to save their life will lose it."[403] He went on to give an example with his own life when he said, Mark 10:45 (NLT), "For even the Son of Man came not to be served but to serve others and to give his life as a ransom of many."

I can illustrate the principle of generativity in my own life when I found out that helping others has affected my life and became a source of joy. Reflecting on my ministry as a Christian minister, I can recall occasions when I was spiritually down, feeling deflated, and beginning to think that I was of no use and doubting whether I was in the right place or whether I should throw in the towel. On each occasion, the Lord miraculously encouraged me. One such time God uplifted me through an anonymous letter, in which the writer asked me to forgive him or her for not signing the letter. I treasure that letter to this day. That letter uplifted me so much that I nicknamed it "letter from God himself." To this day, I do not know who wrote the message because the writer stated that they wanted it to remain anonymous. However, that letter uplifted me and restored my soul, giving me the confidence I needed at that time, to continue in ministry. The note left me wondering how anybody knew the turmoil I was going through, and I had not shared it with anybody. Through that letter, I feel to this day that God intervened directly to encourage me and restore my confidence in His ministry. The words contained in that letter were precisely what I needed at that time. My dominant thought was whether I was useful in that appointment, and the letter stated that since my arrival at that church, my ministry had made a significant impact on that person's life.

On the second occasion, I was actually on compassionate leave following similar circumstances from one of my churches, my feelings were raw, and I was at the lowest I have ever been in my entire Christian ministry. Feelings ofbeing useless were dominant in my thoughts at the time. I had started to wonder what I had achieved. Then this happened, I heard a beep on Messenger; one of the social media applications on my iPhone, it was a call from overseas requesting me to turn on my video call application from Winnie Ndumu, this was unique because although we kept in touch through the social media, she had never expressed interest on face –to - face conversation. I felt it must be important, and I turned on the video call, and there she was. Winnie calls me her dad in the faith, for she became a Christian through a Christian rally where I was preaching. She said, dad, I just wanted to see your face after all those years and bless you for the blessings you brought in my life and invite you to stop and see us at our home next time you come to Kenya. I had not seen her for nearly forty years. Winnie developed in leaps and bounds in her Christian formation, she got a scholarship, went, and studied theology in the US; she went back as lecturer in one of the universities in Nairobi, is now working for Life Ministries, and keeps sending me encouraging videos and pictures of evangelistic campaigns she is involved in with her husband. Through that video link conversation, I felt an Elijah moment; inspired by that video call reminding me of the great spiritual achievements the Lord has accomplished through my life. A person the Lord used me to influence four decades ago uplifted me at her unawares. Around the same time, I received an uplifting email from a fourteen - year - old girl who worshipped in one of the churches, a place I had pastoral oversight in my care from where I had transferred from over three years to that day. We met with her family when I arrived at that church five years previously, so she was five years old when I first met her at the church.

The email read, "Message from Zoe, Hi Daniel, its Zoe (your little pink girl). I hope you and Margaret are all right. It has been so long since we last saw each other, and I have missed you greatly and have thought about you a lot. I truly hope you are well. Your little pink girl is not so little anymore! I have finally exceeded mum height-wise, and I am turning 14 at the beginning of May. I thought you might be pleased to know that I have chosen to study ethics, philosophy, and religion as one of my GCSE subjects because a lot of it is based on Christianity as well as considering morals. When I was younger, I was lucky enough to have strong influences on Christianity and morals, thanks to you, your inspirational services, and other members of the Methodist church. I was also wondering if you had the time that you could explain a bit about confirmation, as it is something I may be interested in. However, I am not really sure what it is even about, and you seemed like the perfect person to ask! I really hope to see you soon. All my love and best wishes, your little pink girl." The sentiments from this little girl's email much uplifted me. When she was younger, she attended church usually dressed in pink hence the nickname, little pink girl." Mentoring people is quite rewarding, and its results usually come back to the mentor unawares as it did in my case on these two occasions.

Going back to consider reticence to mentoring, the final reason I would slightly mention is by people shying away from undertaking mentoring, perceiving it as a lot of work. From my own experience, the role of mentoring is both passive as well as a proactive activity. There are those people that we influence unawares and those whom we proactively engage in a mentoring relationship. On reading testimonies from people who have been involved in a mentoring relationship, their responses resonate with the parable Jesus gave about the final judgment and in particular, the surprising responses, Matthew 25:39-40 (GW), "When did we see you sick or in prison and visit you? Whatever you did for one of my brothers and sisters, no matter how unimportant they seemed, you did it for me." There is a lot of passive mentoring that happens as Christians live their daily lives, and others observe how they live. Mentoring is an opportunity to invest in kingdom values, and every Christian must welcome it. Whenever an opportunity arises for mentoring, Christians should carefully and prayerfully consider it before turning it away; for whatever supposedly good reasons or excuses, heeding the caution in a saying attributed to Thomas Edison, "Opportunity is missed by most people because it is dressed in overalls and looks like hard work."[404] For those who turn away mentoring fearing that it is hard work, they may do so because of the mistaken understanding of mentoring. The art of mentoring does not all depend on the mentor; it is a two-way process; the person mentored plays a vital role. "A mentor is like a man flying a kite. The kite does the flying, and the wind creates the lift. All the man has to do is hold the string with just the right balance of pull and give. If he draws the string too tightly, he puts stress on the kite, and that can rip it apart. But if he lets out too much line and the wind dies, the kit will begin to fall."[405]As a two way process, the mentor could learn a lot from the person mentored, if the relationship is working well. My wife and I are both computer literate, she has diplomas in IT, and we are both touch typists having learned to type at college. However, as we entered the IT and Dot.com generation, we have found ourselves heavily dependent on our youngest son, who is a Millennial in most of the electronic gadgets we have purchased. We have also discovered his opinion as a Millennial quite profound, giving the youth world perspectives. His political interpretation during the recent American campaign for the election of President Trump and the UK Brexit helped us see a point of view we would have missed. Mentoring is a two-way process, "and just as you (as a mature person) can help interpret what the world has been to your protégé, he can help interpret what the world is becoming to you. He can be a tremendous source of information, keeping you up-to-date on current issues, questions, problems, opportunities, developments, and trends."[406] Mentoring others is like an investment that one draws joy from in later years as one sees the multiplication of one's life through the lives of others. Mentoring, like Eric Erikson, demonstrated in his theory of generativity, gives a sense of confidence, having made a difference in the lives of others. Hendricks sums it up thus:

Two lines run through a man's life, a lifeline, and a purpose line. The lifeline marks biological progress; the purpose line marks the spiritual progress. Once the purpose line begins to taper off, it is just a question of time before the lifeline does the same. What a tragedy, then that for many men, we can already write their epitaph. 'Here lies John. Died, aged 39. Buried, age 69'.[407]

Mentoring helps out the mentors live purposeful lives. The most important lesson that I have learned from mentoring others is that it is like harvesting water into a cistern, whereby as my well of happiness and encouragement dries out, I find water in what I have invested in others. Observation from nature teaches us that essential things, do not live for themselves. The sun does not shine for itself, and the flowers do not spread their fragrance for themselves. Neither do rivers drink their own water. Living for others emulates nature. Life is at its best when others are happy because of you. Mentoring others might appear to be hard work, but its benefits are out of this world.

Mentoring and the Wesleyan Tradition

The Wesleyan Holiness movement started with the work of John and Charles Wesley. John Wesley was convinced that "the Church is in the business of producing Christian character. Christians are called to be saints, called to perfection – i.e., the maturity of thought and faithfulness of lifestyle."[408]It began as a revival movement that initially came to be known as Methodism. It was borne out of John Wesley's creative and courageous response to the institutional malaise in the established Anglican Church. According to John Wesley, the key purpose of the church was "to form a community of faith and practice that responds in its life together and witness to the world, to the presence of Jesus Christ."[409] In Mentoring, there are two aspects necessary for spiritual formation:- Firstly: Face-to-face groups in Christian nurture. Such groups are best illustrated in the Wesleyan heritage of small-group ministries, which became the genius of Wesley that he imparted to the Holiness Movement. Secondly, mentoring helps cultivate a discipline of mutual encouragement, strengthening, accountability, and growth. To date, no one has yet improved on John Wesley's plan for pastoral care. Its bountiful success in caring for converts, building up believers, and leading Christians into the experience of sanctification demands our attention in our quest for spiritual formation and ministry development. Most of the believers who found sanctification as a discipline in Wesley's time did so in a small-group meeting. Through his spiritual guidance and teaching, he structured what came to be known as Christian Conference. Therein, people experienced mutual spiritual guidance in classes, bands, societies, families, in "twin soul" and faith mentoring pairs. The society in the Methodist Connexion was at first a religious organization within the Church of England. Societies held no meetings or services that would conflict with the Anglican worship schedule. Eventually, the society became a sort of local congregation meeting in chapels, halls, and homes. The society had four meetings. On Sunday evenings, service was held consisting of preaching, Scripture reading, exhortations, testimonies, and hymn-singing. The society also had a 5 a.m. meeting on a weekday morning. The workday started at 6 a.m., the Methodists went to the factories, and the mines armed with a fresh religious experience. The societies also held a joyous watch night service monthly on Saturday night. It came at the full moon so the members would have moonlight by which to walk home. The societies also held the Love Feast, a service that began with a meal of bread and water, preceded by opportunities to mend relationships, and ended with testimonies and praise. The Class Meeting is hailed as Wesley's most significant contribution. D. L. Moody called it "the greatest tool for discipling converts ever devised."

The society was subdivided into classes of about 12 persons each. Every member of the society was required to join a class that met weekly. The class meeting was a more or less democratic forum where rich and poor, old and young, the educated and the illiterate could meet as peers. At first, "class meetings met in homes, shops, school rooms, attics—even coal pits—wherever there was room for ten or twelve people to assemble. The leadership of classes was open to both genders. In its infancy, the class meeting was the only significant leadership role for women in Britain in a male-dominated culture in the wider society. David Michael Henderson calls the class meeting an instructional group. Methodist doctrines and practices, along with the Sunday sermons, were explained, but the class was also an arena of *koinonia* (fellowship). Acceptance, love, and mutual commitment were the keynotes. After an opening hymn, the typical meeting would then see the class leader share the problems and victories in his or her spiritual life. Class members would then voluntarily follow suit. Answers to prayer, spiritual lessons learned from experience as well as temptations, griefs, backslidings, and the like were shared. In this context of prayer, trust, and confession, spiritual growth was accelerated.[410]Wesley summarized the function of the classes in the regular publication of the Arminian Magazine. The objectives of the class meetings were:-

a. To know who continues as members of the society;
b. To inspect their outward walking;
c. To inquire into their inward state;
d. To learn what are their trials; and how they fall by or conquer them;
e. To instruct the ignorant in the principles of religion; to repeat,
f. To explain and to enforce what was said in public preaching.

The class meeting also ensured that they have a definite, full, abiding conviction that without inward, complete, universal holiness, no man shall see the Lord.

When the Wesleyan revival went to America, the first noticeable feature was rampant revivalism, and, as it developed, the success of the Sunday school shoved the class meeting into the background. Today, in American Methodism, what is left of the heritage of the class meeting is expressed in adult Sunday school classes, in small-group Bible studies, and membership classes. Mentoring did not end with the class meetings. It continued in what was known as the bands: The bands were same-gender groups of five or six persons committed to each other and the holy life. They met to help each other on the road to Christian perfection. The aim for the bands was more in-depth Christian life development among peer groups, and only about one-third of the typical society joined, or was invited to join the bands where they shared their spiritual journeys without reserve and disguise. John Wesley called this close conversation. He felt that Methodism was closest to the New Testament ideal in the band meetings. Wesley said he saw one man who learned more about the spiritual life in one band meeting than he had in 10 years of listening to public preaching.[411]The entry qualification to join the band was by answering eleven questions five of which read as follows:-

1. Have you the forgiveness of sins and peace with God through our Lord Jesus Christ?
2. Have you the witness of God's Spirit within your spirit that you are a child of God?
3. Has no sin, inward or outward, dominion over you?
4. Do you desire to be told all your faults?
5. Is it your desire and design to be, on this and all other occasions, entirely open to speaking everything that is in your heart without exception, without disguise, and without reserve?

Each band meeting started with five questions that Wesley himself wrote.

These were:-

1. What known sins have you committed since our last meeting?
2. What temptations have you met with?
3. How were you delivered?
4. What have you thought, said or done, of which you doubt whether it is a sin or not?
5. Have you nothing you desire to keep secret?[412]

These questions adapted in today's contemporary language would read as follows:-

1. What spiritual failures have you experienced since our last meeting? What known sins, if any, have you committed?
2. What temptations have you battled with this week? Where do you feel vulnerable right now?
3. What temptations have you been delivered from this week? Please share with us how you won the victory.
4. Has the Lord revealed anything to you about your heart and life that makes you want us to join you in taking a second look at what might be sinful attitudes, lifestyle, or motivations?
5. Is there any spiritual problem that you have never been able to talk about to us or even to God?

Looking at these questions repeatedly every week, firstly, we notice peer mentoring illustrated at its very best among trusted friends. We encounter life-on-life mentoring at a deeper level. Most of these questions would be deemed offensive in our modern society whose motto is live and let live. Also, due to the permeation of permissive ethics and the slogan that the truth for you is not the truth for me, asking such questions would be a non –starter. However, as the saying goes, where there is a will, there is away. It is possible to reformulate these questions in a nonoffensive language, a kind of - culturally dynamic equivalent to foster similar fellowship to band meetings. As it was in Wesley days, peer mentoring and development of social and spiritual accountability are paramount to Christians today. There is a hole in the middle of our social and spiritual engagement in which we too often go to church and look at the back heads of our fellow believers' heads during public worship, exchange pleasantries, and social courtesies and never see into each other's hearts. The revival and camp meeting emphasis in America diminished the Band Meeting in the 19th century and early 20th century. And with the Sunday school then charged with almost all the Christian nurture duties, the ministry of the bands faded in most Methodist churches in America. The genius of the band was, however, rediscovered when covenant groups surged through the religious and secular culture in the last three decades of the 20th century. The Wesleyan and Wesleyan-Holiness groups could have embraced the covenant group work, but they had all but discarded the band ethos in favor of revivalism and Sunday school work. There was also a strong desire to emulate Southern Baptists, who were deemed to be successful. The willingness to ape and follow the Baptists in terms of church culture in the Holiness Movement contributed to the loss of the class and band meeting heritage. The Holiness Movement churches had to relearn the covenant and support group ethos by borrowing from the culture and digging into their all but forgotten heritage. Today covenant groups operate as vestiges of the DNA of the Wesleyan-Holiness Movement. The mentoring in discipleship in the Holiness Movement in pursuit for entire sanctification drove the movement to initiate what was known as the Penitent Bands, which could also be called the "backsliders' band" designed especially for sincere people who, for some reason, kept being recaptured by some besetting sin. They wanted to do right but had not found the strength and discipline to utterly forsake their sins and stay on the path to perfection. For the persons in that category, the penitent band met on Saturday nights. It enabled people to open confession of sins with the desire for assistance to spiritual restoration. One wonders what would happen to the spiritual temperature in our churches if those with persistent spiritual problems and failures could, without disgrace or losing face, go to a regular meeting for people just like them? What a celebration when someone would graduate from the penitent band![413] The principle of the band meetings has been adopted by Alcoholics Anonymous (AA) in the UK to help alcohol addicts recover from their addiction. Other similar secular, self-help groups use the principles of the band meetings with a measurable degree of definite success of rehabilitation. What a legacy from the Wesley movement!

In the Wesleyan tradition, Spiritual formation and mentoring were also engendered in what was known as the Select Society: This was a small group for leaders in the Methodist Connexion. Only the most faithful and dedicated were invited. The Select Society had no rules and no order of service. It had no official leader. Even if John Wesley himself was present, he did not preside. Any topic or concern of the leadership team could be discussed. Wesley's first experiment with this structure aimed at helping people advance in perfection. It also enabled them to love each other more, improve every leadership talent. In his own words, Wesley said, "to have a select company, to whom

I might unbosom myself on all occasions, without reserve; and whom I could propose to all their brethren as a pattern of love, of holiness, and good works." In the Select Society, there were no rules, but it had three directions: - Firstly, everything discussed was in confidence.

Secondly, in indifferent matters or opinions regarding non-essentials, members were to abide by the arbitration of the senior minister among them. Thirdly, everyone gave to the common stock of offerings of money and goods for the poor. Such giving was in harmony with the directive for all Wesleyan small-groups meetings—each group was to give an offering for the poor in every session, without any exceptions. In modern church life in the UK, this is known as the benevolent fund sustained through the second collection after communion. In wealthier societies, this is replenished by directly drawing from the general church fund to lessen constant appeals for funds. In less affluent societies, requests to contribute to the benevolent fund are necessary to maintain the fund. Wesleyan studies and visits to the birthplace of the Wesley brothers at The Old Rectory in Epworth would reveal that the Reverend Samuel Wesley and his wife Susanna brought up their nineteen children in family worship. The visitors would discover the room in which Susanna educated these children. My several visits to the rectory and the guide to the home of the Wesley brothers left me with the impression that, while Samuel Wesley was the reverend of the Parish, Susanna Wesley was the reverend at home in the rectory. She had a profound influence on the way her children planned out in their lives, and she mentored them in their early spiritual formation in the family worship that she took sole charge. The Methodical way in which the Wesley brothers developed their church life must have been influenced and mentored by Susanna. She was a staunch believer in family worship as a vehicle for mentoring. She was leading a large Bible study in the house as a non- ordained person that her husband Samuel confronted her about it. In her response as recorded in her Journal she asserted thus: "if after all this you think fit to dissolve this assembly, do not tell me you desire me to do it, for that will not satisfy my conscience; but sent your positive command in such full and express terms as may absolve me from all guilt and punishment for neglecting this opportunity for doing good when you and I shall appear before the great and awful tribunal of our Lord Jesus." Susanna Wesley took face-to-face mentoring of her children seriously, such that in her journal, she went on to say: "I am a woman, but I am also the mistress of a large family. And though the superior charge of the souls contained in it lies upon you, yet in your long absence, I cannot but look upon every soul you leave under my charge as a talent committed to me under a trust... take such a proportion of time as I can spare every night to discourse with each child apart. On Monday, I talk with Molly on Tuesday with Hetty, Wednesday with Nancy, Thursday with Jacky, Friday with Patty, Saturday with Charles."

From such family upbringing, we find that one of the essential groups during Wesley's time was—the family. Family worship and study was recommended twice daily, morning, and evening. It was one of the engines that fuelled the Methodist revival. The emphasis on this was great. On top of this, Thursday night was given to the one-on-one parent to child instruction. On Saturday night, the family would review all that they had learned during the week. To help with the family worship and religious education, Wesley provided A Collection of Prayers for Families, Prayers and Devotions for Every Day of the Week, Prayers for Children, Lessons for Children, and Instructions for Children on Christian living. To help parents who had little experience with family worship, Wesley devised an 8 –part methodical family worship composed of:

1) 1 A short extemporaneous (impromptu) or read a prayer.
2) 2 Psalm singing.
3) 3 Bible study. A parent was to read the Scripture for the day and explain it. Then the children were to describe the Bible passage back to the parents.
4) Family Prayer using both written and spontaneous prayers.
5) Singing of the Doxology.
6) A parent gave the benediction.
7) The Blessing. The parent laid hands on the head of each child and blessed the child in Jesus' name, a tradition I found among the Maasai of Kenya in which the greeting to a child is by laying hands on the child's head. I discovered this when I went to visit a Maasai family with one of the parents, Rosalyn Pakine, who was my student in the MA program. When the children opened the door, they stood in front of me with their heads bowed down, waiting for me to lay my hands on them. I did not know what to do until the parent realized my embarrassment and performed the ritual on my behalf!

Wesley gave instructions that the blessing in Jesus' name, was never to be omitted no matter how bad the child had behaved that day. This form of mentoring is quite powerful even for the ill-behaved child for being blessed in Jesus' name by a parent every day—even on days when the child's conduct did not deserve it must have had a substantial impact on teaching how we receive means of grace from God. It would boost a child's self-esteem and their spiritual health and formation.

To summarize, mentoring help in spiritual formation and ministerial development in several ways: - Firstly, face-to-face, the life-on-life offer of companionship on the spiritual journey.

Secondly, face-to-face groups form an essential part of the Church as a community of faith.

Thirdly, developing the skills and disciplines of face-to-face discipleship is vital in spiritual formation and life development and ministry skills and spiritual practice in ministry. Fourthly, class meetings, band meetings, and special society meetings help in developing the disciplined skills of accountability.

Fifthly, this mentoring enables development in the skill of encouragement to others.

Sixthly, the class meetings form of mentoring provides the discipline not only of fellowship but also a sense of belonging. Too many Christians have no one to talk to about their most profound spiritual battles and needs. Granted that in today's society, we may not be able to reproduce John Wesley's precise structures, we can ferret out valuable gems from it and apply in our situations because, as mentioned earlier, we are all one-winged angels and as such must embrace each other so that we can fly. There is merit to heeding the words of John Wesley, "It is a blessed thing to have fellow travelers on the road to the New Jerusalem. If you do not find any, you must make them, for none can travel this road alone."[414]

The above discussion underscores the importance of mentoring in spiritual formation, whether on a one to one basis or in small groups. The vestigial remains of the discipline of mentoring is often expressed among modern Christians in the language of "watching each other in love" but its practical implication is usually lacking and as such allows to set in the dry rot of decline in most Wesleyan Holiness Movement through deliberate abandoning its DNA of spiritual care, nurture and mentoring. If the Wesleyan Holiness Movement were to rediscover its DNA, it ought to perhaps consider asking the following questions:-

1. What are face-to-face group experiences in place in the past year that mirrors one of the early Wesleyan groups?
2. What follow up groups are there to help converts experience face-to-face mentoring?
3. Are other nurture groups there for the community in the life of the local church?
4. What plans are there to improve the sense of belonging for all in the life of the local church? How is it monitored to make sure all feel included?
5. What is the dynamic equivalent of Wesleyan face-to-face groups in modern society?
6. If we were to start a covenant group something like Wesley's bands, around what would it be organized in the context of the local church?
7. To recover their DNA, what needs to change in the mindset and life of the local church?
8. The role of one-to-one spiritual guidance as a means of grace is of paramount importance in spiritual formation. Serving as spiritual friends and faith mentors is one way of practicing the priesthood of all believers. We serve as "God's ushers" to each other.

There is ample literature[415] on spiritual mentoring, which helps us discern the Wesleyan model of spiritual friends and faith mentors and what soul friends and faith mentors look like today.

By God's usher, we are referring to the ministry of faith mentors and spiritual friends. They usher the one they serve into the presence of God. It is the ministry of ushering friends down the paths of righteousness, truth, and peace, where God can reveal himself through His Word and the Holy Spirit. It is part of the Reformation doctrine of the priesthood of all believers. We are talking about a ministry of mediation in which faith mentors and soulmates in peer mentoring mediate grace, the love of God, discernment, self-knowledge, and a sense of vocation or calling[416]. This discipline cannot be compared, let alone equated with preaching to 1,000 people, nor is it like teaching a class of 20. The one-to-one; or life-on-life ministry is crucial and more fundamental for Christian growth and discipleship. If the Christian faith is to prosper in the post-Christian age, it will require spending more time with fewer people and in investing and developing one-to-one relationships. Mass appeals still have their place, but society and culture have changed, making these less productive. Mass evangelism in the Western World has had its day; in God's economy of time, it seems to have given way to friendship evangelism if we could coin such a term. By that, I mean, befriending people to mentor them for their benefit and God. In today's egalitarian society, one to one mentoring and outreach becomes more amenable and commendable in terms of contextual mentoring in teaching Christian values. The ministry of coaching, nurturing, and teaching should be done in small groups and one-to-one ministry. More time with fewer people seems to be the more commendable modus operandi of our modern society. The Wesleyan spiritual disciplines of community involvement through friendships, mentoring pairs—one-to-one relationships commend themselves as being the way forward for the future. Faith mentoring is the ministry of an experienced, mature, established Christian to a new convert, a young Christian, or even a not-yet-converted person. Mentoring is the spiritual equivalent of an apprentice relationship. John Wesley called them "spiritual fathers" and "nursing mothers." This phraseology was not original to Wesley; it is found in Pauline epistles addressing the Thessalonian Christians.[417] Twin souls are the term Wesley used to describe two mature spiritual friends who met with each other regularly as equals, giving to each additional support, accountability, discerning insight, concerned counsel and love as they serve as God's usher to one another. Perhaps this is the most neglected ministry among Wesleyan-Holiness people today. The mature Christian is always called to serve, serve, and serve some more, but who is it that helps, the ministers, and the more experienced Christian? When I started as a trainee counselor, it was stressed that I needed to have a supervisor to practice. I thought it was because I was a novice, only to discover that even my supervisor was required to have a supervisor! The principle was that one could not receive emotional baggage of other people without one being able to off-load and ventilate and process one's own emotions triggered by the receiving in the process of counseling. The question of who cares for the carers has guided the work of social services. What a pity that in Christianity too often, those who minister to others are left alone to fend for themselves. Such faithful believers need a soul friend with whom they can share the spiritual life "without reserve and disguise." The Bible has plenty of passages that support the concept and discipline of mentoring. For example, Paul, as Faith Mentor for the Thessalonians said: 1Thessalonian 2:7 (NRSV): "So deeply do we care for you that we are determined to share with you not only the gospel of God but also our own selves because you have become so dear to us. We were gentle among you, like a nurse tenderly caring for her own children. Paul went on to say, 1Thessalonian 2:11-12 (NRSV) "We dealt with each one of you like a father with his children, urging and encouraging you and pleading that you live a life worthy of God, who calls you."

Faith Mentoring takes the form of coaching, teaching, and sharpening skills, encouragement, and accountability. When Jane Hilton, a new Christian under the mentoring of John Wesley, was devastated by a withering temptation, he wrote to her, "Christ is yours, and He is wiser and stronger than all the powers of hell. Hang upon Him . . . lean upon Him, the whole weight of your soul."[418] Her faith mentor would not let her give up. The way Wesley dealt with his struggler should inspire us to want to do the same for others. It also takes the form of modeling, as mentioned earlier. "You became imitators of us and the Lord."[419] The modeling is not cloning but objectively modeling in integrity and truth and always pointing to Christ. As the person being mentored grows, their eyes become fixed on Jesus, the perfect model, to be like Jesus is at the heart of mentoring. Faith mentoring also hands down the gems of the Christian faith to the younger generations. Sometimes a mentor acts as a mapmaker in helping the person mentored gain a long-range view of their past life and future possibilities. From this comprehensive view of the person's past, along with a realistic understanding of the present, the mentor can help the person-mentored map out attainable goals[420]. Another image of a mentor is that of a sponsor in which an older Christian walks along with a younger Christian. In one of the churches I ministered, whenever young families brought their children to be baptized, the church appointed an appropriate sponsor from the main body of the church to act on behalf of the church in helping that child grow in the Christian faith. In this program, each young person seeking to be "confirmed" is publicly assigned a sponsor whose role is publicized for all the church to be aware of: Firstly, as a model of how a person of faith lives in today's world. Secondly, as a friend who knows the child and eventually gets to know the family and can witness to the maturing faith of that child before the community. Thirdly, the sponsor acts as a guide and confidant, providing an early opportunity for the mentoring relationship to develop, if and whenever it is desired. Fourthly, sponsors offer themselves as learners interested in their personal growth as they walk the faith journey with the sponsored youth. Sponsor offer themselves as one who invites the candidate into fuller participation in church life and service. There is also the concept of Midwife of the Soul, implying that the faith mentor is often dealing with another person who has yet to discover, understand, and claim the spiritual realities of God. The faith mentor in Celtic literature is sometimes described as the midwife of the soul—aiding the birth of the spiritual life. The one being taught is shown the deep needs and possibilities of his or her own heart and soul. New birth includes discovering how his or her spiritual yearnings connect with the Spirit of God. Mentoring spiritual births and rebirths require patience, love, and discernment.[421] A faith mentor also may assume the role of advocate or guarantor in the loose sense of the word, whereby they may need to defend, explain, or protect the person mentored. Hendricks[422] relates an example of such a case in which a young person, Julius, was rescued from arrest by the police by his mentor Jerry vouching for him. Jerry had lost his sixteen-year-old brother in tragic circumstances and determined 'to love somebody else's brother,' a determination that made him have a youth ministry through mentoring. Where mentoring takes formal engagement, the mentor may make any of the following pledges:-

1. Promise to spend the time it takes to build an intensely bonded relationship with the person mentored.

2. Commit to the task of visualizing and articulating the possibilities and potential of the person mentored.
3. Promise to be honest, yet affirming, in confronting the errors, faults, prejudices, and immaturities of the person mentored
4. Make an undertaking to be transparent, own failures and brokenness, strengths, and successes as part of a relationship of integrity with person mentored.
5. Commit to standing through trials and hardships with the person mentored, even if they are self-inflicted, by ignorance, error, or deliberate mistakes.
6. Commit to helping a person mentored set spiritual, life goals, and share dreams.
7. Commit to assisting the person in mentored objectively and evaluate progress toward their goals.
8. Commit to being a living example.
9. Commit to openness to learn from the person mentored and allow them to be themselves and the person God wants them to be.

Most of the discussion has so far majored on a mentor as someone older guiding a younger person. If that is all, there was in mentoring, then the question "Who cares for the carers?" would surface. I mentioned earlier that in the counseling industry, every person, counselor, or supervisor, must be supervised. There is a great need for mentors themselves to be mentored. In society and especially in the church, there is a gaping hole in the scarcity of mentoring at the collegial, fraternal level. In their book, *The Essential Guide to Burnout: Overcoming Excess Stress*, Andrew and Dr.Elizabeth Procter discuss causes of burnout, among which they identify workaholism. They cite workaholism as "an addition, and like all addictions, it blocks creative energy. To recover our creativity, we must learn to see workaholism as a block instead of a building block."[423]They also discuss and suggest many possible solutions, among which they suggest, spiritual accompaniment[424] but also recommend supportive friends. " It is good to talk with trusted friends. They care about you; they can be candid to you. It has a great advantage that they know us best and will want the best for us."[425]The Hendricks briefly mention Peer-Mentoring[426]giving the examples of Jonathan and David in the Old Testament and Barnabas and Paul in the New Testament.[427] Other authors referred to Peer Mentoring as "Twin Souls and Spiritual Friends"[428]This refers to maturing Christians who commit to helping each other live a holy life growing in Christlikeness. The name is attributed to Celtic Christianity in which Saint Brigit (ninth century AD) told her foster son, "Go forth and eat nothing until you get a soul friend, for anyone without a soul friend is like a body without a head." In the 12th Century, Aelred of Rievaulx celebrated the blessing of a soul friend. This mentoring is engendered by feelings of security, openness, and joy of sharing with someone you trust and allowing them to sharpen you as you sharpen them to borrow the imagery from Proverbs 27:17. Peer- Mentoring is powerful and most needed in spiritual formation. It develops in the context of friendship; Proverbs 27:6 says the wounds of a friend can be trusted. Fear of criticism is the number one reason why people shy away from mentoring, but such fear is overcome by entering into peer mentoring. John Wesley never described it as peer-mentoring, He nevertheless talked of,

> What happiness, what security, what joy to have someone to whom you dare to speak on terms of equality to another self; one to whom you need have no fear of confessing your failings; one to whom you can unblushingly make known what progress you have made in the spiritual

> life; one to whom you can entrust all the secrets of your heart.[429]

John Wesley believed that all Christians need the support of spiritual friendship and guidance. To Frances Godfrey, whom he addressed as "My Dear Fanny," he wrote, "It is a blessed thing to have fellow travelers to the New Jerusalem. If you do not find any, you must make them, for none can travel this road alone."[430]

Even wealthy bankers like Ebenezer Blackwell needed spiritual friends. Wesley wrote to him, "I am fully persuaded if you had always one or two faithful friends near you who could speak the very truth from their heart and watch over you in love, you would swiftly advance."[431]

To Mary, Bosanquet Wesley wrote, "You need a steady guide and one that knows you well."[432] Wesley's letter to Ann Bolton, written when he was 82 years of age, shows both the need and the qualities Wesley expected in a spiritual friend.

> My Dear Nancy—It is undoubtedly expedient for you to have a friend in whom you can fully confide that can always be near you or at a small distance, and ready to be consulted on all occasions. The time was when you took me to be your friend, and (to speak freely) I have loved you with no common affection. I "have loved you"—nay, I still do; my heart warms to you while I am writing. But I am generally at too great a distance so that you cannot converse with me when you would. I am glad, therefore, that Providence has given you one whom you can more easily see and correspond with. You may certainly trust her in every instance, and she has . . . understanding, piety, and experience. She may, therefore, perform those offices of friendship which I would rejoice to perform

> were I near you. But whenever you can, give me the pleasure of seeing you.[433]

In recent times, Emile records the experience of prayer and about how God sends a soul friend at just the right times.

> "To 'find' a spiritual friend is truly to be found, to be chased down, smoked out of one's hiding place in the corner of existence and brought into the centre, swept into the blazing presence of God. . . . This love . . . is . . . the friendship of the saints in heaven and on earth."[434]

Most denominations across the world have experienced great scarcity and lack of ordained ministers to lead churches. One of the reasons has been ministerial burnout and drop out. The primary cause of this is loneliness and disillusionment, and the most glaring reason for this is the lack of peer mentoring. Spiritual ministry is a battlefield because ministers are at the forefront of the spiritual warfare of which the Bible describes thus: "For we wrestle not against flesh and blood, but against principalities, against powers, against the rulers of the darkness of this world, against spiritual wickedness in high places."[435]In this respect, it is dangerous and suicidal to try to engage in spiritual ministry as a lone ranger. Given this nature and perspective of Christian ministry, the Christian minister should at least enlist a prayer partner. Someone to cover one's back to use the imagery we used earlier about the Roman army marching as a phalanx.

I cannot emphasize enough, the importance of the ministry of mentoring for spiritual formation and growth; suffice to say we neglect it at our peril. Whether in ministry or just living out our Christian faith, it is prudent at least to identify a soul-spiritual friend, and your spiritual formation and ministry will blossom.

Individualism is the worst enemy to spiritual growth. Remember Jesus sent his disciples in pairs, the police patrol in pairs, and the great saints worked in this way: Paul and Barnabas, Paul and Silas, John and Charles Wesley. If we do, likewise, our personal growth, ministry, and spiritual formation will prosper.

Grace and the use of sacraments.

What is grace?

The final discipline that we have identified as a pivotal pillar for spiritual and ministerial formation is grace. What is grace? It is a robust word rich in meaning that extends into both everyday usages in the English language and Biblical theology. The non –theological understanding of the word grace translates in a variety of words: The English dictionaries have two primary definitions. Firstly as a description of an action: elegance or beauty of form, manner, motion, or action. Secondly, as a noun: mercy, compassion, or pardon. In tracing some of the secular usages of the word grace in the English language, Philip Yancey cites the following: "We are grateful for someone's kindness, gratified by good news, congratulated when successful, gracious in hosting friends. When a person's service pleases us, we leave a gratuity. A composer of music may add grace notes to the score. Though not essential to the melody – they are gratuitous – these notes add a flourish whose presence would be missed. British subjects address royalty as "Your grace." Students at Oxford and Cambridge may "receive grace," exempting them from specific academic requirements. Parliament declares an "act of grace to pardon a criminal."'[436]These secular synonyms are well known; equally too are the antonyms, and Yancey cites a few of these: "Fall from grace"; "we insult a person by pointing out the dearth of grace: "You ingrate!" or worse, "you're a disgrace!" or persona non grata – person without grace.[437]

"Absurdity of grace"!

In spite of all these popular expressions about grace, it remains a mystery to the secular mind that has not fully experienced God's grace and forgiveness to be able to appreciate the meaning of grace. Even among nominal Christians who choose to be religious rather than seek intimacy with God, find grace to be puzzling such Christians preach grace but live by the law, hard-hearted, unforgiving, demanding an eye for an eye and a tooth for a tooth in the endeavor to get even. Religious Christians tend to be legalistic and find it hard to live by grace, to give grace and its twin sibling known as forgiveness. Their thinking resonates with a God of anger and revenge more than a gracious God who does not judge humanity harshly according to its sinfulness, a God of second chances, the long-suffering God. They preach grace but practice earning favor with God through good works. They deify doing and downgrade being when it comes to religious practice. They prefer to be religious rather than be in a relationship with God through His son, whom he sent to redeem the world. They prefer doing Christian work through self-effort rather than dependence on the Holy Spirit. They trust their religious judgment rather than being guided and directed by the Holy Spirit. In Christian theology, two theologians, Augustine and Pelagius and their schools of thought known as Augustinianism and Pelagianism, represent these two strands of Christian practice. Augustine espoused grace early in his spiritual formation after having a sinful beginning in his formative years in which he squandered his youth living immorally. Pelagius, on the other hand, was religiously pristine, meticulous in working out how to please God and developed his theology in that light.

In contrast, Augustine discovered his depravity and passionately pursued God seeking to live by his grace. Yancey aptly puts it this way: "Christians tend to be Augustinian in theory but Pelagian in practice. They work obsessively to please other people, even God."[438]Earlier in this book, we discussed original sin as the major hindrance to spiritual development and formation that emulates God's love and grace. Yancey comments that "like spiritual defects encoded in the family DNA, ungrace gets passed on an unbroken chain."[439]One of the difficulties for the modern mind in understanding grace is that it goes against the grain; for every advertisement of free things tends to have strings attached. My sister in law, Esther, has developed a state of the art line dealing with cold –callers telephone sales trying to sell her things over the phone, offering something free. Her standard line is this: "How can you offer me something for free, and you do not know me from Adam?" Secondly, we live in a society that worships self-effort and achievement. We wear T-shirts depicting our heroes and heroines in our chosen sport. Society lauds Self-determination and self-aggrandizement more than grace and humility. This trend of social mores has its roots in the Enlightenment and is epitomized in the Frank Sinatra single: "I did it my way." Grace and humility are not in vogue in modern society. The misunderstanding of grace is partly promoted by faulty theology that presents the gospel as a freebie of grace. Such a theology ignores and fails to take the doctrine of atonement seriously. The gospel is only free because of the vicarious death of Jesus Christ on the cross. We celebrate Easter morning only because of what happened on Good Friday. "Grace is free only because the giver himself has borne the cost."[440]

Grace in Biblical Theology.

When we turn to historical Christian theology, the simplest definition for grace is God's unmerited favor, unearned kindness. The word translated grace in Hebrew is (חן –Chen) appears about sixty times in the Old Testament. In the New Testament, the keyword in Greek is χάρις – Charis; mainly found in Pauline writings but appearing a few times also in the gospels in both cases its literal meaning is a favor, to bend or stoop in kindness to another, usually a superior to an inferior. Colin Brown traces grace in pre-Christian literature and its derivate charisma to have the ultimate meaning of "gracious gift, a donation from God to men; it denotes the stronger coming to the help of the weaker who stands in need of help because of his circumstances or natural weakness. "[441] Brown estimates that the word translated grace is used about one hundred and ninety times in the Old Testament and one hundred and fifty-five times in the New Testament, one hundred of which are found in the Pauline Epistles.[442]

Although Jesus never used the word grace, he exemplifies it in his teaching in the gospels, as we shall see later. The three most obvious of his parables that demonstrate and illustrate what grace is are the parable of the prodigal son,[443] the laborers in the vineyard[444], and the great supper.[445] We will look later into Jesus' teaching on grace. In Christian theology, the word has also had various mnemonics; one of the most popular is **G**od's **R**iches **A**t **C**hrist's **E**xpense. Quite often, grace, mercy, and blessings tend to be mixed up. I came across on the Internet this description that distinguishes the three: "Grace is when God gives us good things that we do not deserve. **Mercy** is when He spares us from bad things we deserve. **Blessings** are when He is generous with both."[446] The overarching definition in Christian historical theology for the word grace is the condescension or benevolence shown by God toward the human race. In his article, Andrew H. Trotter Jr. has given a fair summary of the word grace in both the Old and New Testament.[447] When Jesus was asked about the commandments, he reduced them into two: Love God and Love, your neighbor.[448]Jesus' call into discipleship could equally be reduced to two injunctions "Come" and "Go." Come and be with me and learn from me as one who came full of grace and truth[449], then go and make other disciples by imparting the grace you have learned from me. The first is an invitation into intimacy and the second an injunction or a command into activity. Spiritual formation is about coming and going. The psyche of human beings craves intimacy, and intimacy with God is the gateway to all other forms of intimacy with self, spouse, and with others. There is a vacuum in every human heart that yearns for its maker as aptly put by Augustine, "Thou hast made us for thyself, O Lord, and our heart is restless until it finds its rest in thee."[450]Jesus called his first disciples into a life of intimacy with him; he told them, "I have called you my friends because I have made known to you everything that I have heard from my father."[451]In his book, *Rhythms of Grace*, Tony Horsfall puts it this way, "His call is to a relationship based on grace, grounded in his unconditional love for us and guaranteed by the unchanging nature of his character...Grace, therefore, leads us to intimacy, and intimacy is what the Christian life is all about. It is a love relationship."[452]

Being and Doing: To understand grace, one needs to consider the question: Which does God prefer, being or doing? My answer to this question is that God requires both in proportion. The cumulative Biblical teaching seems to suggest that our being should inform our doing. But if there were to be a choice, we should choose to be to doing because "our being" always informs and sustains "our doing." After spending time with God and received his grace, we discharged a ministry imbued with grace and unction – anointing from the Holy Spirit that touches people's hearts. In the Old Testament, "being" is preferred to "doing" (by which I mean one's standing with God and serving God) in these words: "it is better to obey than sacrifice."[453]In the New Testament, similar sentiments are echoed in Jesus' words: "If you bring your gift to the altar and there remember that your brother has something against you, leave your gift before the altar. First, be reconciled to your brother, and then come and offer your gift."[454]What Jesus in effect was teaching by saying leave your sacrifice (doing) and go sort out your relationship with your brother and inevitably with God (being) is that being is more important than doing. It is by being with Christ that we learn compassion and gets the compulsion to go. Once we are soaked and saturated by the love and grace of God, we naturally emulate the Apostle Paul and say, "the love of Christ compels us." The injunctions into the discipleship of "come" and "go" teach us that coming should take a priority. "Being" should take precedence to "Doing" and immersion into busyness. It is by being with God that He lets his glory shine to the people we serve. It is by spending time with God first that his servants deliver anointed sermons and services full of unction that touch people. The Old Testament illustrated this when Moses spent time with God on Mount Sinai the Bible says, "When Moses came down from Mount Sinai with the two tablets of the covenant law in his hands, he was not aware that his face was radiant because he had spoken with the LORD."[455]By spending time with the Lord on Mount Sinai, Moses' face shone, and his ministry to the people of Israel was enabled. The ministry of the first apostles was noticed not because of their brilliance but because they had spent time with Jesus.[456]The grace of God is an essential tool that makes a difference in the believer's inner life but also enables the ministry of believers. Horsfall puts it this way: "The two great gospel words are "come" and "go,"; the one a word of invitation, the other a word of command. The first speaks of intimacy, the second of activity. Both are important in the Christian life, but coming to Jesus must always precede our going out for him. For many, there has been too much "going" and not enough "coming," resulting in lives that are spiritually impoverished and lacking in both depth and passion. At this time, the Spirit is reminding us that the gracious invitation of Jesus to intimacy with himself remains his priority and is the foundation of everything else in the Christian life."[457]The grace of God exhibits itself in the life of a Christian in pursuit of holiness, in which the goal of living for the believer is to become like Christ and to express that Christ-likeness in daily living, not by trying harder, but by the grace of God.

The question might arise, how do we know when God's grace is at work? The one incidence that comes to mind goes back approximately twenty-five years ago. I was not sure what God wanted me to serve him in the UK. I had completed my doctoral studies and preparing to return to Africa, where I felt my ministry lay. For five years, these preparations encountered upsets and frustrating circumstances. Opportunity to join the UK Methodist Conference kept presenting itself, but I did not even entertain exploring such for fear of being tied down to a contract. Owing to problems following the birth of our second son, I offered to serve for one year to hasten my preparation to return to Africa, and immediately, an appointment was made for me to serve a huge congregation in an upmarket community for the one year I had requested. As I took the appointment, I laid a fleece to the Lord as follows. I told the Lord that if He wanted me to serve him in the UK, he should confirm this by having one person come to faith through my witness or ministry. Although I was fully qualified with a doctorate in theology and whenever I took services, the feedback I got was that my sermons were inspirational and uplifting I still had a crisis of confidence and felt inferior to serve in the UK. I arrived at this appointment in September, and there was a community hall where an interdenominational ecumenical coffee morning was held once a month with a guest speaker to give an evangelistic address to invite people to come to faith. I attended the September meeting to hear the guest. Then the organizers asked me to take the next meeting in October, and I agreed. I preached on John chapter 4 about the Samaritan woman, how she met Jesus and became the conduit of the conversion of the entire Samaritan village. I then gave my testimony and ended the service without giving an altar call or invitation for people to respond mainly because inwardly, I did not feel anyone would respond! As I was looking for a table to sit on for my coffee, a woman by the name of Dorothy approached me and asked, "Daniel is it possible to know God in the intimate personal way you have told us because both your message and your testimony have touched me." I replied, "O yes, would you like to?" To my surprise, Dorothy said yes, please. So I stopped the order of coffee that I had placed and led this woman to the Lord. In the end, the woman said to me, "Daniel I am going to disappoint you, although I have committed myself to the Lord, I will not be attending your church I want to attend the parish church." I replied it does not matter where you attend worship; the most important thing is that you have received Jesus Christ into your life. As I walked from that meeting, I felt a small voice in my heart saying, "Daniel, do you now believe I can use you here in the UK?" At that, I remembered the fleece that I had laid and had forgotten all about it! For Dorothy, that was prevenient grace, grace that goes before to arrange situations and circumstances for God to meet needs and accomplish his purposes. For me, it was God's grace giving me confirmation and confidence that God, in spite of my weaknesses and feelings of inadequacy and inferiority, could use me, and that confirmed to me to serve him in the UK. As I look back over the years and what God has accomplished through me in those years, only one word comes to mind, grace. Many a time when I have been asked to give my testimony given my humble background, I have based it on the words of Apostle Paul, "I am what I am by the grace of God."[458]I then go on to talk about my humble background growing up in a grass-thatched mud house in Africa in abject poverty. I then go on to talk about God's grace which turned me from pagan boy to preacher box, from peasant to a pastor, from poverty-stricken home and a school dropout to doctoral studies and life in the UK including shaking hands with Her Majesty the Queen and Prince Philip and Princess Diana in Buckingham Palace. A school drop - out who ends up studying Greek for seven years and Hebrew for three years besides speaking three other languages. God is real and reveals himself to people by his grace. When the psalmist says, "Be still and know that I am God,"[459]it means three things: first, intimacy with God is possible because he invites us to it through His word. Secondly, God is knowable personally because He reveals himself to individuals, and thirdly, the means to accomplish the knowledge of God is by being still in his presence and allowing his grace to permeate through our lives. God's grace works in our lives as we learn to rest in him. By rest, I mean repose or condition of rest. Its root meaning comes from the Hebrew word, מָנוֹחַ (manowach) in the Old Testament, and the New Testament, a similar meaning is picked up in the letter to the Hebrews chapter four. Resting in God means that we rely on his grace for both his protection and provision for serving him. The words of James Hudson Taylor: epitomized confidence in God's grace, "God's work done in God's way will never lack God's supply." Relying and resting on God's grace as a means of spiritual development and ministry skill is captured in the paraphrased words of the Irish hymn writer, Jean Sophia Pigott (1845-1882), in her hymn: "Jesus I am resting in the joy of who your. I am finding out the greatness of your loving heart. By your transforming power, you have made me whole. I know your wealth of grace and your certainty of promise have made it mine. Simply trusting you, Lord Jesus, your love so pure, so changeless has satisfied my heart. Keep me ever trusting, resting, fill me with your grace." [460]

In this chapter, we explore grace as a means of sustaining spiritual life development and development of ministry skills, neither of which can be self -manufacture but require dependence on God. The Apostle Paul beautifully sums it up this way: (Ephesians 2:8), "it's all by grace, which is a gift of God." Centuries of Christian experience teach us that even though a believer has been born again and has forsaken the life of sin, an inner bent toward sin remains. Though the believer is done with deliberate acts of sin, an inward principle of sin still resists God's will.[461]

The Wesleyan tradition teaches that God can cleanse the heart and fill it with divine love until entire sanctification is a reality and making it possible for believers to love God with all their heart, mind, soul, and strength, and their neighbors as themselves. Such love is the gift of sanctifying grace. According to Albert E. Day,

> "On this, I will venture my eternal salvation—if you will make the purity of God your indefatigable quest, the God of purity will give himself to you in such fullness, that

> your questions will be transcended in the splendor of the experience that has overtaken you."[462]

We need to bear in mind that "before the splendor of that experience overtakes the Christian pilgrim, sin remains within—though it does not rule. Still, the believer on the road to full sanctification can appropriately confess his or her need for inner cleansing, for the baptism with the Holy Spirit.[463] John Wesley taught that the holiest among us, "the most perfect . . . need the blood of the atonement, and may properly say, 'Forgive us our trespasses.'"[464] The point is that "the holiest among us" are members of a fallen race and the fountain of a thousand infirmities. We cannot change that, but it inclines us towards falling short of God's holiness, God's perfect will again and again.

"Our judgment is flawed, our reason inadequate, our knowledge deficient, and our performance of duty sometimes erratic—even though we intend to do only the right."[465] Often-neglected teaching of Wesley and the Holiness Movement is that these shortcomings, infirmities, faults, and failures that dog us because of our fallenness, while they may not properly be called sins, still need the atoning blood of Christ to make us acceptable to God. Therefore, even the holiest person needs to confess the need for grace to cover inherent mistakes and failures. Closely related to this is the need for the on-going cleansing by the Holy Spirit. Holiness is dynamic, not static. When we receive the baptism of the Spirit, that is, the experience of sanctifying grace, God does not give us a lifetime supply of holiness that we can store away like a bag of flour or shopping in a freezer. The cleansing and filling of the Spirit are not once and for all. Instead, we are kept holy by moment by- moment grace, on-going cleansing of the blood of the Saviour. According to John Wesley's teaching, every Christian needs the power of Christ every moment to help maintain the spiritual life and without which, notwithstanding our present holiness, we should be devils the next moment. Christians need constant confession of the need for atoning grace for the faults and failures endemic in fallen human nature as well as the need for on-going, moment-by-moment cleansing by the Holy Spirit as an on-going process. D L Moody illustrated this principle in the famously quoted incident when once asked why he urged Christians to be continuously filled with the Holy Spirit. "Well," he said, "I need a continual infilling because I leak!" He pointed to a water tank, which had sprung a leak. "I'm like that!" he said. It is a fact that is living in this sinful world; we do need to be replenished by the Spirit.[466]Formation of a Christ-like character is a lifetime commitment. Similar to pursuing grace is the doctrines of sanctification and its central teaching on spiritual formation, life development, and ministry skills. The following are some of the salient points: - The key to comprehending the doctrine of sanctification lies in the recognition that Christ sanctifies believers working through the Holy Spirit. In a word, our sanctification comes through our union with Christ. John Webster explains: 'A Christian dogmatic of holiness is not metaphysics, because the holy God, reaching out into the world in Son and Spirit, is the sanctifier; nor is it mysticism (or moralism), because human reality is holy only in dependence upon the Spirit of the Son who makes holy.'[467]

Although many Christians affirm such belief in practice it is an underappreciated truth that requires that we understand the doctrine of sanctification in its broader context: "understanding the relationship between sanctification and the *ordo salutis* (especially the relationship between justification and sanctification), and the *historia salutis* (the already and not-yet). We should not confuse the forensic and transformative aspects of our redemption.

What Christians must grasp is that the source of sanctification is through union with Christ. Our sanctification lies not in our works, good intentions, or efforts to be holier, but in seeking Christ by faith alone.[468]

To say that sanctification is by faith alone should not in any way imply a diminution of the importance and necessity of good works. The historical Reformed theology has always asserted that while we are justified by faith alone, our faith is not alone: 'Faith... alone is the instrument of justification: yet is it not alone in the person justified, but is ever accompanied with all other saving graces, and is no dead faith but works by love.'"[469]

The following literature helps in striking a balance between the importance of good works in pursuit of holiness and seeking Christ by faith alone through the means of grace (word, sacraments, and prayer).[470] The gospel and union with Christ is the source of Christian holiness and hence of good works.

Grace in the teaching of Jesus

When I studied hermeneutics at the London School of Theology, we had a visiting lecturer, Kenneth Bailey, who made the parables of Jesus come alive. He came to give us a lecture on understanding Parables from the perspective of those people who lived in Palestine at the time of Jesus when they heard the parables first time from the lips of Jesus. Kenneth Bailey is renowned for his knowledge of cultural studies in the Middle East and for shedding light on the New Testament through Middle Eastern Eyes.[471] When he came to give this lecture, he had published his book, *Poet and Peasant and Through Peasant's Eyes.*[472]In this lecture, Bailey explained how the story of the prodigal son read in Lebanon to an audience in a culture similar to Jesus' audience would receive gasps of surprise at the father agreeing to the request from his son to have his inheritance and agreeing straightaway because that was similar to the son wishing his father dead! How the audience would gasp at the father running toward his son instead of walking in a dignified way.[473] The gasps would teach us that the main point of this parable was not about the son but the father, who did an extraordinary thing. It is a parable about a gracious father who had two lost sons: Firstly, the younger son who had run away and wasted his life through reckless living; and secondly, the older son who remained at home and equally was lost through grudging self-importance. It is a lesson on what grace looks like and what it does. Jesus' parable of the prodigal son is given as the last in a triplet: with the lost sheep and the lost silver coin.[474]The context of these three parables was the grumbling of the Pharisees and scribes about Jesus receiving and eating with tax collectors and sinners. The lesson in its original setting (Sitz – im – Leben) and to the first audience was to correct the notions they had and that some people have today about God and who deserves his love. "The key lesson in the three parables about the lost sheep, the lost silver coin, and the lost son emphasize the finder's joy.[475]The first audience would have wondered what kind of father is this because, in reality, rebellious sons would have been not a shocking story, notorious children would be an uncommon phenomenon, but the shock would have been in the behavior of the father in the parable! Jesus, in this parable, portrays a gracious father. The parable of the workers in the vineyard conveys the same message."[476]It is not about the complaining servants for equal payment but about the vineyard owner who decides to show grace to those hired last. It is about showing mercy to those undeserving. For the primary audience who heard Jesus tell the parable, the punch line would have been what kind of master it is who shows such extravagant of goodness! What grace is that! The same is right about the Parable of the unmerciful servant who is showed mercy by having his debt canceled and failed to show mercy to a debtor who owes him money.[477]The same is also true of the Parable of the great banquet.[478] Yancey commenting on these parables puts it this way:

> At the centre of Jesus' parable of grace stands a God who takes the initiative towards us: a lovesick father who runs to meet the prodigal, a king who cancels a debt too large for any servant to reimburse, and employer who pays eleventh-hour workers the same as the first-hour crew, a banquet-giver who goes out to the highways and byways in search of undeserving guests.[479]

And commenting on the parable of the workers in the vineyard, he points out that:

> Jesus' story makes no economic sense, and that was his intent. He was giving us a parable about grace, which cannot be calculated like a day's wages. Grace is not about finishing last or first; it is about not counting the cost. We receive grace as a gift from God, not as something; we toil to earn, a point that Jesus made clear through the employer's response. The main point in the story is that 'God dispenses gifts, not wages. None of us are paid according to merit, for none of us comes close to satisfying God's requirements for a perfect life. If paid based on fairness, we would all end up in hell...Jesus did not give the parables to teach us how to live. He gave them to correct our notions about who God is and who God loves.[480]

There are other stories in the Gospels in which Jesus' teaching implied grace: How many times we should forgive when wronged - seventy times seven times which repeatedly means without limit[481]; the washing of disciples' feet[482]; Jesus reinstates Peter[483]; Jesus' forgiveness of the thief at the cross.[484]

Jesus' explicit and implicit teaching on grace resonates with some Old Testament teaching delving into the detail of which is outside the scope of this book. We could, however, cite an example to illustrate the Old Testament teaching on what grace is. The story of Prophet Hosea further shows God's grace. His wayward wife Gomer left Hosea went and worked as a prostitute, lived with another man, and God commanded Hosea to take her back in these words: "Go show your love to your wife again, she is loved by another and is an adulteress. Love her as the Lord loves the Israelites, though they turn to other gods. Gomer did not get fairness, even justice; she got grace."[485]Therefore, in the New Testament, grace is greatly expounded and widely used in the epistles, mainly in the Pauline epistles. In the gospels, although Jesus does not use the word grace in his teaching, he told numerous parables that illustrated what grace is all about. Yancey summarises the Biblical teaching on grace this way:

> Are you Saul envious because I am so generous to David? Are you Pharisees envious because I open the gate to gentiles so late in the game? That I honour the prayer of a tax collector above a Pharisee, that I accept a thief's last-minute confession and welcome him to Paradise – does this arouse your envy? Do you begrudge my leaving the obedient flock to seek the stray or my serving a fatted calf to the no-good prodigal?[486]

As regards Jesus' teaching on grace, Yancey observes that "Jesus gave us these stories about grace to call us to step completely outside our tit-for-tat world of ungrace and enter into God's realm of infinite grace...the economy of undeserved grace has primacy over the economy of moral deserts."[487]

Therefore, the seventh pillar that underpins spiritual development and formation is grace. Learning to live daily depending on God's grace and dispensing the same to our fellow human beings, whatever their reaction or behavior towards us. Jesus endorsed this way of spiritual formation and behaving in the manifesto of his kingdom, the Sermon on the Mount, when he said, "Unless your righteousness surpasses that of the Pharisees and the teachers of the law you will certainly not enter the kingdom of heaven."[488] How grace works in practical living is illustrated by Bob Gass as follows:

> Jesus told His disciples, 'Since I, your Lord and Teacher, have washed your feet, you ought to wash each other's feet. I have given you an example to follow.'[489]Whose feet did He wash? Peter, who denied Him; Thomas, who doubted Him; Judas who betrayed Him and all the others who would desert Him. In other words, 'Give the grace you have been given. You do not endorse the deeds of your offender when you do, Jesus did not endorse your sins by forgiving you. Grace does not tell the daughter to like the father who molested her. It does not tell the oppressed to wink at injustice. The grace – the defined person, still sends thieves to jail and expects an ex-spouse to pay for child support. Grace is not blind. It sees the hurtfull well. However, grace chooses to see God's forgiveness even more. It refuses to let hurt poison the heart. The Bible says, 'See to it that no one falls short of the grace of God and that no bitter root grows up to cause trouble and defile many.'[490]Where grace is lacking bitterness abounds. Where grace abounds, forgiveness grows. 'Grow in the grace and knowledge of our Lord.'[491] Growing in Bible knowledge is a lot easier than growing in grace towards

> those who hurt you. The first requires a good memory; the second requires a Christ-like character. So how do you 'grow' in grace? By practicing it with everybody you meet, in every situation you find yourself.[492]

Therefore, the pivotal foundation pillar of God's grace underpins Spiritual formation and development. It also underpins spiritual practice in ministry.

The Sacraments as means of grace.

If grace were to be thought of as salt that spices and seasons Christian lives, its dispenser could be considered of as the sacraments. The doctrine of the sacraments is extensive indeed, and giving a detailed account is outside the scope of this book. What we would do, however, is to provide a summary of the sacrament as means of grace as a constant reminder of how God deals with us and expects us to deal with our fellow human beings.

The question is, what is a sacrament?

The observance of sacraments is the dividing line between Roman Catholicism and Protestantism. In the Catholic Church and many of the Orthodox churches, they observe seven rites that they define as sacraments: baptism, confirmation, the Eucharist, penance, anointing of the sick, ordination and matrimony. The majority of the protestant churches, however, to the contrary observe only two: baptism and the Eucharist, commonly known as the Lord's Supper. The Protestants argue that these two are the only ones that Jesus himself commissioned, and he observed. They are considered by most churches to be solemn rites to symbolize or confer grace. The Oxford dictionaries trace the etymology of the word sacrament from Latin *Sacramentum*, meaning solemn oath, taking its root meaning from the Latin verb *sacrare* – to hallow, also used as a translation of the Greek word *musterion*-mystery. The Merriam – Webster dictionary defines a sacrament as a Christian rite that is believed to have been ordained by Christ, and that is held to be a means of divine grace or to be a sign or symbol of a spiritual reality. In this book, we will briefly highlight the means of grace in the two sacraments mainly observed by most Protestant churches: Baptism and the Eucharist.

Baptism

Earlier in this book, we discussed the dynamics of spiritual formation and argued that baptism is deemed to formulate the entrance into the body of Christ the church. In this section, we look at baptism as a means of grace. To understand it as such, we need to look at its root meaning, "washing," and its cognate meaning of "purifying." All Christians observe the sacrament of baptism as a command of Jesus and, as practiced by the Early Church, signifying forgiveness of sins and the gift of the Holy Spirit. Baptism to Christ is baptism to the church, to be a member of the body of Christ, is an embodiment of the gospel of grace."[493]On that 13th day of August 1967 when I received my baptism by immersion, I felt something special to belong to the household of faith, to have my name written in the Lamb's book of life. I thought I belonged to something universal. Since that time, my outlook in Christian life has always been international, interdenominational, and ecumenical in perspective. I sometimes wonder how it feels like to belong to one denomination because this is a luxury I have never had. In my Christian ministry, so far, I have served in three main denominations and trained in an Anglican college and an international - interdenominational school of theology. During my formative years in secondary school, I grew up and served the Kenya Student Christian Fellowship that left an indelible mark on my Christian outlook; I perceive myself to be a Christian first and a member of a local denomination second. Since my days in high school, I have never suffered from denominationalism. From the date of my baptism, I have always felt that I belong to the body of Christ international because of my baptism into Christ's body. My wife and I had both our children dedicated as infants. When Andrew grew up, he was attending Smithbridge Methodist Church. After he completed the Youth Alpha with other young people, he decided to be baptized before he went to Crompton House Church of England School. The baptism took place in an open-air service at Hollingworth Lake. We had arranged that his mother would give his testimony, but when the time came, Andrew grabbed the wireless microphone I was holding while standing in the water from my hands and said, "I want to be baptized because I am a friend of Jesus," and he handed it back to me. It was a great joy to baptize my son by immersion on that Sunday evening. Baptism conveys that sense of belonging to Christ as a means of grace, as I felt at my baptism. Brown sums up baptism as follows: "The coincidence of divine action for faith and in baptism presumes that God's gracious giving to faith belongs to the context of baptism that his gift in baptism is to faith."[494]

The Eucharist

The second means of grace is the sacrament of Eucharist, also known as the mass, communion service, or the Lord's Supper; it is observed by most denominations in the Christian Church. Its central element is breaking and sharing bread, symbolizing sustenance by Christ by feeding on his body for our spiritual nourishment and the pouring and sharing of wine among worshippers to remember and commemorate Jesus' shedding of his blood for the forgiveness of sins. The regular enactment of this religious rite has the internal significance of union and renewal through grace – God's manna to sustain spiritual lives also God's atonement of sin, reminding Christians of perpetual need for sanctification through the blood of Christ. Most Christians take this sacrament very seriously as a means of grace, imparting God's renewal through His grace. "The Word eucharist is taken from the Greek, ευχαριστία - eucharistia which means thanksgiving or gratitude and which was used by the early Christians for the Hebrew word ברכה -berakhah meaning a blessing such as a table grace."[495]

We may, therefore, conclude that Christians who take their spiritual formation seriously would like to underpin it with strong pillars of Christian disciplines, and the discipline using the means of grace in baptism and the Eucharist are strong such pillars. As the liturgy of the Eucharist encourages, we observe the Eucharist, to remember Christ until he comes again. The words of the hymn writer Pratt Green beautifully summarize the sentiments of what happens at the Eucharist: The first stanza sets up the tone of the whole hymn, "Lord, we have come at your own invitation, Chosen by you to be counted your friends. Yours is the strength that sustains dedication. Ours a commitment we know never ends." [496] The hymn goes on to talk about the seal of forgiveness and grace, the renewing of vows, restoration of courage, and increasing glory of learning what it means to accept Jesus as Lord. All these are aspects of what happens when Christians celebrate Holy Communion.

Chapter 5 Notes

235 Matthew 12:28-30 The Message Translation

236 Richard J Foster, *Life with God: Reading the Bible for Spiritual Transformation*, (HarperCollins e-Books, 2014), See also http://rbdigital.oneclickdigital.com

237 Kenneth Boa, *Conformed to His Image*, 89 citing 2Timothy 3:16-17

238 See Brainyquotes Accessed April 19, 2017 .https://www.brainyquote.com/quotes/quotes/t/thomasdewa142165.html.

239 Kenneth Boa, *Conformed into His Image*, 89

240 Ibid. p.89-90

241 These were suggested by Tremper Longmans, in M Robert Mulholland, *Shaped by the Word: The Power of Reading Scripture in Spiritual Formation*, Nashville, Tenn: Upper Room Books, 1985

242 Robert Mulholland warns against this in his book, *Shaped by the Word: The Power of Reading Scripture in Spiritual Formation*, Nashville, Tenn: Upper Room Books, 1985

243 For more on this theme see "What It Means to Me" by Walt Russell, in Leadingham, E. *Discover the Word: Reading the Bible for all its Worth* . Kansas City, MO: Beacon Hill Press, 1997, chapter 8, 83-90.)

244 According to Explorer's Method Chapter 12 of *Reflecting God*, "Nurtured by the Light of the Word,"in Wesley Tracy, *Reflecting God*. (Kansas City: Beacon Hill Press Christian Holiness Partnership, 1747 reprinted 2000)

245 See Gary Cockerill, Wes Tracy, Donald Demaray, and Steve Harper, *The Reflecting God*, (Kansas City: Beacon Hill Press, 2001), 70-72,) where it presents "a Step into the Scene exercise "based on Paul's first letter to the Thessalonians.

246 Gass, Bob. *Word For Today*, 10 March 2018

247 Mike Devries, "Prayer as breathing." Accessed November 3, 2017. *Christianity.com*

248 Kenneth Boa,

249 Ibid. citing John Piper, *The Pleasures of God: Meditations on God's delight in Being God*, (Colorado Springs, Colorado: Mutnomah Publishers, 1991 revised 1992

250 Richard Foster, *Prayer Finding the Heart's True Home*. (San Francisco: Harper San Francisco, 1992)

251 R T Kendall, *The Sermon on the Mount*, (Oxford: Monarch Books, 2011), 206

252 See, David Watson, *Called & Committed*, (Harold Shaw Publishers, Wheaton, IL; 1982), 83 also cited by Kenneth Boa, *Conformed to His Image*, 94

253 Brainy Quotes, Accessed April 19, 2017. https://www.brainyquote.com/quotes/quotes/s/sorenkierk107355.html

254 Kenneth Boa, *Conformed to His Image*, 94

255 Mark 14:36

256 Romans 8:15; Galatians 4:6

257 Psalm 116:1-2; Jeremiah 33:2-3

258 Mark 1:35; Numbers 11:2; 1Kings 18:36-37
259 Luke 18:1; Ephesians 6:18; 1Thessalonians 5:16-18; 1Timothy 2:1
260 Psalm 37:3-6; 63:1-8 & Ephesians 1:16-19
261 John 16:23-24; Philippians 4:6-7
262 2Corinthians 12:7-9
263 John 15:5; Luke 11:9-10; Acts 4:31; Ephesians 3:16; Colossians 4:2-4; Hebrews 4:16; James 5:16-18
264 Colossians 1:9-11
265 Matthew 17:1-9; Mark 9:2-20 and Luke 9:28-36
266 Ibid. (NIV translation)
267 Luke 9:29 (The Message Translation
268 Brian Hoare, *Singing the Faith*, hymn number 21, London: Hymns Ancient and Modern Ltd, 2011
269 Kenneth Boa, *Conformed to His Image,* 94
270 Steve Beard, "The Spiritual discipline of fasting", *Good News Magazine,* (United Methodist Church, USA)
271 Jonathan Crowther, *A Portraiture of Methodism or The History of the Wesleyan Methodists, (*London: Richard Edwards, 1815)
272 Steve Beard, "The Spiritual Discipline of fasting", *Good News Magazine,* (United Methodist Church, USA)
273 "What does The Methodist Church say about fasting?" Accessed May 29, 2018. http://www.umc.org/what-we-believe/what-does-the-united-methodist-church-say-about-fasting
274 Matthew 6:16-18.It also has references in Psalm 1:2 and in Isaiah 30:15-16, 58:3.
275 R T. Kendall, *The Sermon on the Mount,* (Oxford: Monarch Books, 2011), 276
276 Leviticus 23:26-32
277 According to Acts 13:2-3
278 Acts 14:23
279 Exodus 24:18.
280 Joshua 20:26; 2 Sam. 1:12, 2 Chr. 20:13 and Ezra 8:23).
281 Luke 18:12
282 Kenneth Boa, *Conformed to His Image,* 84
283 Adele Ahlberg Calhoun, *Spiritual Disciplines Handbook: Practices that Transforms* Us,(Downers Grove, Illinois: 2015), 246
284 On the subject of fasting, the following resources would take the reader deeper into the subject:
Baab, Lynne M. Fasting: *Spiritual Freedom Above Our Appetites,* Downers Grove, Ill.:IVP Books, 2006
Foster, Richard J. and Helmers, K A. *Celebration of Discipline: The Path to Spiritual Growth.* London: Hodder and Stoughton (first edition, 1980); San Francisco: Harper – Collins, 1998 edition
Johnson, Jan, *Simplicity and Fasting*: Leicester: IVP 2003

Piper, John. *A Hunger for God: Desiring God Through Fasting and Prayer*: Wheaton, Illinois: Cross Way Books, 2013

Thompson, Marjorie J. *Soul Feast,* Louisville: Westminster John Knox Press 1995

285 Adele Ahlberg Calhoun, *Spiritual Disciplines Handbook,* 255.

286 Bob Gass,"On his law he meditates day and night" (Psalm 1:2) in The UCB Word for Today, 7 Nov 2017

287 Matthew 4:1-11; Mark 1:12-13; Luke 4:1-13

288 Mark 1:35

289 John 6:15

290 Matthew 14:23

291 Luke 5:16

292 Matthew 4:1-11

293 Luke 6:12-13

294 Matthew 26:36; see also Kenneth Boa, *Conformed to His Image,* 87

295 Ibid, p.83

296 Ibid p. 84

297 Ibid. p. 88

298 Ibid p.92

299 Ibid p.93

300 Ibid p.91

301 Ibid.p.91

302 Joshua 1:8; Psalm 1:2-3; John 6:63; John 15:4-8 (the concept of abiding); Colossians 3:1-2; Philippians 4:8 and Romans 8:5

303 Boa, op cit. p.92

304 Proverbs 23:7

305 Boa, Ibid. p.93

306 Psalm 63:6 & Proverbs 6:22

307 Boa, op cit. p.93

308 Marjorie J Thompson, Evan B Howard, *Soul Feast: An Invitation To The Christian Spiritual Life.(*Westminster John Knox Press, 2005), 24

309 *Lectio divina,* Accessed April 19, 2017. http://www.gotquestions.org/lectio-divina.html

310 Pope Benedict XVI *On Lectio Divina PDF,* Accessed April 19, 2017. http://www.sfcatholic.org/dwc/Files/OfficeofRespectLife/Marriage/Divina.pdf

311 Jean Leclercq, *The Love of Learning and the Desire for God*, Translated by Catharine Misrahi. (New York: Fordham University Press, 1982) also cited Kenneth Boa, *Conformed to His Image,* 175

312 Psalm 119:18

313 Psalm19:14

314 Kenneth Boa, *Conformed to His Image,* 178 refers to the work of the Holy Spirit in the believer Romans 8:26-27; Galatians 4:19; Joshua 1:8 & Psalm 1:2

315 Ibid. p.178 see also 1Corinthian 2:16

316 Hebrews 4:12-13

317 Boa, op cit. p.182

318 Rudolf Otto, *The Idea of the Holy*.Trans. John W. Harvey, (Oxford: Oxford University Press, 1923; 2nd ed., 1950 (*Das Heilige*), 1917)

319 Kenneth Boa, *Conformed to His Image*, 183

320 Hosea 4:6,

321 1 Peter 5:8

322 2 Corinthians 11:14

323 2 Timothy 3:16

324 Psalm 19:7-14

325 Kenneth Boa, *Conformed to His Image*, 184

326 Richard Peace, *Spiritual Journaling: Recording Your Journey Toward God*. (Colorado Springs, Colorado: NavPress, 1998)

327 Ibid. 7; see also Ronald Klug, *How to Keep a Spiritual Journal: A Guide to Journal Keeping for Inner Growth and Personal Discovery*, A Fortress E-book, Fortress Press.com; 2002, Augsburg Fortress, Minneapolis.

328 Huck Finn, Holiness Today, June 1999, 27

329 C.Lewis, *The Four Loves*, (New York: Harcourt, Brace, 1960), also cited in http://AndiLit.com/2009/07/31/cs-lewis-on-friendship/

330 Mary Fishback Powers, *Foot prints in the sand Poem*, 1939, Accessed August 1, 2019 http://www.onlythebible.com/Poems/Footprint-in-the-sand poem.htmal. April 26, 2010

331 Susan A.Muto, *Pathways to Spiritual Living* Petersham, (MA: St. Bede's Publications, 1984), 96.

332 E Stanley Jones. Quoted by Klug, 25. From Wesley Tracy, *Reflecting God*, page 9.

333 Susan A. Muto, *Pathways*, 99. From H. J. Cargas and Roger Bradley, *Keeping a Spiritual Journal* (Garden City, NY: Doubleday, 1981), 8.

334 Robert Louis Stevenson. *From The Upward Call*, Beacon Hill Press of Kansas City, 1994, p. 115

335 From Peace, 44.

336 Robert Wood, *A Thirty Day Experiment in Prayer*,Nashville: The Upper Room, 1978, 14).

337 Ibid.

338 *The Works of John Wesley*, ed. Thomas Jackson, 3rd ed., 14 vols. (London: Methodist Book Room, 1872; reprint, Kansas City: Beacon Hill Press of Kansas City, 1978), 4:91-92.)

339 An excerpt from book 8 of his journal, *The Confessions of St. Augustine*, trs. Edward B. Pusey, (New York: Washington Square Press, Inc., 1960), 145-48.

340 Matthew 4:19 ; Mark 1:16-20

341 Matthew 11:29-30

342 Matthew 11:28-30, The Message Translation

343 Joseph Stowell – Pastor of the Moody Church, Accessed 19 April, 2017. https://www.sermoncentral.com/sermons/follow-me-and-i-will-make-you-fishers-of-men-john-hamby-sermon-on-basics-of-christianity-61418

344 Paul Harvey, op cit.

345 Hendricks, Howard and William. *Building Character in a Mentoring Relationship; As Iron Sharpens Iron*, (Chicago: Moody Press, 1995), 87

346 Mark 3:14-15

347 Barclay, William. *The Gospel of Mark,* (Edingburgh: St Andrews Press, 1954), 156-7 also cited by Tony Horsfall, *Rhythms of Grace*, (Eastbourne: Kingsway Publications, 2004), 68

348 1Corinthians 11:1 see also 1Cor 4:16 "I exhort you therefore to be imitators of me"; 1Thes.1:6 "became imitators of the churches of God in Christ Jesus that are in Judea; Hebrews 6:12 & 13:7"imitators of the faithful"

349 Ephesians 5:1

350 1Peter 1:15-16

351 John 5:19-30

352 1John 4:16; John 3:16

353 Howard and William Hendricks, *Building Character in a Mentoring Relationship; As Iron Sharpens Iron*, (Chicago: Moody Press, 1995) ; Ted Engstrom, *The Fine Art of Mentoring*, (Brentwood, Tenn.: Woldermuth & Hyatt, 1989)

354 This is a disputed saying attributed to Chinese, Native American, Italian, Indian, Lao-Tzu, Maimonides or even Mao Zedong adage. Accessed 19 April 2018. https://quoteinvestigator.com /2015/08/28/fish

355 Hendricks, *As Iron Sharpens Iron*, 111

356 Hebrews 12:2 (God's Word Translation.)

357 John 21:3

358 Philippians 2:12

359 Paul uses the same phrase in 2Corinthians 7:15 encouraging Corinthians to receive Titus with fear trembling meaning receive him with great humility and respect for his position as a minister of the gospel.

360 Howard and William Hendricks, *As Iron Sharpens Iron*, 13

361 Proverbs 27:17

362 Hendricks, p.18

363 Ibid.p.28

364 1 Samuel 3:1-21

365 Acts 9:27

366 Hebrews 13:7

367 Matthew 7:3

368 Philippians 3:13-24

369 Hebrews chapters 11 and 12

370 Hendricks, op cit. 114

371 Ibid. p.114

372 Ibid.p.115
373 Ibid. p.120
374 Ibid. p.77
375 Ibid. p.78
376 Ibid. p. 120
377 Ibid. Chapter 5, p.59-72
378 Matthew chapters 5-7
379 Matthew 7:18
380 Hendricks, op. cit. 61
381 Revelations 3:20 NLT
382 Hendricks, op. cit. p.61
383 1Thessalonians 2:8
384 Ibid. p.66
385 Ibid. p.67
386 Howard and William Hendricks, *As Iron Sharpens Iron*, 271
387 *I wish I could be a brother like that,* Accessed April 19, 2018. https://www.epm.org/.../Sep/11/i-wish-i-could-be-a-brother-like-that
388 Gordon MacDonald in the foreword to Ted Engstrom, *The fine Art of Mentoring*, (Brentwood, Tenn.: Wolgemuth & Hyatt, 1989), ix-x. Alos cited by Hendricks, *As Iron Sharpens Iron*, 120
389 Ibid. p.120
390 Hendricks, op. cit pp.127-238
391 Ibid p.119
392 Hendricks, *As Iron Sharpens Iron,* 131 citing Michael Medved, "Holywood Vs. Religion" video tape produced by Chatham Hill Foundation, Dallas, Tex. 1994 distributed by World. Inc.
393 Ephesians 4:11-12
394 Colossians 3:16; 2Peter 3:18; See also other Biblical injunctions in Mark 3:14; Luke 6:40b; 1Corinthians 4:16; 1Corinthians 11:1; Philippians 3:17; 4:19; 1 Thessalonians 1:6-8; 1 Timothy 4:12; 2Timothy 3:10; Titus 2:7-8; Hebrews 13:7; 1Peter 5:3; 3John11
395 Hendricks, op. cit. p.138
396 Matthew 28:19
397 Hendricks, Ibid. p.139
398 Ibid. p. 149
399 Psalm 118:23
400 Hendricks, Ibid. p.153
401 Ibid.
402 *Generativity vs. Stagnation: Erikson's Seventh Stage* - Verywell Mind. Accessed March 12, 2018. https://www.verywellmind.com/generativity-versus-stagnation -2795734
403 Matthew 16:25 (NIV)

404 Brainy quote, Accessed April 30, 2018. https://www.brainyquote.com/quotes/thomas_a_edison_104931

405 Hendricks, op. cit. p.140

406 Hendricks, p.147

407 Ibid. p.152

408 William H. Wilmon& Robert L. Wilson, *Rekindling the Flame: Strategies for a Vital United Methodism,* (Nashville: Abingdon Press, 1988 2nd edition), 41, 42

409 William H. Wilmon& Robert L. Wilson, *Rekindling the Flame,* 30

410 See *Zion's Herald*, Boston, November 30, 1825. (Designated as a reprint from the Arminian Magazine).

411 See From Wesley, *Works,* 8:272.

412 Question five is not always included in the early Wesleyan accounts of the bands.

413 See Wesley, *Works, 8:261.*

414 See, John Wesley, Letters, 8:158

415 Laurent Daloz, *Effective Teaching and Mentoring* (San Francisco: Jossey-Bass, 1987), 200-245. ; Ron Lee Davis, Mentoring: *The Strategy of the Master,* (Nashville: Thomas Nelson, 1991), 11-224. ; Wesley Tracy, et al., *Reflecting God,* ad. loc

416 *Upward Call* (Kansas City: Beacon Hill Press of Kansas City, 1994), 135-191; Wesley Tracy, et al., *Reflecting God* (Kansas City: Beacon Hill Press of Kansas City and Christian Holiness Partnership, 2000), 127-134.

417 1 Thessalonians 2;7-11

418 See Wesley, Letters, 5:87.

419 1 Thess 1:5-6, (NRSV).

420 *"Faith Mentoring in the Faith Community,"* unpublished Ph.D. dissertation, Claremont School of Theology, 1986, 62.

421 Wesley Tracy, *Upward Call,* 185.

422 Howard and William Hendricks, *As Iron Sharpens Iron,* 21-23

423 Andrew and Elizabeth Procter, *The Essential Guide to Burnout: Overcoming Excess Stress,* (Oxford: Lion Books), 2013, 163; see also Julia Cameron, *The Artist Way: A Course in Discovering and Recovering Your Creative Self,* (London: Pan Books,1993), 166

424 Ibid. p.148

425 Ibid. p.134

426 Hendricks, *As Iron Sharpens Iron,* 32-34

427 Jonathan and David, "Jonathan made a covenant with David because he loved him as his own soul 1Samuel 18:3 The relationship between Barnabas and Paul it found in Acts 9 when Barnabas introduced Paul to the Apostles and disciples in Jerusalem who were afraid of Paul because of his past having persecuted the church as a Pharisee. We later encounter the two in Acts 13 when they were partners in mission.

428 See Wesley Tracy, *Reflecting God*, op.cit. p. 134. Quoted by Edward C. Sellnor, *Mentoring: The Ministry of Spiritual Kinship*, Mahwah, NJ: Paulist Press, 1989, 156.

429 See John Wesley Letters, 8:158; 3:94-95; 5:187.

430 Ibid.

431 Ibid

432 Ibid

433 *John Wesley Letters*, (San Francisco: Harper & Row, 1984), 55.

434 Emilie Griffin, *Clinging: The Experience of Prayer*, (New York: McCracken, 1994)

435 Ephesians 6:12

436 Philip Yancey, *What's so Amazing About Grace?*, (Grand Rapids, Michigan: Zondervan, 1997), 12-13

437 Ibid. 13

438 Ibid p.71

439 Ibid. 79

440 Ibid. 67

441 Colin Brown, ed. *The New International Dictionary of the New Testament Theology*. Vol.2. (Exeter: IVP, 1976), 115-116

442 Ibid. p.118

443 Luke 15:11-32

444 Matthew 20:1-6

445 Luke 14:16-24

446 Spirit food, Accessed May 20, 2018. http://www.facebook.com/spiritfoodft,

447 Andrew H. Trotter Jr. https://www.biblestudytools.com/dictionary/grace/

448 Mark 12:30-31

449 John 1:14

450 "Augustine of Hippo Confessions" in *The Confessions of St Augustine*, translated by F. J. Sheed, (London: Sheed and Ward, 1944)

451 John 15:15 AMPC

452 Tony Horsfall, *Rhythms of Grace, 25*

453 1Samuel 15:22

454 Matthew 5:24

455 Exodus 32:29

456 Acts 4:13

457 Horsfall, op cit. p. 20

458 1Corinthians 15:10

459 Psalm 46:10

460 *The hymn Jesus I am trusting trusting*, Accessed May 22, 2018. https://www.hymnal.net/en/hymn/h/579

461 Albert Edward Day, *Discipline and Discovery*, (Nashville: Disciplined Order of Christ, 1961), 89.

462 Ibid.

463 Confession in the Prayers of the Sanctified From "The Repentance of Believers" in " *Sermons on Several Occasions, (*London: Wesleyan- Methodist Book Room, n.d.), 185.

464 *The Upward Call*, 87.

465 *The Upward Call,* 87.Also "Our Lord's Sermon on the Mount, Discourse III," *Sermons on Several Occasions, p. 32.*

466 Filling by Holy Spirit, Accessed May 26, 2018. https://www.sermoncentral.com/sermon-illustrations/2970/d-l-moody-was-once-asked-why-he-urged-christians-by-owen-bourgaize

467 John Webster, *Holiness,* Grand Rapids: Eerdmans, 2003, 7.

468 G. C. Berkouwer, *Faith and Sanctification,* (Grand Rapids: Eerdmans, 1954), 21, 33, 43.

469 Reformed Faith (11.2; cf. 16.2).

470 John Webster, *Holiness* (Grand Rapids: Eerdmans, 2003)
Walter Marshall, *The Gospel Mystery of Sanctification: Growing in Holiness by Living in Union with Christ.* A New Version, (Eugene: Wipf & Stock), 2005
Walter Marshall, *Gospel Mystery of Sanctification,* Grand Rapids: Reformation Heritage, 1999
G. C. Berkouwer, *Faith and Sanctification,* Grand Rapids: Eerdmans, 1954
Lewis B. Smedes, *Union with Christ,* Grand Rapids: Eerdmans, 1983.
John Murray, *Redemption Accomplished and Applied,* Grand Rapids: Eerdmans, 1955

471 Kenneth Bailey is an author and lecturer in Middle Eastern New Testament studies. He spent forty years living and teaching New Testament in Egypt, Lebanon, Jerusalem and Cyprus. He has written many books in English and Arabic including. *Poet and Peasant, The Cross and the Prodigal Son, Jacob and the Prodigal, Jesus through Middle Eastern Eyes* and *Paul Through Mediterranean Eyes.*

472 Kenneth E Bailey, *Poet and Peasant and Through Peasant's Eyes.* Grand Rapids: Eerdmans, 1976

473 Ibid. pp. 161-164; 181

474 Luke 15:3-32

475 Yancey, Philip. *What's so Amazing About Grace,* 80

476 Matthew 20:1-16

477 Matthew 18:21-35

478 Luke 14:15-24

479 Yancey, op. cit. p.91

480 Ibid p. 61-62

481 Matthew 18:22

482 John 13:1-17

483 John 21:15-19

484 Luke 23:43

485 Yancey, op. cit p.66

486 Ibid. p.61

487 Ibid. p. 64

488 Matthew 5:20

489 John 13:14-15 NLT

490 Hebrews 12:15 NIV

491 2Peter 3:18

492 Gass, Bob, "Responding with Grace (2 Peter 3:18)", in *Word For Today,* UCB. 9 June 2018

493 Colin Brown, ed. *The New International Dictionary of the New Testament Theology, Vol. 1,* (Exeter: IVP 1976), 147

494 Ibid. p. 148

495 Eliade Mircea, *Encyclopaedia of Religion.* Vol.5 (New York: McMillan Publishing Company), 185

496 Fred Prat Green (1903-2000), *Singing the Faith.* Trustees for Methodist Church Purposes, London: Hymns Ancient & Modern Ltd, 2012, Hymn number 595; *Hymns and Psalms number* 700.

Six Chapter
Spiritual formation in the Wesleyan –holiness movement

> My brother Wesley acted wisely, the souls that were awakened under his ministry he joined in class, and thus preserved the fruits of his labor. This I neglected, and my people are a rope of sand."
>
> (George Whitfield)

The Wesleyan Holiness Movement owes its roots in the 19th century Revival movement started by the Wesley brothers, John (1703-1791) and Charles (1707-1788). They were both ordained ministers in the Church of England who had become disenfranchised by dead religion and set out in search of the religion of the heart as opposed to philosophical religiosity and speculation. They founded what initially was known as the "Holy Club" fellowship in prayer and Bible study during their student days at Oxford University, which was so methodical in its praxis that it became the foundation of Methodism. Initially, the word "Methodist" was pejorative, a nickname denoting their systematic approach to spirituality. Out of this movement has sprung up evangelical denominations and other church-related organizations, all unified by the pursuit of the religion of the heart, once described by Wesley as "strangely warmed heart" on his conversion day celebrated on the twenty-fourth of May. The Wesley brothers repudiated ultra Calvinism that emphasized the Sovereignty of God in matters of Christian belief and self -abandonment to God almost to the exclusion of human response and responsibility. The Moravians whose certainty of faith influenced Wesley, and the love of God brought Wesley to a theological paradigm shift, a kind of "Damascus Road experience similar to Apostle Paul that made him recognize the importance of the cooperation of human will and responsibility espoused in what came to be known as Armenian theology.[497] Their shift was influenced by reading a book: *The imitation of Christ: Serious Call to a Devout and Holy Life* by William Law. Wesleyan Holiness Movement traces its roots in the Reformation, Pietism, and Puritanism, emphasizing individual spirituality and the responsibility to live a holy life. The central tenet in the Holiness Movement is a belief in a second blessing or work of grace after regeneration and the commitment to pursue the experience of entire sanctification that enables the believer to live a holy life entirely without willful sin. In his book, *Plain Account of Christian Perfection*, John Wesley defined holiness not as achieving sinless perfection but as having one's heart fully fixed on God, setting aside all other affections—"perfect love."[498] Wesley's teaching on holiness combined William Law's ideas and the Moravian emphasis on felt assurance of salvation (which Wesley extended to include sanctification), and the Puritan insistence on microscopic examination of conscience coupled with sanctified action in all spheres of life. The Wesley brothers developed a disciplined approach to spiritual growth and formation that was deemed methodical. It is this that laid the foundation stone of Methodism and its derivative denominations. These are: African Methodist Episcopal (1814); Keswick Convention (1875); Salvation Army (1880) founded by William Booth (1829-1912), Christian and Missionary Alliance (1887); Church of God (1897); Pentecostal

Movement in 1901-1906 led by William Seymour (1870-1922); Church of the Nazarene (1907); Pentecostal Assemblies (1907); Assemblies of God (1914); Foursquare Gospel (1927); Calvary Chapel (1965); Vineyard Ministries (1983). The main emphasis was on personal holiness and the possibility of entire sanctification and Christian perfection.

Spiritual formation, as a discipline, finds fertile soil and ground within the Wesleyan Holiness Movement. The seven disciplines discussed in this book would resonate with Christians within the Holiness Movement. As it developed in both England and America through the Wesley brothers in England and Francis Asbury in the USA, the class meetings were *sine quo non*, for growth and spiritual formation.

What is the significance of class and band meetings in spiritual formation?

The Wesleyan Holiness Movement tradition started as a renewal movement in the 18th century. Its DNA was the transformation of individual people's lives, their communities, and broader society. Its motto was to spread scriptural holiness throughout the land. The key to this transformation was the weekly mid-week meetings that came to be known as:

The class and band meetings.

The class and band meetings composed of a small group of people who met weekly to check the state of their souls. The critical focal question in the class meeting was: **"How is it with your soul?"** The goal of the class meeting was essentially the same as that of early Methodism itself, "to be transformed by the grace of God, to become an altogether Christian. Today, the class meeting more closely resembles an archaeological artifact of the history of the early Wesleyan movement than a lived practice, which is a great loss."[499] What is lost is the continual experience of daily transformation in people's lives as a means of Christian nurture and growth into discipleship with the sad result of stagnant spiritual development and growth. The second significant loss is fellowship and mutual support, and with it, the loss of personal spiritual accountability. The class meetings were small accountability groups that helped each participant to do right and resist temptation on a daily, weekly basis.

In England and America, there have been marked a decline in class meetings because of changes in postmodernity societies and their core belief, "the truth for you is not the truth for me," coupled with permissive ethics in defining morality. The class meeting, could, however, be revived with modification to fit in modern society in which the leader, who is possibly trusted by the group could engage in a peer-mentor relationship with each member on a one to one basis to engender accountability giving space for Bible study for Christian nurture and social engagement.

As regarding the origins of the class meeting, cynics and critics of Wesley see it as a by-product of a fundraising effort. Initially, the class meeting started when Wesley sent the leaders of the class meetings to individuals to collect a penny for the New Room Chapel in Bristol, which stands to this day. "With Wesley's characteristic genius, he saw that this was an opportunity for spiritual formation as well. The leader began to inquire of their spiritual status as well as to collect an offering."[500]

Kevin M. Watson's work is the most authoritative account, extensive work in-class meetings.[501] According to Watson: "The class meeting was started in 1742 when a group of Methodists was trying to figure out how to pay off a building debt in Bristol. Captain Foy suggested that the Bristol society is divided up into groups of 12 people. One person in each group would be designated the leader and would be responsible for visiting each person in their group every week to collect one penny from them. By this means, Foy believed the building debt could be retired. Someone raised a concern that this would prevent the poorest Methodists from being involved. Captain Foy responded by volunteering to take the 11 poorest members of the Bristol Society into his group. He said that he would visit them each week and ask them if they could contribute. If they were unable, Foy would pay their penny on their behalf. Then, he challenged the other people at the meeting to do the same thing.

In trying to practice this plan, it became apparent that many Methodists were not keeping the "General Rules," which were: do no harm, do good, and practice the means of grace (i.e., prayer, searching the Scriptures, receiving Communion, etc.). Almost immediately, Wesley realized that the class leaders (who were the ones that had initially been committed to making the weekly collection) were ideally suited to address the lack of discipline in keeping the General Rules amongst Methodists. In the General Rules, Wesley described the primary duty of the class leader to make sure that the members are working out their salvation. The society divided into small companies, called classes, according to their respective places of abode. There were about twelve persons in every class, one of whom it was the Leader. It is his or her business,

> To see each person in his class once a week at least, in order to inquire how their souls prosper; to advise, reprove, comfort, or exhort, as occasion may require; to receive what they are willing to give toward the relief of

> the poor. To meet the Minister and the Stewards of the society once a week; in order to inform the Minister of any that are sick, or of any that walk disorderly, and will not be reproved; to pay to the Stewards what they have received of their several classes in the week preceding; and to show their account of what each person has contributed.[502]

Initially, the class leader met each person at his or her own house. For practical reason, however, it was easier for the entire class to meet together once a week; and this became the standard practice. Wesley reported in *A Plain Account of the People Called Methodists* that at the class meeting, "Advice or reproof was given as need required, quarrels made up, and misunderstandings removed: And after an hour or two spent in this labor of love, they concluded with prayer and thanksgiving." Wesley further reported on what he believed were the fruits of the class meeting:

> It can scarce be conceived what advantages have been reaped from this little prudential regulation. Many now happily experienced that Christian fellowship of which they had not so much as an idea before. They began to 'bear one another burdens,' and naturally to 'care for each other.' As they had daily, a more intimate acquaintance with, so they had a more endeared affection for each other. And 'speaking the truth in love, they grew up into Him in all things, who is the Head, even Christ; from whom the whole body, fitly joined together, and compacted by that which every joint supplied, according to the effectual working in the measure of every part, increased unto the edifying itself in love.[503]

The class meeting, then, quickly developed into a much more crucial tool for enabling Methodists to "watch over one another in love," to support and encourage one another in their lives with God. John Wesley thought the oversight and support that the class meeting provided was so meaningful that it became a requirement for membership in a Methodist society. To be a Methodist meant that you were involved in a weekly class meeting.

So what happened during these weekly meetings?

Classes were intended to have between 7 to 12 members in them. They had both women and men in the classes, and class leaders were both women and men. Classes were divided primarily by geographical location. In other words, you would have attended a class meeting with the Methodists in your neighborhood. From what we have seen above, the class meeting seems to have focused on three things. First, it held people accountable for keeping the "General Rules." Second, the class meeting was a place where every Methodist weekly answered the question, "How is it with your soul?" More recently, the Methodist historian Scott Kisker has rephrased this question to "How is your life in God?" Third, it was a place where Methodists were encouraged to give weekly to the relief of the poor.

The phrase that I believe best captures what the Methodists believed was so important about the class meeting was "watching over one another in love." Early Methodists were asked to invite others into their lives and to be willing to enter deeply into the lives of other people so that together, they would grow in grace. They were committed to the idea that the Christian life is a journey of growth in grace, or sanctification. And they believed that they needed one another to persevere on this journey."[504]

Watson,[505] in his analysis of Rack[506]on the decline of the class meetings, points out that: "The decline of the class meeting in the United States, at once more swift and pervasive, is a study in itself. As Methodism moved into America, the social development of early American Methodism, which changed its focus in the nineteenth century to rural and frontier evangelism. The topography was more conducive to the camp meeting than that of the class. There was also the move towards a parish oriented form of the pastorate, rather than the circuit system, which relied more heavily on the class leader. He further points out that American appeal to retain the class meeting indicate this office had come to be regarded primarily as that of a sub-pastor-a subtle change of emphasis, but profoundly different from its original purpose and function. Literature review shows that the motivation and the purpose of the founding of the class meeting were for practical discipleship in light of Wesley's understanding of the doctrine of justification by faith and of sanctification. The current debate at the time was whether justification by faith meant that good works were unconditional. The hardcore Lutheranism maintained that good works were not a condition of faith, but that good works followed from faith. Luther contended that good works were a condition of continuing in that faith, stating that "although acceptation to everlasting life is conjoined with justification, yet our good works be necessarily required to the attaining of everlasting life."[507] This could be summed up as "juxtaposition of grace freely given, and good works as a subsequent obligation."[508]The overarching concern was on stressing human accountability and good works, for Wesley accountability was paramount to Christian discipleship, and the class meetings were the means of achieving and maintaining discipleship discipline. The second major doctrinal drive to the establishment of the class meeting was Wesley's understanding of Christian perfection after the Aldersgate Experience with God. The doctrine of perfection is closely tied to Wesley's understanding of the discipline of spiritual self-examination that he believed was important in Christian discipleship. Wesley came to believe that the pursuit of personal holiness was pertinent to Christian living, and he strongly believed that this was engendered in the class meetings. He asserted that "It is by discipline that every good soldier of Christ is to "inure himself to endure hardship" It is through "daily care", albeit by the grace of God in Christ that the Christian purges "the inmost recesses of the soul from the lusts that before possessed and defiled it". The Christian who does not run the race in this way, who do not practice such self-denial, fights the fight of faith to little purpose and merely "beateth the air."[509] There is a sense in which the class meetings were means of efficacious means of prevenient grace through practicing personal accountable Christian disciplines. The minutes of the 1744 Conference urged the Methodist preachers to use all the means of grace, "instituted" and "prudential," and to "enforce the use of them on all persons." The prudential means were the various personal disciplines for growing in grace – watching, self-denial, the exercise of the presence of God – and regular attendance at class or band meeting."[510] In developing Methodist discipleship, Wesley restricted justification to moment by moment sense of pardon experienced by faith; Wesley infused a divine immediacy into the whole of the Christian life. He found in the richness of Methodist religious experience, a spiritual growth that was analogous to birth, childhood, and coming of age, leading to what he came to regard as a "second blessing."[511] But when the second blessing was taken for granted, however, there was a falling away – even by most mature. Obedience could not, for one moment, be neglected.[512] The critical question for Christian discipleship, therefore, was how to permit God's grace to foster a maturity of constant obedience, so that sanctifying grace might work with an unimpeded love. It was Wesley's theological understanding of this question, which led him to adopt what at first seemed an unbelievably simple solution: a weekly meeting of like-minded persons who would exercise mutual accountability for their discipleship. This prudential means of grace was as profound as it was simple. In adopting the class meeting as a basis for early Methodist polity, Wesley was practical. The dynamic of early Methodist discipleship was established at the very beginning of the movement on the solid theological principle of distinctive justification – how not to resist the immediacy of God's gracious initiatives. It remains the most important contribution made by Wesley and by Methodism, to the Christian tradition." There are other resources on the subject of class meetings.[513]

What are the benefits of class meetings?

In Western societies where we have what has come to be known as the missing generations in church, the resurrection of class meetings or its dynamic cultural equivalent is very much necessary as a means of evangelism, Christian nurture, and spiritual growth. For several main reasons:

1. The response of a person who has been "de-churched" for years, accepting an invitation to attend a mid-week meeting possibly in someone's house than to invite them to a church meeting, is more likely. People who have lost contact with the church or never had a connection with the church would respond more positively to a personal invitation. In this sense, class meetings are practical tools of personal evangelism and outreach.
2. The personal nature of one to one encounters is less intimidating and more conducive to a Western society where isolation, individualism, and breakdown of community cohesion are a real impediment to outreach.

The house-church movement, the cell church movement, and the Alpha church movement have utilized variants of the class meeting to great advantage in their church growth. In African societies, the class meeting finds dynamic cultural equivalent and resonates with the tribal and clan systems that quickly engender a sense of belonging and solidarity.

3. Christian care and nurture through the catchphrase, "watching each other in love."
4. Spurring each other into intimacy with God and learning about holiness in practice.
5. Works of mercy arc encouraged in these small meetings through encouraging loving deeds towards the neighbor. The small group at Oxford, which was known as the methodical "Holy Club," out of which the term Methodist developed engaged in works of mercy in the hospital and prison visitation. As Methodism developed, it found fertile soil among the poor, factory workers, farmers, and miners.
6. A safety net for those who have been hurt in church and find it hard to attend church. The small class meeting provides a means of fellowship and model reconciliation.
7. The most important benefit is the development of spiritual accountability.

The band meetings.

Similar to the class meetings, the Band meetings were meant to assist in the pursuit of holiness together and provide mutual accountability based on trust where spiritual sojourners and friends would confess sins before each other without fear of condemnation. The band meetings were organized in peer groups according to gender and marital status. The band meetings acted as catalysts to spiritual growth in providing discipleship model of growing in love through accountability in a small group of similar persons. The main focus of the band meeting was a confession of sin for the sake of growth in holiness that was crucial in advancing the early mission of the movement to "spread scriptural holiness." Francis Asbury Journal emphasizes the seriousness of the band meetings as follows, "Both the class and band meetings were important for helping people become entire Christians who give the DNA of early Methodism and the Holiness Movement."

The Wesley's Rules for Band-Societies that were drawn up December 25, 1738, stated as follows:- The design of our meeting is to obey that command of God, "Confess your faults one to another, and pray one for another, that ye may be healed. To this end, we intend.

1. To meet once a week, at the least.
2. To come punctually at the hour appointed, without some extraordinary reason.
3. To begin (those of us who are present) exactly at the hour, with singing or prayer.
4. To speak each of us in order, freely and plainly, the true state of our souls, with the faults we have committed in thought, word, or deed, and the temptations we have felt since our last meeting.
5. To end every meeting with prayer suited to the state of each person present.
6. To desire some person among us to speak his own state first, and then to ask the rest, in order, as many and as searching questions as may be, concerning their state, sins, and temptations.

Some of the questions proposed to everyone before he is admitted among us may be to this effect:-

1. Have you the forgiveness of your sins.
2. Have you peace with God through our Lord Jesus Christ.
3. Have you the witness of God's Spirit with your spirit, that you are a child of God.
4. Is the love of God shed abroad in your heart?
5. Has no sin, inward or outward, dominion over you?
6. Do you desire to be told of your faults?
7. Do you desire to be told of all your faults and that plain and home?
8. Do you desire that every one of us should tell you, from time to time, whatsoever is in his heart concerning you?
9. Consider! Do you desire we should tell you whatsoever we think, whatsoever we fear, whatsoever we hear, concerning you?
10. Do you desire that, in doing this, we should come as close as possible, that we should cut to the quick, and search your heart to the bottom?
11. Is it your desire and design to be on this, and all other occasions, entirely open, so as to speak everything that is in your heart without exception, without disguise, and without reserve?

Traditionally there were five questions to ask during a Band Meeting. These were

1. What known sins have you committed since our last meeting?
2. What temptations have you met with?
3. How were you delivered?

4. What have you thought, said, or done, of which you doubt whether it is a sin or not?
5. Have you nothing you desire to keep secret?

These five questions have been modified to fit modern times as follows:-

1. Have you had any spiritual failures recently? Have you been disappointed with yourself lately, spiritually speaking? How can we be most helpful in restoring or supporting you? When we pray for and with you today, at what point should we focus our prayers?
2. What temptations or spiritual problems have you been battling lately? At what points in your life do you feel most vulnerable? Most weak right now? Most under pressure?
3. If you have been delivered from any temptations lately, would you share with us how the victory was won? Would you share with us how you have endured and survived recent trials?
4. Has the Lord revealed anything to you about your heart and life that makes you want to take a prayerful second look at your attitudes, lifestyle, service, or motivations?
5. Is there a spiritual problem so deep or so personal that you have never been able to talk to anyone about it? Can you even talk with God about it? Are you carrying excess baggage from the past that still today keeps you defeated and depressed? Would you like to share it with us, your spiritual partners? Or, at least let us pray for you about it - would you set a time each day (or this week) when you are going to pray about this matter so we can at that very same hour pray for you wherever we are?[514]

There are two main recent books on the Band Meeting. The first is by Kevin M. Watson and Scott Kisker, *The Band Meeting: Rediscovering Relational Discipleship in Transformational Community.* The second book is by Kevin M Watson, *Pursuing Social Holiness: The Band Meeting in Wesley's Thought and Popular Methodist Practice.* Kevin's book reveals the meaning and significance of the band meeting. Its blurb reads as follows: "Kevin M. Watson offers the first in-depth examination of an essential early Methodist tradition: the band meeting, a small group of five to seven people who focused on the confession of sin to grow in holiness. Watson shows how the band meeting, which figured significantly in John Wesley's theology of discipleship, united Wesley's emphasis on the importance of holiness with his conviction that Christians are most likely to make progress in the Christian life together, rather than in isolation. Watson explores how Wesley synthesized important aspects of Anglican piety and Moravian piety in his version of the band meeting. Pursuing Social Holiness is an essential contribution to understanding the critical role of the band meeting in the development of British Methodism and shifting concepts of community in eighteenth-century British society."

The importance of the class meetings and the band meetings is high lighted by an entry in Francis Asbury's journal at the beginning of his ministry in America, ten years before his ordination, and before he was the leader of the American Methodism. He stated: -

> In meeting the society at night, I spoke plainly of some who neglected their bands and classes; and informed them that we took people into our societies that we might help them become entire Christians, and if they wilfully neglected those meetings, they thereby withdrew themselves from our care and assistance."[515] The closest

> equivalent to the band meeting in our modern society is what is known as peer mentoring based on the bible verse: "As iron sharpens iron, so a man sharpens the countenance of his friend.[516]

There is a popular saying that Methodism was born in song referring to the Wesleyan hymns and their influence, nevertheless, the one indisputable legacy that the Wesleyan movement bequeathed to the world is the class meetings and the band meeting. "The Class meeting is the most appropriate entry point for transformation driven small groups for people who do not have much experience within them."[517] The real genius of the Wesleyan movement is harnessing the dynamics of small groups. In reflection on Wesley's class meeting and band meeting structure and their usefulness, George Whitfield who was a contemporary of John Wesley once said:- "My brother Wesley acted wisely, the souls that were awakened under his ministry he joined in class, and thus preserved the fruits of his labor. This neglected and my people are a rope of sand." An expanded version of this was recently cited as follows:-

> "John Wesley was not the greatest preacher of his day. His occasional friend and sometime nemesis George Whitefield were that. "My brother Wesley acted wisely," Whitefield said. "The souls that were awakened under his ministry he joined in societies, and thus preserved the fruit of his labor. This I neglected, and my people are a rope of sand." .... Wesley himself used the image to describe the Christianity against which his people reacted in eighteenth-century England: "Those who were desirous of saving their souls were no longer a rope of sand, but clave to one another, and began to watch over each other in love. Societies were formed, and Christian discipline was introduced in all its branches." .... There

> are no Whitefieldian societies now. But there are tens of millions of Wesleyan believers around the world."[518]

In the United Methodist Church of the USA, in its mission statement, it emphasizes "making disciples of Jesus Christ for the transformation of the world." Attendance to class meetings in early Methodism was mandatory. Admission to the larger society meeting required a ticked from a class leader, validating one's faithful participation in class meetings. As noted earlier, it began with small groups that crystallized to class meetings, which defined what it meant to be a Methodist. Historically class meetings ensured that every Methodist was connected to other Methodists, so no one was left out, ignored, or overlooked. According to Kevin Watson, "they relentlessly focused every Methodist on the current state of their relationship with God. And they connected people to others who were at different stages of their Christian life."[519]From the very beginning, the Holiness Movement developed the culture of mentoring as a normal way of living the Christian life. The formation of these small groups was the organizational stroke of genius of John Wesley in birthing Methodism. Although this was not John Wesley's patented idea, he had borrowed it from the Moravians he borrowed it and perfected it to the fine art of mentoring and discipleship. It became the principal concept in the Revival of the church that is associated with him. The genius was in developing mentoring through "Class Meetings for support, correction, and encouragement to live out the Christian life in a hostile world environment aimed to make the people who in their daily living resembled Christ."[520] As George Whitfield admitted it is the class system that made John Wesley supersede George Whitfield, his contemporary evangelist by establishing a discipleship movement that kept the Holiness Movement growing century after century to the current 70 million Methodist membership worldwide not mentioning membership in other denominations within the Holiness Movement (Pentecostalism, Church of the Nazarene or even the Salvation Army). It is an obvious factor that where the Holiness Movement has remained true to its DNA in operating the class system in mentoring or its dynamic equivalent as Wesley intended, the decline has remained beta noir and to the contrary where the class system has declined into social care parse church decline has been inevitable. By abandoning the class system as an agent for mentoring, making disciples, developing spiritual Biblical holiness and growth, any church in any denomination runs the risk of ceasing to be a discipleship movement and descending into mutual admiration societies void of spiritual vitality let alone the desire to evangelize or reach out to others spiritually. The class system is a Methodism legacy to the world which has been adopted by some of the new church movements, especially the House Church Movement, and who, as a result, has seen exponential growth in their church membership. The converts from John Wesley Mission developed into what was known as "local societies," which in modern language would refer to local congregations. The societies further divided into smaller groups known as "classes of twelve people or more each having its leader, who received the contributions of the members and served as sub-pastor. In this context, class referred to an assembled group of people to receive instructions and engage in fellowship and mutual support as opposed to social status. To appreciate the influence and impact of the class meeting on the growth of the Methodist movement, one needs to compare and contrast John Wesley Movement and his contemporary George Whitefield. It is not an exaggeration to posit that in terms of oratory, public speaking and preaching, the evidence seems to suggest George Whitefield was a more gifted public speaker and preacher than John Wesley. George Whitefield (also known as George Whitfield) was a contemporary of John Wesley born on 27 December 1714 in Gloucester and attended Pembroke College at Oxford University, where he met the Wesley brothers.

George Whitfield, together with the Wesley brothers, John and Charles, was part of the "Holy Club" at the University of Oxford. He was one of the founders of Methodism and the evangelical movement generally. When the Wesley brothers went for their mission in Georgia, Whitefield became the leader of the Holy Club Movement in Oxford.[521] There is a sense in which George Whitefield could be the Wesley brothers' mentor in that, in 1738, he went to Savannah, Georgia, in the American colonies, as a parish priest. While he was there, he decided that one of the high needs of the area was an orphan house. He then decided this would be his life's work. He returned to England to raise funds, as well as to receive priest's orders. While preparing for his return, he preached to large congregations. At the suggestion of friends, he preached to the miners of Kingswood, outside Bristol, in the open air, where the Wesley brothers later operated their new movement. Because he was returning to Georgia, he invited John Wesley to take over his Bristol congregations and to preach in the open air for the first time at Kingswood and then at Blackheath, London.[522] Whitefield accepted the Church of England's doctrine of predestination and disagreed with the Wesley brothers' views on the theory of the Atonement and Arminianism. As a result, Whitefield did what his friends hoped he would not do—hand over the entire ministry to John Wesley.[523] Whitefield formed and was the president of the first Methodist conference. But he soon relinquished the position to concentrate on evangelical work.[524]

There are three churches in England established in his name – one in Penn Street, Bristol, and two in London, in Moorfields, and Tottenham Court Road – all three of which became known by the name of Whitefield's Tabernacle. The society meeting at the second Kingswood School at Kingswood, a town on the eastern edge of Bristol, was eventually also named Whitefield's Tabernacle. Whitefield acted as chaplain to Selina, Countess of Huntingdon, and some of his followers joined the Countess of Huntingdon's Connexion, whose chapels were built by Selina, where a form of Calvinistic Methodism similar to Whitefield's was taught. Many of Selina's chapels were built in the English and Welsh counties, and one was erected in London—Spa Fields Chapel.[525] George Whitefield, like John Wesley, also preached on horseback. He preached nearly every day for months to large crowds of sometimes several thousand people as he traveled throughout the colonies, especially New England, in the USA. His journey on horseback from New York City to Charleston was the longest then undertaken in North America by a white man.[526] The Anglican Church did not assign him a pulpit, so he began preaching in parks and fields in England on his own, reaching out to people who usually did not attend church. Like Jonathan Edwards, Whitefield developed a style of preaching that elicited emotional responses from his audiences. But Whitefield had charisma, and his voice (which according to many accounts, could be heard over five hundred feet, his small stature, and even his cross-eyed appearance which some people took as a mark of divine favor all served to help make him one of the first celebrities in the American colonies.[527]

Like John Wesley, George Whitefield used media to publicize his ministry. He employed print systematically, sending advance men to put up broadsides and distribute handbills announcing his sermons. He also arranged to have his sermons published. The popularity of George Whitefield reached the Whitehouse in the USA, and president Benjamin Franklin attended a revival meeting in Philadelphia, Pennsylvania, and was much impressed with Whitefield's ability to deliver a message to such a large group. Franklin had previously dismissed, as an exaggeration, reports of Whitefield preaching to crowds of the order of tens of thousands in England.

When listening to Whitefield preaching from the Philadelphia courthouse, Franklin walked away towards his shop in Market Street until he could no longer hear Whitefield distinctly. He then estimated his distance from Whitefield and calculated the area of a semicircle centered on Whitefield. Allowing two square feet per person, he computed that Whitefield could be heard by over thirty thousand people in the open air[528]. Franklin admired Whitefield as a fellow intellectual but thought Whitefield's plan to run an orphanage in Georgia would lose money. He published several of Whitefield's tracts and was impressed by Whitefield's ability to preach and speak with clarity and enthusiasm to crowds. People remember Whitefield as one of the first to preach to the enslaved. Phillis Wheatley wrote a poem in his memory after he died. In an age when crossing the Atlantic Ocean was a long and hazardous adventure, he visited America seven times, making thirteen ocean crossings in total. It is estimated that throughout his life, Whitefield preached more than 18,000 formal sermons, of which seventy-eight were published. In addition to his work in North America and England, he made fifteen journeys to Scotland—most famously to the "Preaching Braes" of Cambuslang in 1742, where a crowd Whitefield estimated at 30,000 heard him preach. He also made two journeys to Ireland, and one each to Bermuda, Gibraltar, and the Netherlands. He went to the Georgia Colony in 1738 following John Wesley's departure, to serve as a colonial chaplain at Savannah. In this sense, George Whitfield influenced John Wesley, the founder of the Holiness Movement, and was also his mentor. It is also the observable fact that in terms of preaching, Whitfield was a better preacher and gifted orator. The significant difference, however, seems to lie in John Wesley's organization of his converts into classes and actively promoting mentoring among his followers. As noted earlier in this chapter, Whitfield himself admitted this and lamented regrettably in these words: "Brother Wesley acted wisely," he said. "The souls that were awakened under his ministry he joined in class, and thus preserved the fruits of his labor. This I neglected, and my people are a rope of sand."[529]By promoting mentoring in small groups, Wesley provided an opportunity for in-depth discipleship and growth in spiritual holiness. One of the significant works of the subject of Wesley "Class Meetings" has been done by Henderson.[530] He and other scholars on Wesleyan's study credit the success of Wesleyan Revival and the establishment of the Methodist Church and later the Holiness Movement and its derivate denominations to John Wesley's genius in developing and establishing the class meetings. "The genius of Wesleyan revival was an instructional tool more so than a theological distinctive or an organizational structure. The "method," which gave Methodism both its name and its overwhelming effectiveness, was the class meeting. It was this "method," which gave Wesley and his associates the ability to provide minute supervision to a vast army of growing Christians. As the architect of a well-disciplined movement, he was able to assimilate large population blocks into his organization in a short time, train them effectively in the rudiments of Christian discipleship, and mobilize them into an ardent corps of social change agents."[531]

To understand John Wesley and why he chose the skill of mentoring from the very beginning, one needs to understand his intentions and objectives. "Wesley was disillusioned with the emptiness of "paper religion," especially that speculative theology laced with philosophy so popular at Oxford."[532]As a scholar from one of the leading seats of learning, he had observed the effects of purely academic knowledge and philosophy void of the Word of God and the Holy Spirit and what it had done to the Church of England in which he was a minister. "Wesley's goal was to spread scriptural holiness throughout the land. Methodism was born out of the context of a society gripped in a vice of poverty, disease, and moral decay. Society had dismissed Puritanism; the church had "drifted into a trifling worldliness. The clergy generally tended toward deism in theology and polite indulgence in lifestyle. Religion had lost any real impact on the daily lives of the people."[533] John Wesley had observed how, since the Reformation, the English aristocracy had legislated and pressured and coerced the general populace toward uniformity and regularity in religion, in reaction against the excesses of the Puritan commonwealth. There is a sense in which John Wesley could be termed as the father of the Pentecostal movement. Some Methodist churches who have adopted the respectability and high churchmanship that had set in the Anglican before Wesley tend to shy away from anything emotional. What they need to realize is that early Wesleyan Methodism was passionate and enthusiastic.

"The most dreaded malady of the religious establishment was what they termed "enthusiasm" – an epithet that connoted not only personal fanaticism but also that sinister mesmerism which was thought to excite the unstable masses toward anarchy and rebellion."[534]

It is the enthusiasm that made early Methodists to be persecuted for their faith and eventually ostracised from the Anglican Church. The very foundations of the Wesleyan movement were missional, evangelistic, designed to nurture personal spirituality, Christian development, and spiritual growth.

Chapter 6 Notes

497 Roger E Olson, *Armenian Theology: Myths and Realities*, (Downers Grove, Ill.:IVP, 2009), 25

498 Wesley on perfectio, Accessed April 4, 201. http://www.ccel.org/w/wesley perfectio/perfection.html

499 Class meeting, Accessed April 4, 2018.www.seedbed.com/how-to-reclaim -wesleyan-class-meetings?

500 Class meeting, Accessed April 4, 2018. https://Secure.wesleyan.org/4088/ how-wesleys-class-meetings-really-started.

501 Watson, Kevin M. *The Class Meeting: Reclaiming a Forgotten (and Essential) Small Group Experience.* (Franklin, Tennessee: Seedbed Publishing, 2014).

502 John Wesley, *A Plain Account of the People Called Methodists*: In a letter to Revd. Mr. Perronet, Vicar of Shoreham in Kent. (London: Printed by H. Cook, 1755)

503 Ibid. II.7

504 The Methodist Class Meetings for the 21st century: The Foundation in Accountability, Christian Living, Methodist History, Ministry, Wesley, Accessed April 19, 2018. https://vitapiety.com/2020/07/30/ the-methodist-class-meeting-for-the-21st-century-the-foundation.

505 David Lowes Watson, *The Early Methodist Class Meeting: Its origins and Significance,* (Nashville TN: Discipleship Resources, 1985), 182, footnote 35

506 Henry Rack, "The Decline of the Class-Meeting and the Problems of Church-Membership in Nineteenth-Century Wesleyanism,"in *Proceedings of the Wesleyan Historical Society 39* (1973-74), 12-21

507 Neelak S Tjernagel, *Henry VIII and the Lutherans: A Study in Anglo-Lutheran Relations from 1521-1547,* St (Louis: Concordia Publishing House, 1965), 263.

508 Watson, *The Class Meeting*, 41

509 Ibid. p. 48 see also Wesley, *The Sermons* 1:272ff

510 Ibid. p.57 citing Wesley, *Minutes 1:5*

511 Ibid. p.64 citing, Wesley, *Letters, 3:212; 5:333; 6:116*

512 Ibid. p. 65

513 These include: Miley, John. *A Treatise on Class Meetings*, (Cincinnati.The Methodist Book Concern, 1851);

L Rosser, *Class Meetings: Embracing their Origin, Nature, Obligation and Benefits*, Richmond: Published by the Author, 1855. Charles W Ferguson, Methodists and the Making of America: Organizing to Beat the Devil, 2nd ed, (Austin, Texas: Eakin Press, 1983), 69-77,149f ; Frank Baker, *Wesley to Asbury:Studies in Early American Methodism. (*Durham, NC: Duke University Press, 1976), 7 6, 104 J Artley Leatherman, "The Decline of the Class Meeting"in Samuel Emerick, ed., *Spiritual Renewal for Methodism,(*Nashville: Methodist Evangelical Materials, 1958), 44

514 Wesley Tracy, *Herald of Holiness*, (February, 1991), 28.
515 Asbury June 12, 1774, *vol. I Journal*, p. 118)
516 Proverbs 27:17 NKJV
517 Band meetings, Accessed April 19, 2018. https://vitalpiety.com/tag/bandmeeting
518 Rope of Sand, Accessed April 4, 2018. https://milewis.wordpress.com/2015/12/19/whitfield-wesley-rope-of-sand/
519 "How is your spiritual life?:The class meetings today"in A UMC.org by Joe Lovino 17/8/2015
520 William H. Wilmon& Robert L Wilson, *Rekindling the Flame*, 41
521 Chapter V: The Holy Club". Wesley Center, Oxford.
522 Whitefield's Mount". Brethren Archive. Retrieved 21 November 2015
523 Warren W Wiersbe, *50 People Every Christian Should Know*, (Michigan: Baker Books, 2009), 42–43,
524 Holy Women, Holy Men: Celebrating the Saints, (New York :Church Publishing. 2010), 680
525 Coldbath Fields and Spa Fields". in *Old and New London: Volume 2* (London, 1878), 298-306. *British History Online*, Accessed November 21, 2015. http://www.british-history.ac.uk/old-new-london/vol2/
526 "George Whitefield". Digital Puritan. Accessed November 2, November 2015. digitalpuritan.net/george-whitefield/
527 "George Whitefield: Did You Know?". Christian History. Accessed November 21, 2015. digitalpuritan.net/george-whitefield/
528 Franklin Autobiography, 163–64
529 A "Rope of Sand" in Wesley Tracy, *The Upward Call*, 139.
530 Michael D Henderson, *John Wesley's Class Meeting: A Model for Making Disciples*: (Nappanee, Indianapolis:Evangel Publishing House, 1998 &2005).
531 Michael D Henderson, *John Wesley's Class Meetings*, 15
532 Ibid. p.22
533 Ibid. p.20
534 Ibid. p.20

Seven CHAPTER

Practical Application

Image Illustration by David Barrett Wilkinson

Matthew 14:28-29 (NIV)

"Lord, if it's you... tell me to come to you on the water.... Come".

The title of this book: "To be like Jesus" expresses a desire for a deep longing to be transformed into Christ-likeness. We want to conclude it with similar desire and longing represented by one of Jesus' disciples, Peter: "Lord let me emulate you and walk on water like you." There are a various rendering of the Greek translations of the text in (Matthew 14:28),[535] but the underlying meaning of the verb translated (tell me, call me, order me) is a request to emulate Jesus and walk on water as He did. The desire to be like Jesus and imitate His example is not dreaming; neither is it absurd, nor is it "wishful –thinking." Jesus said: John 14:12 (NIV) "Whoever believes in me will do the works I have been doing, and they will do even greater things than these." Therefore the desire to be like Jesus and the deep longing to emulate him in our spiritual formation is consonant with His will and promise for his real followers. To be like Jesus is the ultimate goal of Christians, who are justified by faith, changed daily in an encounter with God in His word and dependence on the Holy Spirit to apply means of grace in the Christian life. The ongoing work of the Holy Spirit in a Christian's life produces sanctification. The scriptures say that Christ left an example in His life and ministry for Christians to follow.[536]The scripture illustrates this in the washing of disciples' feet during Jesus' farewell party.[537]Those who say they are Christians should endeavor to walk the way Jesus walked.[538]During His earthly life, Jesus showed an example of utter dependence on God; at one time, he continued all night in prayer to God.[539] Newton Conant, one of my tutors, commenting on 2Peter 3:18, says: "the transforming of our lives into the image of Christ is done by the Holy Spirit and not by self-effort but by beholding on the Lord are changed into the same image by the Holy Spirit…The measure, therefore, in which the Holy Spirit can make the believer like Christ is dependent upon the believer earnestly beholding the glory of Christ in the Word of God."[540] The importance of prayer in the life of a Christian who wants to be conformed into the image of Jesus Christ cannot be overemphasized; it is a sine qua non. Conant bluntly puts it this way: "Haphazard and careless prayer life is the pathway to spiritual failure...prayerful life must be observed faithfully if we are to follow the example of our Lord."[541]

What about the storms of life?

We observed earlier in this book, the call to follow Jesus is a call to rest from heavy burdens laid upon the Christian either by themselves through foolishness in indulgence to sinful behavior or by organized religion with its rules and regulations void of God's grace. It is also a call to experience life in its fullness.[542]It is a call that might help Christians avoid and minimize self-inflicted pain and suffering but not a call to exempt pain and suffering in totality. As human beings Christians, all share in human pain and suffering in the world. The main difference is that Christians go through the pain and suffering from the one who has called them, Jesus Christ, bearer of human pain and suffering. Two texts in the Bible illustrate this point. The first is from the Old Testament, the story of Daniel and his three colleagues in Babylon when they defied the pagan orders of king Nebuchadnezzar. Three of them were thrown into the fiery furnace, but God intervened and saved them to the amazement of the king: Daniel 3:24-26 (NKJV) "Then King Nebuchadnezzar was astonished; and he rose in haste and spoke, saying to his counselors, "Did we not cast three men bound into the midst of the fire?" They answered and said to the king, "True, O king." "Look!" he answered, "I see four men loose, walking in the midst of the fire, and they are not hurt, and the form of the fourth is like the Son of God."

Then Nebuchadnezzar went near the mouth of the burning fiery furnace and spoke, saying, "Shadrach, Meshach, and Abed-Nego, servants of the Most High God, come out, and come here." Then Shadrach, Meshach, and Abed-Nego came from the midst of the fire."

The psalmist gives comfort: Psalm 91:3 (NASB) "For it is he who delivers you from the snare of the trapper and from the deadly pestilence." The prophet Isaiah gives the assurance, Isaiah 43:2 (NKJV) "When you pass through the waters, I will be with you; and through the rivers, they will not overflow you. When you walk through the fire, you will not be scorched, nor will the flame burn you." Isaiah 43:2 (NLT), "When you go through deep waters, I will be with you. When you go through rivers of difficulty, you will not drown. When you walk through the fire of oppression, you will not be burned up; the flames will not consume you." The second illustrations are two passages from the New Testament that pictures the life of the disciples in the midst of the storm in (Mark 4:35-41 and 6:45-41). Although the contexts of these two passages differ, their object lessons are similar. In chapter four, the context follows a lengthy section of teaching on parables about the Kingdom of God, including the parable of the mustard seed, and in chapter six, it follows the feeding of the five thousand. These two passages have three significant similarities. The first is Jesus, who initiated the journey into the storm. Secondly, Jesus acted at the nick of time when his disciples were at the point of panic; he also showed great tranquillity and dealt with the wind. Thirdly, the passages demonstrate Jesus' power over the storms and nature per se. In the first passage, "When evening came, he said to his disciples, Mark 4:35, "Let us go over to the other side." In the second passage, Mark 6:45, "Jesus made his disciples get into the boat and go on ahead of him to Bethsaida."

While in the first passage the Greek words translated "let us" might imply a suggestion, in the second passage it seems to be an order, the verb in the original Greek (ἠνάγκασεν –enankasen) is the imperative-"compelled" and some translation render it as such.[543] Those who know the geography of the area would know that sailing on Lake Galilee towards Bethsaida faces a headwind in the direction of Mt Arbel's high cliffs where winds are funneled through the gap down towards the Sea of Galilee at high speed making roaring the boat nigh impossible. In both cases, the disciples were following directives from Jesus as if Jesus wanted to test their faith in his power. The response in the first incidence implies this summation: "who is this? Even the wind and the waves obey him!"[544] Equally in the second passage, "he climbed into the boat with them, and the wind died down. They were completely amazed for they had not understood about the loaves."[545]In the second passage, it is linked to the feeding of the five thousand directly where he had demonstrated his power. In both incidences, the calming of the storms and Jesus walking on water appears to be some form of what some universities use as a form of teaching – CAT –Continuous Assessment Test. As Christians travel on their journey of faith, they will find themselves amid storms thrown at them. There are five deducible vital lessons from these two passages. The first lesson is that following Jesus does not exempt his followers from storms of life. Secondly, Jesus initiates their life's journey and travels with them in the storms of life, continually reminding us that He is more significant than any storms that life might throw at us. Thirdly, the purpose of the storm is to strengthen their faith in the master of the storms. Fourthly, Jesus' message to his followers amid the storm is always the same, "do not be afraid"; for Jesus is the same yesterday, today and forever.[546] Also, Jesus promises Matthews 28:20 (GW) "And remember that I am always with you until the end of time." Jesus promise echoes God's commitment to the patriarch Jacob Genesis 28:15 (GNT), "Remember, I will be with you and protect you wherever you go...I will not leave you until I have done all that I have promised you." This promise holds to all those who come to Jesus and decide to follow him in discipleship and spiritual formation because those who believe in God of Abraham inherit the same promises. Jesus is the captain of the storms, and he is never late, he watches over the storms and steps in at the right time. In the second passage, "he saw the disciples straining" and stepped into the boat at the right time. Those who engage in the journey of spiritual formation can do so with confidence knowing that Jesus sees every problem they face. None of us chose to be born in this world, none of us chooses to cross over into a new year, it is Jesus who chooses, let us learn to heed to his message amid the storms of life, "do not be afraid!"

The Signs and evidence of Spiritual Formation.

This book started by citing two choruses that influenced my formative years in spiritual formation: *"Let the beauty of Jesus be seen in me"* and *"To be like Jesus."* It is from the second chorus that we drew the title of this book. Throughout this book, I have argued and given both theological and biblical appraisal of what spiritual formation entails. I have also validated that spiritual formation is a journey or process that involves the whole of lifetime commitment and develops by engaging in deliberate disciplines that help in spiritual formation through the journey. I identified seven disciplines that I argued are crucial pillars that underpin the architectural structure of the spiritual temple of spiritual formation.

In life actions proceed from the character, what a person is, is shown by their actions. The same is true in nature species are identified by their nature. In concluding his Sermon on the Mount, Jesus alluded to this truth when he taught that a tree is known by its fruits (Matthew 7:16-20; Luke 6:43-44 also Matthew 12:23). He explained this truth by posing the conundrum: "Do people gather grapes from thornbushes or figs from thistles?" – Every good tree bears good fruit, but a bad tree bears bad fruit. Matthew 7:16 (NLT) says, "You can identify them by their fruit, that is, by the way, they act. Can you pick grapes from thornbushes or figs from thistles and concludes, Matthew 7:20 (NLT) "So then, by their fruit, you will recognize them." Other scriptures attest to this truth: Proverbs 20:11(NIV) "A young man is known by his actions."; 1Samuel 24:13 (KJV). "Wickedness proceeds from the wicked." Matthew 12:23 (NIV). "Make a tree good, and its fruit will be good or make a tree bad, and its fruit will be bad; for a tree is known by its fruits." The epistle of James teaches that faith without good deeds is dead and goes on to repeat the same conundrum posed by Jesus: James 3:12 (NIV) "Can a fig tree grow olives or grapevine bear figs? Neither can salt spring produce fresh water." The Apostle Paul alludes to the same truth by giving the contrast between the fruit of the Holy Spirit in a person's life and the fruits of natural living following the impulses and instincts of the human body. Galatians 5:22-23 (NIV) points out that "the fruit of the Spirit is love, joy, peace, forbearance, kindness, goodness, faithfulness, gentleness, and self-control.

Galatians 5:19 (NIV) contrasts these with the fruits of or the acts of the flesh: "Sexual immorality, impurity, debauchery, idolatry, witchcraft, hatred, discord, jealousy, fits of rage, selfish ambition, rivalries, dissensions, and divisions."

I want to conclude this book by pointing out some signs and evidence of spiritual formation in a person's life.

1. **Grace and gracious living**. The first of these is a life full of grace in contrast to legalistic religiosity or mere religious ritual void of love and forgiveness. If there is one thing that characterized the life of Jesus from which all the rest flowed, it was grace. In his introduction (the prologue) of the person and character of Jesus, the gospel of John 1:17 (NIV) says, "From his (Jesus Christ's) fullness we have received grace upon grace. Moses gave the law, but grace and truth came through Jesus Christ." Throughout his ministry, Jesus behaved graciously and showed grace to all he met. One prominent occasion is when a woman caught in adultery was supposed to be stoned to death, but instead, Jesus intervened, forgave her, and commanded her not to sin anymore.[547]In this incidence, Jesus did not only endorse that forgiveness is preferable to legalistic religious law, but he also exercised grace and truth, which should always go together. The Christian who pursues grace without truth risks being antinomian or libertarian that leads to all sorts of spiritual aberrations like permissive ethics, even subtle heresy that is unleashing in the guise of religious freedom in the twenty-first century. Its mantra is that the truth for you is not the truth for me, leading to immoral behavior promulgated by permissive ethics and expressed under the excuse of new morality and lifestyle espoused in the New Age Movement. The safeguarding balance is to develop and mature in grace, seeking God's truth as Jesus did in the cited passage. In this incident, Jesus holistically dealt with the sinner and the sin. He was gracious to the sinner by pronouncing forgiveness but condemned the sin by commanding that the woman should sin no more. Some would disparage the way Jesus dealt with the woman through misunderstanding what was at stake and why Jesus dealt with it the way he did. Those who accuse Jesus of allowing a sinful woman to get

away scot-free rather than let her face the full weight and the consequences of the religious law, do so through a total misunderstanding of the injustice and manipulation that was at stake. Jesus acknowledged the woman's errant behavior by commanding her not to do it anymore and upheld the truth, that if they were to apply their religious law, they should do so truthfully. The reality is that Jesus stopped an injustice – where was the man? In that culture, the act of adultery could only be committed where two people are involved, man and woman. The law that the Pharisees were trying to apply to condemn the woman to death required that both the man and the woman be stoned to death after a fair trial when two or more witnesses testified of the sin before a judge. The Pharisees in this incidence were breaking their laws. What Jesus dealt with was not only a case of injustice in a society that berated women but could also have been a case of corruption. One could conjecture that the man she was caught in the act with was prominent and perhaps had paid a bribe, otherwise, why did they only bring the woman to Jesus instead of taking her and the man before a judge in compliance with their religious laws? We also know that the context for this passage in the gospel of John is one in which the Pharisees were trying to trap Jesus to find cause to accuse and arrest him. They were breaking their laws and expected Jesus to keep their perverted version, but Jesus showed grace and stood with the truth. Throughout his ministry, Jesus lived, showed what grace is about, and upheld the truth by speaking the truth in love. The same grace characterizes the followers of Jesus in their pursuit of spiritual formation. Jesus' teaching on the Sermon on the Mount is an explication of how grace works in real life. The summary of the Sermon on the Mount in the eight beatitudes spells out the paradox of grace pointing out to the eight attitudes that characterize the evidence of a person permeated by grace. The person filled by grace seeks passionately to live by God's truth that draws the person to love scriptures that complements and commends their gracious living. The person filled by grace finds scripture to be a delight, not a dread. Exercising grace has been the hallmark of the Holiness-Movement from its inception by the Wesley brothers as a holy club to promote scriptural holiness throughout the land. Those within the movement and adhere to its teaching are characterized by a deep passion for sanctification, even entire sanctification, and upholding the truth of scriptural holiness.

2. **Compassion - Meeting people's physical and spiritual needs**. At the beginning of this book, we acknowledged that by growing in an African animist village religious background, I never had Western nursery rhymes during the formative years of my childhood. I, however, pointed out when I eventually joined the church, the chorus *"Let the beauty of Jesus be seen in me,"* started to have an impact in my Christian formation and later on the chorus, *"To be like Jesus."* A third chorus also had an impact on me forming as a Christian that I learned during my Christian development in later teenage years. This chorus used to be one of the top ten sung in Kenya Student Christian Fellowship meetings in which my Christian formation developed. The Chorus went as follows:- *"Everywhere He went He was doing good. Almighty Healer. He healed (cleansed) the lepers. When the cripples saw Him, they started walking. Everywhere He went, my Lord, was doing good."*[548] It is based on the Bible verse in the book Acts 10:38, where Luke is giving an account of the ministry of Jesus. The context of this verse is the conversion of Cornelius Acts 10:1-2, a gentile described as "devout, God-fearing, gave much

alms to the poor and prayed to God always." These were attributes expected of a practicing religious Jew. In this verse, Luke credits Jesus with the ministry of promoting people's well-being wherever he went. Teaching, healing the sick, and meeting physical as well as spiritual needs. At the heart of the ministry of Jesus was blessing people with love, peace, and happiness. Jesus valued people's holistic well-being. He did good in his teaching and healing to all who had a need. His compassion was all-embracing, self-effacing, and all-inclusive. His ministry included even the enemies, and Jesus calls His disciples to meet the needs of others, including those who hate them.[549] In the story of feeding the five thousand, Jesus' disciples tried to separate his preaching of the gospel and meeting the physical needs of hunger when they implored Jesus to release the crowd so that they could find something to eat. Jesus replied you feed them,[550] implying the gospel and meeting people's physical needs go together. Jesus mandated those who follow him to serve even their enemies without expecting anything in return. This teaching is echoed in Paul's teaching first to the Galatians 6:10 (AMP): "While we [as individual believers] have the opportunity, let us do good to all people [not only being helpful but also doing that which promotes their spiritual well-being], and especially [be a blessing] to those of the household of faith (born-again believers)."To the Thessalonians Christians, 1Thessalonians 5:15 (NLT), Apostle Paul gave the injunction: "See that no one pays back evil for evil, but always try to do good to each other and all people." The author of the letter to the Hebrews echoes similar sentiments Hebrews 6:10. The Christian who is in the process of forming in the image of Christ develops a mantra in life to exercise the choice of offering the gift of God's grace through doing good to everyone they come into contact with as much as it is humanly possible no matter what others do to them. Such a ministry is not only a sign or evidence but the acid test of the Christian transformation in spiritual formation. The letter of James in the New Testament makes doing good to all a Christian imperative James 4:17 (CEV), "If you don't do what you know is right, you have sinned." Showing compassion Jesus' style is contrary to modern culture that is dominated by this mantra: "What is in it for me?" For the Christian, however, it is a sure sign and evidence that one is forming and conforming to Jesus Christ's nature and becoming more like Him. The ministry of compassion was not an "Add-on" to Jesus' ministry; it formed his mission statement right at the beginning of his ministry when He said: Luke 4:18 (ESV), "The Spirit of the Lord is upon me because he has anointed me to proclaim good news to the poor. He has sent me to proclaim liberty to the captives and recovering of sight to the blind, to set at liberty those who are oppressed." In making this declaration, Jesus perceived himself to be fulfilling Old Testament prophecy in Isaiah 61:1-2 about his mission and ministry. He calls his followers to do the same. As Christians form in personal spirituality and ministry, they will be characterized by the same compassion that was found in Jesus' ministry and exercised in his life. Jesus showed compassion in two areas: spiritual and social action. In his ministry, he showed compassion in addressing both the physical and social needs. In dispensing compassion to both, Jesus showed liberal –all-embracing extravagant grace that touched all in need that he met. In exercising the ministry of compassion, the key question is: How do we see people? When a politician sees a crowd of people, he sees potential voters. When a businessperson sees people, he sees potential customers, and when an executive of a large corporation sees people, he sees potential purchasers of their merchandise, but according to Matthew 9:36, when Jesus Christ saw people, he was filled with compassion over their spiritual and physical needs. Strong passion for God's unconditional love, fuels compassion for people's needs. As the Apostle Paul moved from region to region-establishing churches in his missionary journeys, he described the force behind his drive in these words: 2Corinthians 5:14 (KJV), "For the love of Christ constrains (compels) us." The love of Christ is the constraining force behind ministries of compassion. According to Romans 5:8, the love of God demonstrated in Jesus Christ is towards those who are undeserving. Grace ignites the fire of unconditional love that drives the wheels of compassion ministries. In John 4:4-42, compassion drove Jesus to meet both the spiritual and the social needs of the Samaritan woman as well as the outcast demon-possessed person from Gadarene Mark 5:19. When Jesus met Matthew (Levi) as a tax collector, much hated by Jews seen as collaborators with the oppressive Roman Empire, Matthew was not the celebrity that he became as Jesus' follower; he was a despised, outcast publican.[551] God's unconditional love drove Jesus to call Matthew as an apostle. When Matthew threw out a party in response to Jesus' favor, the religious elite (Scribes and Pharisees) complained to Jesus for associating with sinners the likes of Matthew.[552]Similarly, Jesus showed compassion to another despised social outcast – wealthy Zacchaeus.[553] In these passages, compassion drove Jesus to the borders of the social divide, where he builds social bridges rather than barriers. To demonstrate what compassion is like, Jesus told the parable of the Good Samaritan.[554]From this parable, we learn four lessons about compassion. First, compassion feels something, empathy on the part of the subject of compassion.

Secondly, compassion does something it moves from feelings to action. Thirdly, compassion is based on need, not worth. The beaten bleeding man in the story was in need no matter his worth the response towards his need was driven by his need, without questioning who he was. Fourthly and finally, compassion costs something. To be like Jesus is to dispense compassion to those in spiritual, social, and physical needs to all those whom God will put on our path.

3. **Prayerful Life**. The third sign or evidence that spiritual formation is or has taken place in a person is prayer life. To be like Jesus entails that those who desire to be like him would be characterized by a deep desire for prayer life like Jesus did. Jesus led a busy life, he was a man in high demand, he had a mission to fulfill, a kingdom to inaugurate and build in three years, yet he never allowed busyness to deter him from deep prayer life. There are at least three things we can glean from Jesus' prayer life:
    a. **Jesus devoted much time to prayer**. Jesus' prayer life included "praying all night."[555]Such commitment to prayer implies sincere heart-searching prayer but also means intimacy with God. Some Christians find spending an hour in prayer too long, let alone praying all night. If we understood prayer as a two-way process where we talk to God and allow him space to speak to us, it shows that Jesus treasured spending time with God and valued fellowship with God. This intimacy echoes in other passages in the gospels.[556]During my time in pastoral ministry in three continents, Africa, America, and Europe in the UK, the worst attended church meetings are prayer meetings. A typical caricature is a story the late Paul Nzimbi, father to the former archbishop of the Anglican Church of Kenya, told me. Paul was a devout man, and we used to spend a

lot of time talking while I studied at St Charles Lwanga secondary school, his wife shared parentage with my maternal grandfather. Paul used to tell me stories about his Christian formation. One that stuck in my mind was an incidence when he attended a prayer meeting, and on his way back, he met a scoffer who mockingly asked him, how many participated in the prayer meeting. Paul, who had a deep sense of humor, he replied we were five. In astonishment, the scoffer asked who those five were. Paul replied, there was me, God the Father, God the Son, God the Holy Spirit, and the devil who never leaves alone God's people! A cynic once remarked, if you want to know the strength of a church, do not take the count in the Sunday morning worship, but take the count in the mid-week prayer meeting. Christians who desire spiritual formation are desperate for a deeper prayer life.

b. **Jesus scheduled time for prayer**. When I was in the Sales industry, I recall our branch manager saying that the meaning of the phrase, "I haven't the time is it is not important enough." He went on to explain that we always make time for what is important to us. Jesus' pattern is that he scheduled first thing in the morning to be his quiet time with God.[557]Anything important always takes the priority of our time, and we make time for it. By not scheduling times for prayer, we plan to fail in having prayer times.

c. **Jesus prioritized prayer time**. Even when busyness loomed, Jesus' prayer life came first. "When it was time for prayer, it was more important for Jesus that he keeps this appointment than it was to preach to crowds of people. He sent the multitudes away or withdrew from them to make time for private prayer."[558]The first event to enter the diary of a Christian who wants to be like Jesus daily should be prayer time.

4. **Dependence on Scripture and the Holy Spirit**. Any Christian who is seriously pursuing Spiritual Formation would show a lofty view of scriptures and reliance on the guidance of the Holy Spirit.
   a. **Jesus' dependence on Scripture**: Jesus inaugurated his ministry based on scripture.[559] He understood his ministry as a fulfillment of the Old Testament prophecy.[560] At the beginning of his ministry, during his temptation, Jesus utterly relied on scripture. His loft view of scripture pervaded his earthly ministry. In his conversation with Nicodemus, a reputable Jewish theologian, Jesus cited one of the most disputed miracles in the Old Testament, the lifting up of the serpent in the desert by Moses.[561]In his teaching, it is evident that he believed one of the most ridiculed Old Testament miracles by modern theologians, the story of Jonah. Jesus said that he was going to re-enact the story of Jonah, referring to his death and resurrection.[562]In this teaching, Jesus talked about the effect of Jonah's message to the Ninevites after spending three days in the stomach of a whale that it would resonate with his death and on the cross, spending three days in the tomb and its effect to the world to the power of the resurrection in repentance.[563] Jesus also gave credence to the miracle of manna from heaven that is disputed by most Bible critics. In his teaching after the feeding of the five thousand,[564]Jesus referred to himself as the manna from above. Jesus' high loft view of scripture is shown when he validated the historicity of the account of the flood that is discredited and discarded by Bible critics as a fairy tale.

Jesus, however, compared the end times and His second coming as resonating with the story of Noah.[565]When Jesus spoke to the disappointed, discouraged disciples on the road to Emmaus after his resurrection, he explained it from scriptures.[566] Christians who are serious with their spiritual formation and development would similar to Jesus develop a high loft view of scripture and seek to emulate his example of the dependence on scripture. My once tutor in college, Conant sums it thus: "It seems that the entire Christian life is, in a sense, just a continuing revelation from the Word of God to us of our helplessness in ourselves and also of our abundant resources in Christ. Our spiritual growth is dependent upon seeing ourselves daily as we are before God. We must see ourselves increasingly in the Word of God as weak vessels, defeated and empty apart from Christ. We must also see ourselves in the Scriptures as crucified with Christ, raised with Him, His life our life, His grace sufficient in our weakness.[567]In my short Christian pilgrimage and coming from the non-Christian background, I have been amazed to come across Christians with a low view of scriptures yet seeking to grow in their Christian faith. God uses His written word to communicate to His children through His Holy Spirit. When God's children barricade themselves from reading scriptures and rely on human reasoning unleashed by the philosophical epoch of Enlightenment, they barricade themselves from God's grace mediated by the Holy Spirit through His written word. Mahatma Gandhi a Buddhist challenged the Christians who do not hold aloft view of scripture saying: "You Christians look after a document containing enough dynamite to blow all civilization to pieces, turn the world upside down and bring peace to battle-torn planet, but you treat it as though it is nothing more than a piece of literature."[568]The Bible is one of the greatest pillars (source of spiritual vitamins) of our spiritual formation and transformation. Dwight L Moody once said, "The Bible was not given for our information but our transformation."[569]Talking about its ability to stabilize and sustain Christian life, Charles H. Spurgeon said, "A Bible that's falling apart usually belongs to someone who isn't."[570]Those of us born before the Facebook, Myspace, and Tweeter Era would remember saving sweet letters from our school sweethearts. My wife and I would celebrate our ruby wedding anniversary next year, God willing, and I still keep and treasure her love letters written in those pink notepads; some arrived smelling sweet talcum powder! We possibly would recall how often we would open those letters and soak our thoughts and emotions and savor those sweet moments of past years with nostalgia. We treasure them as love letters. That is what the scriptures should be to Christians. The Bible is a love letter from a loving father to his dear children, encouraging and directing them on how to happily live their lives and avoid painful pitfalls through making wise decisions. St Augustine of Hippo once said, "The Holy Scriptures are our letters from Home."[571] Two USA presidents recognized the ability of the Bible to impart wisdom and wise counsel. According to President Ronald Reagan, "Within the covers of the Bible are the answers for all the problems men face."[572]While Abraham Lincoln commenting on reading, the Bible said, "Take all that you can of this book upon reason, and the balance of faith, and you will live and die a happier man."[573] The apostle Paul acknowledges the integrity and ability of the

Bible to influence the Christian life, by describing it as two aged sword, living and active, piercing to the soul, spirit, and body,[574]pointing to the dynamism of scripture in dealing with the tripartite nature of human beings. Its reliability and permanence are eternal.[575] The Bible is God-breathed, inspired through the superintending hand of the Holy Spirit, and it is the primary source of finding God's will. It is through God's spoken and written Word, the Bible that we find and encounter, the Living Word, Jesus Christ. To be like Jesus is to be reliant on and to have a loft view of scripture like Jesus did during his earthly ministry. It is from scripture that we learn, "what we are by nature, and what we are in union with Christ."[576]To be like Jesus is to have a lofty view of scripture like Jesus did during his earthly ministry. There are some Christians who would argue that the Bible is hard to understand and as such, find no interest in reading it. To those who hold such a view, the Danish philosopher, Soren Kierkegaard, scathingly would say: "The Bible is easy to understand. But we Christians are a bunch of scheming swindlers. We pretend to be unable to understand it because we know very well that the minute we understand, we are obliged to act accordingly."[577] For those Christians who want to be like Jesus and who want the beauty of Jesus to be seen in their lives: all his tender compassion and purity, the Bible is the place to turn to as Martin Luther put it, "The Bible is the cradle wherein Christ is laid."[578]On discovering this truth, John Wesley said: "I want to know one thing, the way to heaven, how to land safely on that happy shore. God himself has condescended to teach the way for this very end; he came from heaven. He has written it down in a book! O, give me that book! At any price, give me the book of God! I have it: here is knowledge enough for me. Let me be: A man of one book."[579]

b. **Dependence on the Holy Spirit**. It has been said that the book of Acts of the Apostles could be nicknamed or should have been called the book of the Acts of the Holy Spirit. This assertion is made on account of the following reasons: This is because of four major reasons:- Firstly the outpouring of the promised Holy Spirit and the commencement of the proclamation of the gospel of Jesus Christ with spirit-filled evangelism beginning in Jerusalem and spreading in a short space of time to Rome the capital of the Roman Empire. According to Varughese: "In spite of severe opposition in a short space of time into thirty-nine cities and in thirty countries in the first century and the shift from the age of Jesus to the age of the Holy Spirit."[580] Secondly, the Holy Spirit enabled signs and wonders to be performed through the apostles. Thirdly because of the many references of the Holy Spirit in the book of Acts, where he is referred to as he and never as it or force. Fourthly and most importantly, because of the language used on the Holy Spirit directing affairs of early disciples and evangelism. Holy Spirit empowered witness in Jerusalem, Judea, and Samaria.[581] "The Holy Spirit empowered speaking in other tongues at Pentecost.[582] The Holy Spirit empowered Peter's boldness to confront Jewish opposition."[583]'The Holy Spirit stroke dead Ananias & Sapphira for lying to Him."[584] The Holy Spirit witnesses what apostles were doing." [585]'The Holy Spirit spoke through Stephen."[586]'The Holy Spirit directed Philip to witness to the Ethiopian, thus taking the gospel to Africa before it reached Europe."[587] The Holy Spirit encouraged the growth of Churches in Judea,

Galilee & Samaria."[588] The Holy Spirit directed Peter to go to the Gentiles as Peter testified: "Holy Spirit told me."[589]The Holy Spirit through Agabus predicted famine in Antioch."[590]The Holy Spirit directed Barnabas and Paul for the Gentile mission."[591]The Holy Spirit adjudicated in the decision of the first church council, the Jerusalem Council."[592]The Holy Spirit changed the course of Mission from Asia to Europe."[593]The Holy Spirit forbids Paul at Tyre to go to Jerusalem."[594]The Holy Spirit warns Paul at Caesarea about going to Jerusalem."[595]The Holy Spirit's involvement in directing the affairs of the apostles and the growth of the early church makes him the director of evangelism and church mission whenever He is allowed to do so.

Similarly, the way the Holy Spirit was involved in directing the earthly life of Jesus shows that Jesus was utterly dependent on the Holy Spirit. At Jesus' baptism, there was a convergence of the Trinity as he came out of the water, the Spirit of God descending like a dove and resting on him, thus anointing Jesus for the mission that lay ahead. God, the father, uttered his approval in words, "this is my beloved son in whom I am well pleased."[596]Jesus' anointing with the Holy Spirit at his baptism resonated with the anointing of the priest in the Old Testament."[597]Peter testified of this anointing in these words: "God anointed Jesus of Nazareth with the Holy Spirit and power, and how he went around doing good and healing all who were under the power of the devil because God was with him."[598]After his baptism (anointing), full of the Holy Spirit, He was "led by the Spirit into the wilderness to endure his temptation."[599]Mark's account uses even a stronger verb: "immediately the spirit drove him into the desert."[600]Luke reports that Jesus returned from the wilderness in power of the Spirit,[601] at the start of his ministry, Jesus declared "the Spirit of the Lord is upon me he has anointed me to preach...to heal...deliver and to set free.[602]Jesus attributed the power by which he cast out demons to the Spirit of God.[603]

Therefore, the Christian who pursues spiritual formation and is determined to be like Jesus must learn to keep in step with the Holy Spirit. Jesus had emptied himself to be fully human then depended on the Holy Spirit throughout his life and ministry on earth to direct him in all he did. For a Christian who wants to live a powerful prayer life, they must acknowledge that: "the Spirit helps us in our weakness. We do not know what we ought to pray for, but the Spirit himself intercedes for us with groans that words cannot express."[604]For Christian who wants to live a victorious life over sin, they must realize to: "live by the Spirit and will not gratify the desires of the sinful nature."[605]In other words, the conquest over sin is only possible through dependence on the Holy Spirit as Jesus did. The desire to know Jesus Christ is a great and laudable longing for most Christians, but that is only made possible by depending on the Holy Spirit. I once heard a story told by the late Selwyn Hughes about a girl who bought a book in a bookshop and found it hard going and difficult to get into. Then one day, she went to a meeting and met the author. The following day, her mother found her burning the midnight oil reading the book, unwilling to go to bed. When the mother inquired why the girl explained that she met the author of the book, she was finding it hard to understand and get into, but now she has got into the book and does not want to put it down. That is what it is like in terms of getting to know Jesus and his word the Bible; the Holy Spirit reveals both to the Christian.[606]The Holy Spirit guides,[607] and sanctifies and makes the Christian "reflect the Lord's glory, and being transformed into his likeness with ever-increasing glory which comes from the Lord, who is the Spirit."[608]

5. **Dependence on God:** The filial relationship between Jesus and God the father portrayed in the gospels is exceedingly admirable. Its purpose was to give us an example to emulate as God's children. Although this might be psychologically painful for those who have not enjoyed a good relationship with the father figure or for those who have never had a father – figure relationship, it nevertheless shows what such a relationship could have been. Historical theology affirms through, Apostles' Creed, Athanasius Creed, and the Nicene Creed that Jesus was truly human. This creed is the benchmark of orthodoxy and differentiates true Christianity from cults and sects. It distinguishes authentic Christianity from sects that have held and taught the wrong view of Christ's humanity. Throughout the two millennia of Christianity, sects have manifested themselves in various guises to undermine the humanity of Christ; the most prominent was Docetism. Such heresy was one of the earliest Christological heresies on the person of Jesus Christ. It was a branch of a significant philosophical heresy known as Gnosticism that emerged in the second century AD, influenced by dualistic Greek philosophy that taught that the human body was irredeemably evil and concluded that if Jesus was who he claimed to be the son of God; he would have had nothing to do with the physical body. Docetism argued that Jesus Christ's body was not real, but

an apparent phantom of celestial substance. Docetism comes from the Greek verb, δοκειν meaning to seem and its noun δοκησις meaning apparition or phantom. Its central teaching was that the existence of Jesus Christ's historical and all his human forms was not real but mere semblances. It is one of the earliest heresies on the false view of Jesus Christ's humanity. Its central tenet was that Jesus Christ did not have a real natural body during his life on earth, thus denying the Incarnation. Early patristic fathers refuted the Docetism heresy: Ignatius of Antioch in the first century AD. Irenaeus (115-190 AD) also refuted it, and so did Hippolytus (170-235 AD). The council of Chalcedon condemned Docetism in AD 451 that gave the definitive Christological formulation followed by orthodox Christianity to date. The heresy of Docetism on the humanity of Jesus Christ has a twin sibling –Arianism that occupied debates in the first ecumenical church councils, Nicaea and Constantinople. Arianism is a Christological heresy that denied the divinity of Jesus Christ and maintained that Jesus as the son of God was created by God the father and was not co-eternal and consubstantial with the father as taught in the orthodox mainline Christianity. The priest Arius from Alexandria (250 – 336 AD) championed the teaching of Arianism. Essentially, Arianism denies the doctrine of the Trinity, arguing that God created Jesus at a given point in time as a creature distinct from God the Father and subordinate to him. It also denies the Incarnation arguing that Jesus Christ did not always exist with the Father. In the Arian debate, the main contention was the Greek word: "Homoousian," meaning substance. Arianism maintained that Jesus Christ was not of the same substance with God the Father. The Council Nicaea 325AD and council of Constantinople in 381 AD condemned Arianism after prolonged debates in the Early

Church. The principle teachings of Arianism is embraced today in Unitarianism and by the Jehovah's Witnesses. Both these two heresies: Arianism and Docetism, hit at the very root of Christian belief and makes nonsense of the central thesis of this book, to be like Jesus. The Biblical evidence is, however, overwhelming that Jesus was genuinely coeternal and consubstantial with God, but also he was genuinely human after incarnation and lived a perfect life, giving and leaving humanity an example to follow. The balanced view on the human and divine nature of Jesus Christ that he was fully human and fully divine poses a genuine question: How do we account for his divine power when he lived on earth and operated as fully human. The theological, doctrinal explanation is found in the theory of kenosis in which Jesus Christ humbled himself and emptied himself of his divine prerogatives and power to be fully human. The oldest Christological hymn of the incarnation [609] describes the two natures of Christ. Jesus Christ deliberately laid aside his majesty for the sole purpose of winning humanity back to God by showing humanity how it could be done, live divine lives on earth, and by giving his example. In his life and teaching, Jesus Christ demonstrated that by living a life of obedience, dependence on God, it is possible to live a victorious holy life on earth. Scripture gives evidence that Jesus always had at his disposal his heavenly power. A case in point was at his arrest when Peter drew up his sword to defend him. Jesus said, "Put your sword back in its place...Do you think I cannot call on my Father, and he will at once put at my disposal more than twelve legions of angels?"[610]

To illustrate this point, I am going to use the imagery of dual citizenship, which needs not open the old debates of Docetism and Arianism. I am using dual citizenship to elucidate the reality, and the challenge of Christians living conscious of their earthly life and the heavenly life to come was reality is experienced by fixing their eyes on Jesus,[611] the perfect man who operated on both spheres. Taking cognizance of views expressed in Docetism and Arianism, we still believe that the Biblical portrait of Jesus Christ's humanity gives clear evidence that Jesus was truly human. Luke describes Jesus Christ's spiritual and social development as a child[612]by providing an account of him developing in favor of God and man, implying that Jesus as a boy had God's approval and was well-spoken socially in his village. As a boy, Jesus got lost in the crowd, perhaps doing all that was expected of boys of his age. His curiosity as a twelve-year-old boy got him lost in Jerusalem and was found three days later "sitting among the teachers, listening to them and asking them questions, and they were amazed at his understanding and answers."[613] Jesus got tired from the mid-day sun and sat by a well to rest while he sent his disciples to go into the village of Samaria to buy food.[614]Jesus got tired after a day's work and slept in the boat.[615] Jesus got angry at the abuse of God's temple by market traders and cleansed it.[616] Jesus showed human emotions and wept touched by the sorrow of the death of Lazarus.[617] At the cross, Jesus cried in agony, got thirsty[618], and expressed compassion on the care of his mother like all firstborn sons would do.[619] In keeping with all these attributes of humanity throughout his ministry, Jesus showed utter dependence on God, setting an example for his followers to depend on God. Jesus Christ was truly human is not in doubt. Therefore Jesus was truly human and lived a perfect life in total dependence on God, leaving humanity an example to emulate. Those Christians who aspire and desire to form in Christ's image have to go against the grain of modern society's trinity of living that emphasizes self-assertion, self-effacing, and self–dependence and learn to depend on God even when that is not cool in contemporary culture. To be like Christ is to depend on God. Jesus said, John 6:38, 39 (NIV) "For I came down from heaven, not to do mine own will, but the will of him that sent me. And this is my Father's will which has sent me." Jesus further said, John 4:34 (KJV) "My meat (food) is to do the will of him that sent me, and to finish his work." Doing the will of God was paramount to all that Jesus did on earth, he said, John 5:30 (KJV) "I can of mine own self do nothing…I seek not my own will, but the will of the Father which has sent me." He also said: John 5:19-20 (NIV) "I tell you the truth, the Son can do nothing by himself; he can do only what he sees his Father doing, because whatever the Father does the Son also does." The ultimate dependence on God and abandonment to his will by Jesus was in Gethsemane, where he faced the ordeal of dying on the cross. It is in this encounter where he revealed his true humanity. It is human nature to avoid pain and suffering at all costs. The prayer of Jesus at Gethsemane reveals his true humanity but also his determination to depend on God's will. Jesus prayed (Luke 22:42, Matthew 26:42; John 18:11 NIV) "Father if you are willing, take this cup from me; yet not my will, but yours be done." The close filial relationship between Jesus and God is depicted in scripture in Jesus' last week on earth.

When he arrived in Jerusalem, Jesus knew what lay ahead, excruciating death on the cross and said, John 12:27-28 (NIV) "Now my heart is troubled, and what shall I say? 'Father, save me from this hour? No, it was for this very reason I came to this hour. Father, glorify your name!" Then a voice came from heaven, "I have glorified it and will glorify it again." John's account of this incidence goes on to explain that this final exchange between Jesus and God the father was audibled by the crowd who thought that it had thundered, and Jesus explained that the loud voice was for their benefit. What a grand finale to Jesus' life on earth! He lived on earth, depending on and doing God's will. At the beginning of his earthly ministry at his baptism, a voice from God the father was heard confirming Jesus' status (Matthew 3:17, Luke 3:22 NIV) "This is my beloved son whom I love; with him, I am well pleased." Now at the end of his ministry, as he enters the final week, God confirms his pleasure with him and his glorification. What an example for the Christian to follow! Living a life dependent on God and doing His will. A Christian who longs to be like Jesus learns to develop an intimate relationship and dependence on God.

6. **Sanctified victorious living.** Ephesians 6:12 (KJV) "For we wrestle not against flesh and blood, but against principalities, against powers, against the rulers of the darkness of this world, against spiritual wickedness in high places." In chapter two, we demonstrated that one of the hindrances to spiritual formation is satanic warfare through witchcraft and haunting living dead in the African context. Although in that chapter, special reference was to Africa, this hindrance is not limited to Africa, Wiccan, and the occult and psychic crystal ball involvement with the dead are common in Western society too. Spiritual warfare is real and is faced by every Christian wherever they live, whether aware of it or not. The most deadly tactic in warfare is camouflage, and the devil and his demonic forces use camouflage to great effect by convincing Christians that belief in demons and witchcraft are illusions; they are the

only figment of people's imagination. A survey done in 1934 among fifteen hundred ministers in the USA "showed that 54% did not believe there was a personal devil."[620]The devil thrives and relishes on Christian ignorance of his existence. The scripture warns against such ignorance, 2Corinthians 2:11 (NIV) "So that Satan might not outwit us. For we are not unaware of his schemes." The truth is that witchcraft and the occult are international phenomena that exist as an unseen supernatural force that constantly wages warfare against Christian belief. Witchcraft and Satanism are documented in other parts of the Western world in which Satan is openly worshipped. "The liturgy consists of sacrilegious treatments of common prayers, with the substitution of "Satan" for "God," and readings from Milton's *Paradise Lost*, Dante's *Inferno*, and some obscure poems."[621] Other documentation of Satanism dating back over fifty years ago in the USA reported, "Demonism is a growing phenomenon throughout the world. The news media report its rapid spread in England. Some reports are suggesting that Germany now has more witches, wizards, and necromancers than full-time Christian workers. An American pastor with a German-born wife recently described the case of two demon-possessed, black-attire girls "baptized to Satan." Their parents are demon-worshippers.... Demonism today is a further manifestation of man's revolt against God."[622] When a person becomes a Christian, they enlist in spiritual warfare, whether they know it or not. In this warfare, the devil undertakes the task to bring them down in their spiritual pursuit through discouragement and any other form of attack. The Christian life is a battlefield through which Satan extends the same warfare he unleashed to Jesus at the start of his ministry in his temptation in the wilderness using the same trinity of temptation: lust of the flesh, the lust of the eyes and pride of life.[623] The Christian life is constant spiritual combat with demonic spiritual forces of darkness. I once heard a comment by the late Derek Prince[624] that got me thinking. He said power, control, domination, and domineering spirit, the desire to manipulate and dominate people lies in the realm of witchcraft! As I thought about it, I began to realize the truth in that assertion because God is a perfect "gentleman"; He never forces His will on anybody. He has endowed human beings with the free will to choose to obey him or disobey him. In the Old Testament, it says, Isaiah 1:18 (NASB) "Come now, and let us reason together, says the Lord: though your sins are as scarlet, they shall be as white as snow; though they are red like crimson, they shall be as wool." In the New Testament, Jesus never coerced anybody to follow him; he issued the invitation. When Jesus called the first disciples, they asked him where he was staying. Jesus gave no convincing winsome explanations; he said come and see (John 1:38 -41). In the course of his teaching ministry one of his what theologians refer to as 'hard sayings', hid hard to his followers and some turned away from following him, and he turned to the twelve disciples and offered them permission to leave too by asking the question: John 6:67 (NIV) "Do you want to leave too?" Jesus begs for permission or invitation to involve himself in one of the seven churches in Revelation 3:20 (NLT) "Look! I stand at the door and knock. If you hear my voice and open the door, I will come in, and we will share a meal as friends." God respects human free will, let alone seeking to manipulate and dominate them, so should we respect other people's will and choices and not seek to domineer. Prince's assertion also got me thinking in reflecting on experiences in the cause of my Christian ministry stretching a few decades; I have encountered domineering and oppressive people in the life of the church, indicating the possibility of witchcraft in the church. The church throughout its history has been plagued by power struggle and manipulation of people to dominate others. There are many explanations for church splits and cessation in church history, but the common causes were not always doctrinal but a power struggle. When the desire for power and domination of others occurs as the cause of the split, there is, in most cases, something sinister and demonic to substantiate evidence for witchcraft, for in most cases, it involves strong domineering characters. Although my initial reaction to Derek Prince's statement was of shock and denial, my observation and experience of shenanigans in church life, however, indicates that there are Christian wizard and witches that dominate in local congregations, and where they exist at times they are quite subtle and camouflaged as the hardest working people in the congregation. In some situations, no life-changing spiritual mission ever takes place in such congregations. The domineering people are die-hards, resilient, ruthless to anyone who differs from them, even the vicar, minister, or pastor. Their motto is "My way or no way." The oppression and suppression of ministerial authority tend to happen in traditional churches where laity holds the upper hand in leadership and in determining the life of the church. The parody is that it happens in those churches that espouse the democratic running of the church, and because of human frailty, a few manipulate the situation, and they become the democracy. The analogy is also true mainly in modern churches, especially in prosperity gospel churches where the minister or the pastor assumes unfettered authority without checks and balances or even accountability. Such tends to happen in modern churches where the minister or the pastor assumes a role in leadership as the CEO with unrivaled authority that manipulates and dominates the congregation as a personal business. The minister, too, could be used by the devil as a wizard or witch in manipulating, domineering and oppressing people. Apparently, in those churches where the lay holds sway and have swung the pendulum too far, this is the very thing they tried to address only to turn the power to the dominant vocal minority few. We do not find autocratic or democratic leadership in scripture. In the Old Testament, we had theocratic leadership in which God was the leader, and in the New Testament, what we can glean from Jesus' model of leadership is was what has commonly come to be known as "Servant Leadership" borrowed from Jesus' words and teaching.[625]

Stalwarts and Satanic Agents.

To safeguard sweeping, every strong personality in the church with the same broom let me issue a caveat to distinguish between innocent, hard-working stalwarts of the church who expend countless hours of love to their church, chapel, and other places of worship buildings, and Satanic agents. The stalwart might hinder God's work unawares because of ignorance trying to protect all they have known in the life of their church fellowship and wrongly believing that is all there is. Some stalwarts are "generational Christians" who do and defend what they do in church because their parents and grandparents did it; some would even say "it is all in the family" before giving litany account of how many generations of their family were involved with the particular church or chapel. Some of these stalwarts may hinder mission because of their lack of encounter with the risen Christ and absence of what John Wesley referred to as "warmed heart" – the conversion experience. For some, they pile on the role after role because of their love for their chapel to keep it going rather than having malice or desire to dominate. Their opposition to spiritual change could easily be attributable to ignorance rather than evil malice. They behave like cheerleaders loudly shouting what has often been referred to as the seven last words of the church: "We've always done it this way."I think some would even add the words, "and we like it that way."

The Satanic agents, on the other hand, are antagonistic to spirituality but amenable to social activism. They would vehemently oppose efforts to evangelistic endeavors and enterprise but would support entertainment events, including pantomimes on the sanctuary. They hold their local churches at ransom by threatening to resign if things do not go their way. They wield such power that members of the local congregation are afraid of them, even the minister. When left unchallenged, they bleed the life of the church to death and its closure. I once encountered one such person in one of my local churches, and when the person threatened to resign, as the superintendent minister, I called a bluff and accepted the resignation with immediate effect on the spot and told the person; I wanted it in writing in twenty-four hours. In less than twenty-four hours, he sent an envoy, a retired minister, to plead with me that the person had rescinded his resignation. These people are what we might call "Christian wizards and witches" masquerading as most caring and sacrificial for the life of the congregation, but their main desire is power, control, and domination. Their modus operandi is "infiltrate, influence and dominate."

In some cases, they would complain that nobody wants to offer for official roles in the life of the church, but when one researches into the causes, one finds they are the very cause why people do not want to take office for fear of conflict with them. I once encountered such a situation in a local church where senior stewardship rotated between two warring stewards Norah and Bassy (not their real names).

Norah was quite vicious and bullish; sometimes, she even attacked the minister and told him or her what needs to happen! Bassy was quite gentle, amiable, amenable, and lovely she got on well with most people in the church and was very supportive of ministers. Norah was the opposite, wild bull that bullied people around. The parody is that Norah was a tiny little woman and Bassy was well build woman loved by most people in the church as the gentle huggy bear while Norah was like a vicious bull that most people avoided and dared not oppose her for fear of creating an atmosphere or even getting into an argument. When it was Norah's turn to become a senior steward, as the minister, I struggled and hardly got anybody to offer to take on stewarding roles. I managed to persuade Kimberley (note her real name) to become a senior steward. Kimberley was a widow, quite positive bubbly and vivacious and inspirational; she was winsome, always smiling, and got on with most people in the church. She at first resisted telling me that her late husband was a very able steward, and she could never match his standards. I explained to her the situation and why I wanted her to become the senior steward that year to help change the dynamics in the minister's vestry. When she accepted, I went on to ask for other volunteers to the role of stewards. To my surprise and the surprise to everybody, I managed to get two! I recall approaching a young man known as Pius (not his real name). His first question was blunt as a true Yorkshire man, "who will be with me in the minister's vestry," I said Kimberley, and without hesitation, he said yes to my great surprise because I was expecting a firm no. Pius was one of the youngest men in the congregation; he was in his thirties and attended mainly the evening service. By changing the vicious Norah from the vestry, we were able to recruit two new stewards that year and had one of the happiest years working together. Kimberley and her new group of stewards were quite positive and supportive, and in that year, we attempted and accomplished a few spiritual things in the life of the local church. The one characteristic of those who might be termed as "wizard and witches" in the church that makes them susceptible to being satanic agents is that they hardly attend prayer or Bible study meetings but are kingpins of social events in the particular congregations where their power and influence holds sway. At times one may get the impression that they do not want new people for fear of losing their roles, strangleholds, and strongholds of the life of the local church. They oppose every effort for spiritual outreach, and for the most part, the word evangelism is like a swear word; they have no appetite for prayer or reading the Bible.

Whether we agree with Prince's summation about power, control, and domination being in the realm of witchcraft or not, the fact remains that any person that desires to be like Jesus in their spiritual formation must be aware of spiritual warfare. The scriptures assume the reality of spiritual warfare hence the instruction to be on the defensive with appropriate spiritual weaponry.[626] The encouraging thing is that Christians fight from the victory that Jesus Christ has already won. What the Christians need to do is to appropriate this victory by relying on God, submitting to His guidance and obedience in using the provided armory in scripture.[627]There are two types of Christians, those who strongly believe in the existence of demons and spiritual warfare and at times, risk overplaying the presence of the demonic and those who play down the existence of Satan and demons and deny that there is such thing as spiritual warfare. There are two fatal mistakes in warfare, failure to identify the enemies' camouflage, and underestimating the strength of the enemy. To shrug off an enemy as a pushover when he is fully armed, organized, experienced, and dangerous is to vouch for defeat, and that is what the Christians who dismiss spiritual warfare as a myth do. There is definitely, Spiritual warfare, the existence of Satan, and demonic forces that camouflage as angels of light.[628] These forces are real and in constant warfare against the Christian. Steven J Cole comments, "There is a great difference between how God and Satan deal with their followers. God reveals to His followers the strength of the enemy, but Satan does not dare to reveal to his followers the strength of God or they would mutiny."[629]The denial of the existence of personal devil was articulated by Rudolf Bultmann as follows: "It is impossible to use electric light and the wireless and to avail ourselves of modern medical and surgical discoveries, and at the same time believe in the New Testament world of demons and spirits."[630]This thinking is found in many Christians today in the Post Modern era. According to a recent survey,[631] only 52 percent of Baptists, 24 percent of Methodists, and 34 percent of Lutherans believed that the devil is a personal being. Among the clergy, 18 percent of the Methodists deny the existence of the devil altogether, and 36 percent regarded him as an impersonal force; and 34 percent of the public believed in a personal devil. Jesus Christ engaged in Spiritual warfare during his earthly ministry to His death on the cross. Those who follow Christ must prepare for spiritual warfare. Philippians 1:29 (ESV) "For it has been granted to you that for the sake of Christ, you should not only believe in him but also suffer for his sake." To be like Jesus is to live his sanctified victorious life against the worldly anti-God systems vitiated by demonic activities. It is to allow Christ to live His life through us and to echo the words of scripture: Galatians 2:20 (NIV) "I have been crucified with Christ, and I no longer live, but Christ lives in me. The life I live in the body, I live by faith in the Son of God who loved me and gave himself for me."

7. **Balanced World View**

My wife and I have lived in the UK for the last four decades. Most of that time, we were UK residents but Kenyan citizens. Our two boys were all born there and are UK citizens. As our sons became grown-up men and ourselves started getting older, the issue of attaining British citizenship surfaced. The dilemma was, should we continue to live in the UK as Kenyan citizens our country of birth or attain British citizenship where we resided and worked? Four thousand miles separate Kenya and UK! As time went on, we developed strong ties, interests, affinity, and allegiance in both countries for obvious reasons. The saying "East, West, home is best," began to beg the question where home is? It is in seeking an answer to this question that the issue of dual citizenship became real to us. The definition of Dual citizenship is a situation in which a person is concurrently regarded as a citizen of more than one country under the laws of the respective countries. A person with dual citizenship is, in essence, a citizen of two countries at the same time. Dual citizens receive the benefits and privileges of the two countries, primarily in social welfare and travel documents, in most cases, dual passports.

Christians are by nature and default dual citizens. Through the natural birth, the Christian is a citizen on earth, and by the second birth, "being born again,"[632]the spiritual birth the Christian becomes a citizen of heaven, written in the lamb's book of life.[633]There are numerous passages in scripture that attest to the truth about Christian's dual citizenship. In the teaching of the Apostle Paul, 2Corinthians 5:8, (NIV) "to be absent from the body is to be present with the Lord." Also in Pauline teaching, 2Corinthians 5:1 (NIV), "We know that if our earthly house of this tabernacle (the body) were dissolved, we have a building of God, a house, not made with hands, eternal in the heavens." In his teaching and life, Jesus attested to this truth when he said, Matthew 16:19-21 (NIV), "Do not store up treasures here on earth where moths eat them and rust destroys them, and where thieves break in and steal, but store up for yourselves treasures in heaven where moths and rust cannot destroy, and thieves do not break and steal. For where your treasure is, there your heart will also be." In his farewell address to his disciples, Jesus said, John 14:3 (NIV), "I go to prepare a place for you and will come again and receive you to Myself, that where I am you may also be." In his final moments before his death on the cross, Jesus forgave the thief at the cross and said, Luke 23:43 (NIV), "Today you will be with me in paradise." In popular music in the last fifty years or so, this truth has been popularized by Jim Reeves classic song: "This world is not my home I am just passing through."[634] The Arch patriarch of the Christian faith,

Abraham, is referred to in scripture as a wondering Aramean in Hebrew ger, which means a sojourner who is an apt description of the Christian. The Christian life is portrayed in scripture as the life of pilgrimage, traveling to a final destination. In John's gospel, the prologue[635]in describing the Incarnation says that the Word (Logos) understood to refer to Jesus "dwelt among us." The word translated "dwelt" its ultimate meaning is "tabernacled" implying temporary mobile residency resonating with the children of Israel dwelling by pitching and un-pitching tents in the desert. The Apostle Paul in Philippians 3:20 makes it explicit when he says, "our citizenship (referring to Christians in general) is in heaven." Some of the critics of Christianity have criticized some Christians for being so heavenly minded that they are of no earthly good. This criticism is for Christians who focus on their heavenly destination that they ignore their temporary earthly residency and disengage from social actions in the community they live in. In so doing such, Christians forget that they may be citizens of heaven their eternal destiny, but they are still residents on the earth. The Christians require living a balanced life and constantly being transformed to be more like Jesus Christ to maintain a heavenly perspective. They also need to develop and exercise a balanced worldview like Jesus who lived on earth as a citizen of Palestine, then a colony of the mighty Roman Empire, yet as the creator of heaven. For thirty-three years He lived as a faithful sojourner on earth doing well everywhere he went through engaging in social action in societal evils that plagued the society Jesus lived in and doing all he could to alleviate or eradicate them. Jesus did so to give an example of how Christians should live their lives on earth with a longing for heaven. The longing for the permanent heavenly citizenship should inspire faithful urgent living on the short fleeting life on earth. It calls for faithful carpediem –seize the day prayer with the Psalmist, Psalm 90:12 (NLT) "Teach us to realize the brevity of life, so that, we may grow in wisdom." The Psalmist also prayed, Psalm 39:4 (NIV) "Show me oh Lord, my end and the measure of my days, and let me know how fleeting my life is." Jesus demonstrated how to live a balanced Christian life by exercising a balanced view of the present world in light of the world to come (heaven); also how to interpret the temporal events occurring on earth in light of the permanent, eternal world. A Christian who is becoming more Christ-like learns to interpret current world events in light of eternal values as Jesus did. To develop an objective worldview, one has to evaluate it on non-objective personal experience but also by objectively comparing what the scriptures say. For example, when Jesus encountered people's antagonism against God, and his rejection by the Jewish leaders, He saw it in light of scriptures.[636]Jesus foretold the current increased international conflict and warfare as a sign of end times or his second coming and the end of the present age;[637]likewise, lawlessness and crime over the last decades. Since the re-birth or re-establishment of the Jewish nation in Palestine, the conflict has dominated world news ever since. International interventions through the United Nations Organization have not produced any long-lasting solution; perhaps the scriptures do[638] by stating that these are signs of the end times. Another example is that over the last three decades or so, traditional churches in the West have experienced meltdown in church decline. Accompanying the statistics for this state of affairs has been sociological explanations that are farfetched and tenuous, maybe the scriptures[639]provide a plausible explanation that the church in Laodicea is a prophetic symbolism of the church in the end times with its self-sufficiency symbolized by Christ knocking to enter from the outside.[640] A few years ago, the devastation of warfare described in scriptures[641]would easily have been dismissed as deluded phantasy but not anymore in light of the Hiroshima atomic bomb and the current escalation of the cold war and the star wars. The hostilities in the Middle East towards Israel and the Russian involvement may find some socio-political explanations, but maybe the scriptural summation as signs of end times gives a more plausible explanation.[642]Post-modernity gives credence to secularism and assumes that all modern sociological phenomena have a metaphysical explanation without recourse to spiritual, religious assertions. As already demonstrated, a balanced view would give recourse to a religious scriptural explanation as Jesus did. A case in point is Paul's teaching to his protégé, Timothy that today reads like a column in the Times magazine: 1Timothy 4:1 (NIV), "The Spirit clearly says that in the latter times (end times) some will abandon the faith and follow deceiving spirits and things taught by demons." Paul also went on to say 2Timothy 3:1-5a (NIV) "Mark this: there will be terrible times in the last days. People will be lovers of themselves, lovers of money, boastful, proud, abusive, disobedient to their parents, ungrateful, unholy, without love, unforgiving, slanderous, without self-control, brutal, not lovers of the good, treacherous, rash, conceited, lovers of pleasure rather than lovers of God-having a form of godliness but denying its power." The above litany of behavior and social evil reads like a weekly column in the paparazzi, which is quite revealing given that it was written nearly two thousand years ago in the Holy Scriptures. When Martin Luther started the Reformation, its aim was a corrective measure of the abuse of power by the papacy. Martin Luther is lauded and rightly credited with freeing the church from the shackles of abuse of power by the papacy. He also re-established the authority of scripture with his catchphrase "sola scriptura" and the efficacy of grace mediated in reading the Holy Scriptures and in reliance on God for guidance. At the time that Martin Luther published his ninety-five theses over five hundred years ago, corruption, avarice greed, and prelacy were rampant. In light of the current proliferation of new religious movements, one might quip, "What has changed?" The precedent established by the Reformation of individuals differing and breaking away from the established church and start their separate church structure has, in recent times, been abused. Wesley Granberg – Michaelson laments that "The one holy catholic and apostolic church has, in fact, become endlessly and ceaselessly divided into separate denominations."[643]He goes on to assert that:

> The Reformation had unintended consequences that injured the church life and witness, continuing today. Here is our present shameful and sinful state of affairs: Today, there are an estimated 43,800 denominations in the world, often living with sectarian distrust and judgment of one another. This staggering proliferation of divided institutionalized churches could never have been imagined in the first 1,500 years of Christian history. Despite the significant accomplishments of the ecumenical movement over the past 60 years, today, we still assume impunity for ongoing actions that continue to sever the Body of Christ and disobey the consistent, clear, repeated biblical commands to reconcile divisions and live together in unity. Such is a legacy of the Reformation.[644]

The intensity of cessations and divisions of the church has intensified in the last few years. When I researched Christology with special reference to New Religious Movements for my doctoral thesis awarded in 1989, there were an estimated six thousand new religious movements. The exponential proliferation has just occurred in the last three decades. While plausible causes could be found in the socio-scientific sphere of influence, the words of Paul to Timothy cited above strikes at the heart of the matter, greed, and selfishness disguised as the proclamation of the gospel. During Paul's preaching and planting of Christianity similar ill motives existed of which the apostle exclaimed: Philippians 3:15-18 (NIV) "It is true that some preach Christ out of envy and rivalry, but others out of goodwill…(some) preach Christ out of selfish ambition, not sincerely. But what does it matter? The important thing is that in every way, whether from false motives or true, Christ is preached. And because of this, I rejoice. Yes, and I will continue to rejoice." Living a balanced Christian life has been commended by prominent theologians in past generations. The most famous is the esteemed theologian Karl Barth's famous quotation advising ministers of the Word to preach using the Bible on the one hand and the newspaper in the other. In an interview with Time Magazine, Barth stated: "The pastor and the Faithful should not deceive themselves into thinking that they are a religious society who has to do with certain themes; they live in the world. We still need – according to my formulation –the Bible and the Newspaper."[645] In an earlier interview, "Barth recalls that forty years ago he advised young theologians "to take your Bible and your newspaper and read both. But interpret newspapers from your Bible." [646]Jesus lived a balanced life in which he interpreted current events from scripture. A balanced Christian that is growing to be more Christ-like should live a balanced life that sees and interprets world events holistically. It is my prayer what I have shared in this book from the depth of my heart and experience in my short Christian journey will encourage and inspire your journey. It is also my prayer that what I have shared in this book would spur and inspire you to sing with me my three choruses that form part of my nursery rhymes: "To be like Jesus." "Everywhere He went, He was doing good." But above all, to raise an octave higher in singing, "Let the beauty of Jesus be seen in me. His wonderful compassion and purity. O thou Spirit divine all my nature refine, Till the beauty of Jesus is seen in me." That is my prayer, may that be your prayer too?

Chapter 7 Notes

535 The Weymouth Translation renders it: "Master…if it is you, bid me come to you upon the water"; The Living Bible: Sir it is really you tell me to come over to you walking on the water"; Lord if it is really you, call me to come to you on the water"; The God's Word Translation: "Lord if it is you, order me to come to you on the water"; The NIV: "Lord if it is you, tell me to come to you on the water";

536 1Peter 2:21

537 John 13:1-20

538 1John 2:6

539 Luke6:12

540 Newton C. Conant was one of my tutors in 1975 and makes this observation in his book, Conant, Newton C. *Changed By Beholding Him*, (Fort Washington, P.A.; Christian Literature Crusade, 1972), 10

541 Ibid. p.11

542 John 10:10

543 Constrained (KJV); Insisted (NLT); Compelled (Darby Bible Translation); He made (ESV); Obliged (Douay-Rheims Bible)

544 Mark 6:41

545 Mark 6:51-52

546 Hebrews 13:6

547 John 8:11

548 The author of this chorus is somewhat unknown, various people wrote the lyrics to it and various website seem to credit to various people for example, https://www.allmusic.com/…/everywhere-he-went-he-was-doing-good-mt0013035041

549 Matthew 5:44 cf Luke 6:27-35

550 Mark 6:37-44

551 Luke 5:28

552 Luke 5:30-32

553 Luke 19:7

554 Luke 10:25-37

555 Luke 6:12

556 Matthew 14:23

557 Mark 1:32-35

558 Newton C Conant, *Changed by Beholding Him*, 14-15

559 Luke 4:18

560 Jesus read the scroll in Luke 4:18-21 and applied it to himself according to the prophecy of Isaiah 61:1-3

561 Numbers 21:8 cited in John 3:14-16

562 Matthew 12:40 citing Jonah 1:1-3:2

563 Luke 11:30

564 John 6:33-35 & 6:47-50 citing Exodus 16:14, 31 that resonates also with Psalm 78:24, 25.

565 Genesis chapters 7-9 cited in Matthew 24:36-39

566 Referring to Old Testament scripture that pointed to the manner of his death and its purpose in Psalm 22, Isaiah 53 as indicated in Luke 24:25-27

567 Newton C Conant, *Changed by Beholding Him,* 1972, 49

568 D L Moody, *The Bible,* Accessed July 10, 2018. https://www.whatchristianswanttoknow.com/quotes-about-the-bible-25-awesome-sayings/

569 Ibid.

570 Ibid

571 Ibid.

572 Ibid.

573 ibid

574 Hebrews 4:12

575 Isaiah 40:8

576 Newton C Conant, *Changed by Beholding Him,* 50

577 John Wesley, The Bible, Accessed July 10, 2018. https://www.crosswalk.com/faith/spiritual-life/inspiring-quotes/25-quotes-from-influential-christians-about-the-bible.html.

578 Ibid.

579 Ibid.

580 Alex Varughese, and Roger Hahn, *Discovering the New Testament: Community and Faith.* (Kansas City: Beacon Hill Press, 2004), 172

581 Acts1:5,8

582 Acts 2:3,4,6

583 Acts 4:8

584 Acts 5:1-11

585 Acts 5:32

586 Acts 6:10

587 Acts 8:9

588 Acts 9:31

589 Acts 11:12

590 Acts 11:28

591 Acts 13:2

592 Acts 15:28

593 Acts 16:6-7,10

594 Acts 21:4

595 Acts 21:11

596 Matthew 3:16,17

597 Exodus 29:7

598 Acts 10:38

599 Luke 4:1
600 Mark 1:12
601 Luke 4:14
602 Luke 4:16-21
603 Matthew 12:28
604 Romans 8:26
605 Galatians 5:16 compare with Romans 8:13
606 John 16:14, 15
607 Romans 8:14
608 2Corinthians 3:18
609 Philippians 2:5-11
610 Matthew 26:52-53
611 Hebrews 12:2
612 Luke 2:52
613 Luke 2:41-52
614 John 4:6
615 Mark 4:38-40
616 Matthew 21:12-13 cf. John 2:13-25
617 John 11:35
618 John 19:28
619 John 19:26-27
620 Newton C Conant, *Changed By Beholding Him*, 128
621 *Camden Courier Magazine*, Camden County, New Jersey, September 3, 1968
622 *Christianity Today Magazine*, February 17, 1967.
623 1John 2:16 compare with temptation of Jesus Matthew 4:1-11 and Luke 4:1-13
624 Peter Derek Vaughan Prince was a Bible teacher whose daily radio programme, *Derek Prince Legacy Radio*, broadcast around the world in various languages. Derek Prince Ministries is at the forefront of combating spiritual hunger worldwide by making compelling Bible teaching available in over 120 languages. Accessed July 10, 2018. https://www.dpmuk.org/
625 Mark 10:43-45
626 Ephesians 6:11-20
627 James 4:17 teaches that by submitting to God, the Christian resists satanic warfare.
628 2Corinthians 11:14
629 *The Christian in Complete Armour,* Accessed June 23, 2018. https://bible.org/seriespage/lesson-56-why-christians-must-be-fighters-ephesians-6:12-13
630 John R W Stott, *The Cross of Christ*. (Downers Grove, Illinois: IVP, 2006), 12
631 *Christianity Today*, April 18, 1980, 31.
632 John 3:3-21
633 Revelation 20:15-20

634 Jim Reeves, This world is not my home, Accessed July 15, 2018. https://en.wikipedia.org/wiki/This_World_Is_Not_My_Home

635 John 1:1-14

636 Jesus understood John 15:23-35 in light of Psalm 69:4; Matthew 13:14-15 in light of Isaiah 6:9-10: Matthew 15:7-8 in light of Isaiah 29:13: Jesus also interpreted His rejection by the people in Matthew 21:42 in light of Psalm 118:22-23 and Matthew 26:31 in light of Zechariah 13:7

637 Luke 21:25,26

638 In Luke 21:24; Jeremiah 23:7,8; Isaiah 60:9 and Ezekiel 37:1-8

639 In Revelation 3:14-19

640 Revelation 3:20

641 Revelation 6:8 and 9:15

642 Ezekiel 38 and 39

643 Wesley Granberg-Michaelson. "Where Protestantism Went –Wrong: The 500th Anniversary of the Reformation Calls for Repentance as Well as Celebration." In *Sojourners: Faith in Action for Social Action Magazine*, February 2017, 28

644 Ibid. p.28

645 Karl Barth, *Time Magazine* for an interview he gave in 1966

646 *Times Magazine*, Friday, May 31, 1963 cited in http://barth.ptsem.edu/about-cbs/faq

Bibliography

Apostolides, Anastasia and Dreyer, Yolanda, "The Greek Evil Eye: African Witchcraft and Western ethnocentrism" *in HTS 64 (2)*, 2008.

Augustine, St. *The Anti-Pelagian Works of St Augustine Bishop of Hippo* Vol 3. (Classics Reprint), London: FB & C Limited, 2015.

__________. *The Confessions of St Augustine,* (translated by F. J. Sheed), London: Sheed and Ward, 1944.

Baab, Lynne M. Fasting: *Spiritual Freedom Above Our Appetites,* Downers Grove, Ill.: IVP Books, 2006.

Bailey, Kenneth E. *Poet and Peasant and Through Peasant's Eyes.* Grand Rapids: Eerdmans, 1976.

Baker, Frank. *Wesley to Asbury: Studies in Early American Methodism.* Durham, NC: Duke University Press, 1976.

Barclay, William. *The Gospel of Mark,* St Andrews Press, 1954.

Barr, J. *Semantics of Biblical Language,* London: Oxford University Press, 1961.

Barrett, W.E.H. "Notes on the Customs and Beliefs of the Wa-Giriama, etc.,

British East Africa." *Journal of the Royal Anthropological Institute, vol.41,* 1911.

Bascom, William. *The Yoruba of South Western Nigeria.* London: Holt, Rinehart & Winston, 1969.

Beard, Steve. "The Spiritual discipline of fasting," *Good News Magazine*, USA: United Methodist Church, January 30, 2012.

Beattie, John. *Bunyoro, An African Kingdom.* NY.: Holt, Rinehart & Winston, 1960.

Berkouwer, G. C. *Faith and Sanctification*; Grand Rapids: Eerdmans, 1954.

Brown, Colin, ed. *The New International Dictionary of the New Testament Theology.* Vol.2. Exeter: IVP, 1976.

Britannica, *The New Encyclopaedia Britannica*, Chicago, 1995.

Berkouwer, G. C. *Faith and Sanctification.* Grand Rapids: Eerdmans, 1954.

Boa, Kenneth. *Conformed to His Image: Biblical and Practical Approaches to Spiritual Formation.* Grand Rapids: Zondervan, 2001.

Bonhoeffer, Dietrich. *Life Together.* San Francisco: Harper and Row, 1954.

Bonaventure Ed. "The Soul's Journey Into God," *in* Ewert Cousins *Classics of Western Spirituality*; New Jersey: Paulist Press, 1978.

Bounds, E.M. *Power through Prayer.* Grand Rapids: Baker, 1963.

Bower, John. *The Oxford Dictionary of World Religions*, Oxford: Oxford University Press, 1999.

Brunner, Emil. *The Christian Doctrine of the Church, Faith and the Consummation,* (Cairns D. trans). Philadelphia: The Westminster Press, 1962.

Bujo, B. "A Christocentric Ethic for Black Africa" in *Theology Digest, Vol3. No.2,* 1982.

Calhoun, Adele Ahlberg. *Spiritual Disciplines Handbook: Practices that Transforms* Us, Downers Grove, Illinois: 2015.

Calvin, John. *Institutes of the Christian Religion, The Library of Christian Classics,* Vol 20 ed. McNeal, John T. trans. Ford Lewis Battles, Philadelphia: Westminster Press, 1960.

Cameron, Julia. *The Artist Way: A Course in Discovering and Recovering Your Creative Self,* London: Pan Books,1993.

Camden Courier Magazine, Camden County, New Jersey, September 3, 1968.

Campbell, J.Y. "The Christian Use of the Word Ekklesia" in Three New Testament Studies (1965), in *Journal of Theological Studies* 49, 1948.

Campolo, Tony and Darling, Mary Albert. *The God of Intimacy and Action: Reconnecting Ancient Spiritual Practices, Evangelism, and Justice*, San Francisco, CA.: Jossey-Bass, 2007.

Cargas, H. J. and Roger Bradley, *Keeping a Spiritual Journal*. Garden City, NY: Doubleday, 1981.

Carter, Jesse Benedict. "Ancestor-Worship and Cult of the Dead (Roman)." *Encyclopedia of Religion and Ethics*. Vol. 1:461-466. Edinburgh: T & T. Clark, 1909.

Casey, Michael. *Sacred Reading: The Ancient Wisdom of Lection Divina*. Ligouri, Mo:Triump Books, 1995.

_______________.Toward God: *The Ancient Wisdom of Western Prayer*. Ligouri, Mo:Triumph Books, 1996.

_______________. The Undivided Heart: The Western Monastic Approach to Contemplation.Petersham, Mass.: St Bede's Publications, 1994.

Champion, Arthur. "The Agiryama of Kenya," *Occasional Paper No. 25*, John Middleton, ed. London: Royal Anthropological Institute of Great Britain and Ireland, 1967.

Christianity Today Magazine, February 17, 1967., Also April 18, 1980.

Cockerill, Gary.; Tracy, Wes.; Demaray, Donald.; and Harper, Steve. *The Reflecting God*, Kansas City: Beacon Hill Press, 2001.

Cohen, A (ed). *The Soncino Books of the Bible*, London: Soncino Press, 1983.

Collins, Kenneth J. and Tyson, John H. eds. *Conversion and Spiritual Formation in the Wesleyan Tradition.* Oxford: Abingdon Press, 2001.

Conant, Newton C. *Changed By Beholding Him,* Fort Washington, P.A.: Christian Literature Crusade, 1972.

Cracknell, Kenneth, White, Susan J. *An introduction to World Methodism,* Cambridge: Cambridge University Press, 5 May 2005.

Crooke, W. "Ancestor Worship and Cult of the Dead." *Encyclopedia of Religion and Ethics.* Vol. 1:425-432. Edinburgh: T & T. Clark, 1909.

Cross, Frank Leslie, Elizabeth A. Livingstone, "Baptism" in *The Oxford Dictionary of the Christian Church,* Oxford: Oxford University Press, 2005.

Crowther, Jonathan. *A Portraiture of Methodism or The History of the Wesleyan Methodists.* London: Richard Edwards, 1815.

Daloz, Laurent.*Effective Teaching and Mentoring.*San Francisco: Jossey-Bass, 1987.

Dionisopoulos-Mass, R. "The evil eye and bewitchment in a peasant village," In Maloney, C (ed), *The evil eye,* New York: Columbia University Press. 1976.

Davis, Ron Lee.*Mentoring: The Strategy of the Master.*Nashville: Thomas Nelson, 1991.

Day, Albert Edward. *Discipline and Discovery,* Nashville: Disciplined Order of Christ, 1961.

Deeter, Allen C., *An Historical and Theological Introduction to Philip Jacob Spener's Dia Desideria: A Study in Early German Pietism*, Ph.D., Princeton University 1963.

Dieter, Melvin G. et al. *Five Views on Sanctification*. Grand Rapids: Zondervan, 1987.

Dieter, M E. & Berg, D L. (editors) *The Church: Wesleyan Perspective.* Prestonburg, KY: Reformation Publishers, 2008.

Driberg, J.H. *The Lango,* London: T.Fisher Unwin Ltd.,1923.

Dundas, Charles. *Kilimanjaro and Its Peoples*. London: H.F.& G. Witherby, 1924.

Elliott, J H. "Paul, Galatians, and the evil eye." *Currents in Theology and Mission*, 1990.

______. Elliott, J H. "The evil eye in the First Testament: The ecology and culture of a pervasive belief," in Jobling, D, Day, P L & Sheppard, G T (eds), *The Bible and the politics of exegesis*, Cleveland, OH: Pilgrim Press. 1991.

_______. Elliott, J H. " Matthew 20:1-15: A parable of invidious comparison and evil eye Accusation", *Biblical Theology Bulletin 22*, 1992.

Elworthy, F T. *The evil eye.* New York: Julian Press, 1958.

Engstrom, Ted. *The fine Art of Mentoring*, Brentwood, Tenn.: Wolgemuth & Hyatt, 1989

Erb, Peter C. (Ed.) *Pietists: Selected Writings (Classics of Western Spirituality)*, New York: Paulist Press, 2003.

Evans, Pamela. *Shaping the Heart: Reflections on Spiritual Formation and Fruitfulness.* Oxford, Abingdon: The Bible Reading Fellowship, 201.

Evans-Pritchard, E.E. *Theories of Primitive Religion.* London: Oxford University Press, 1965.

Ferdinando, Keith. *The Triumph of Christ in an African Perspectives: A Study of Demonology and Redemption in the African Context. Cumbria*: Paternoster, 1999.

Ferguson, Charles W. Methodists and the Making of America: Organizing to Beat the Devil, 2nd ed, Austin, Texas: Eakin Press, 1983.

Finn, Huck. *Holiness Today,* June 1999.

Finneran, N. "Ethiopian evil eye belief and the magical symbolism of the ironworking," *Folklore* 114, 2003.

Flavel, John. *On Keeping the Heart,* Grand Rapids, Michigan: Christian Classics Ethereal Library, 2002.

Foster, Richard J. *Life with God: Reading the Bible for Spiritual Transformation* (place of publication not identified): HarperCollins e-Books, 2014.

_______. *Prayer Finding the Heart's True Home.* San Francisco: Harper San Francisco, 1992.

Foster, Richard and Helmers, K.A. *Life with God: Reading the Bible for Spiritual Transformation,* London: Harper and Stoughton, 2008.

________. *Celebration of Discipline: The Path to Spiritual Growth*. London: Hodder and Stoughton (first edition, 1980); San Francisco: Harper – Collins, 1998 edition.

Gass, Bob. *Word For Today*, Stoke –on- Trent: United Christian Broadcast, 2017.

Gehman, Richard. *Who are the Living Dead: A Theology of Death, Life After Death and the Living Dead*, Nairobi: Evangel Publishing House, 1999.

Gilmore A. (ed), *Christian Baptism: A Fresh Attempt to Understand the Rite in terms of Scripture, History and Theology*, London: Lutterworth Press, 1959.

Gnanadurai, Daniel Premkumar. "Exploring Conversion and Spiritual Formation as an Ongoing Conversion Process and its Implication to Mission", (Unpublished MA dissertation in Mission and Evangelism). Cliff College (Manchester University): Calver, Hope Valley, Derbyshire.

Goody, Jack. *Death, Property, and the Ancestors: A Study of the Mortuary Customs of the Lodagga of West Africa*. London: Tavistock Pub.,1962.

Gravel, P B. *The malevolent eye: An essay on the evil eye, fertility and the concept of mana*. New York: Peter Lang, 1995.

Griffin, Emilie. *Clinging: The Experience of Prayer*, New York: Harper & Row (1984); McCracken, (1994); Wichita, KS: Eighth Day Books, (2003).

Groeschel, Benedict J. *Spiritual Passages: The Psychology of Spiritual Development*. New York: Crossroad, 1983.

Guthrie, Donald. *New Testament Theology*, Leicester: IVP, 1981.

________. *Hebrews: Tyndale New Testament Commentaries*. Leicester: IVP, 1988.

Hallesby, O. *Prayer*. Minneapolis: Augsburg, 1994.

Hall, Thelma. *Too Deep for Words*, New York; Paulist Press, 1988.

Hanson, R P C. *The Acts (The New Clarendon Bible)*, Oxford: The Clarendon Press, 1967.

Hardie, M M. *The evil eye in some Greek villages and the upper Haliakom valley in west Macedonia*, in Dundes, A (ed), *The evil eye: A folklore casebook*, 1981.

Henderson, David Michael. *"John Wesley's Instructional Groups,"* unpublished Ph.D.Dissertation, Indiana University, 1980.

Henderson, Michael D. *John Wesley's Class Meeting: A Model for Making Disciples*: Nappanee, Indianapolis, Evangel Publishing House, 1998.

Hendricks, Howard, and William. *Building Character in a Mentoring Relationship; As Iron Sharpens Iron*, Chicago: Moody Press, 1995.

Henry, Carl F H. (editor) *Basic Christian Doctrines*, Grand Rapids, Michigan: Baker Book House, 1962.

Hobley, C.W. *Bantu Beliefs and Magic with Particular Reference to the Kikuyu and Kamba Tribes*. NY.: Barnes & Noble, Inc., 1922.

Hopwood, P G S. *The Religious Experience of the Primitive Church,* New York: C Scribner's Sons 1937.

Hornby, S A. and Deuter, M. *Advanced Learner's Dictionary of Current English.*Oxford: Oxford University, 2016.

Horsfall, Tony. *Rhythms of Grace,* Eastbourne: Kingsway Publications, 2004.

________. *Deep Calls to Deep: Spiritual Formation in the Hard Places of Life.* Abingdon: Bible Reading Fellowship, 2015

Idowu, E. Bolaji. *African Traditional Religion: A Definition.* Maryknoll, NY.: Orbis Books, 1973.

Ignatius of Loyola. *The Spiritual Exercises,* Translated by Anthony Mottola. New York:Image, 1993.

Johnson, Jan, *Simplicity and Fasting*: Leicester: IVP 2003.

Keating, Charles J. Who We Are Is How We Pray: Matching Personality and Spirituality. Mystic, Conn.: Twenty-Third Publications, 1987.

Keating, Thomas. *Intimacy with God, Open Mind, Open Heart,* New York: Crossroad Publishing Company, 2015.

Keller, Timothy. *Walking with God Through Pain and Suffering.* New York: Penguin Books, 2016.

Kendall, R.T. *The Sermon on the Mount,* Oxford: Monarch Books, 2011.

Klug, Ronald. *How to Keep a Spiritual Journal: A Guide to Journal Keeping for Inner Growth and Personal Discovery.* Augsburg Fortress, Minneapolis : A Fortress E-book, Fortress Press. com; 2002.

Kreeft, Peter. *Christianity for Modern Pagans.* San Francisco: Ignatius, 1993.

Krige, J. D. "The Social Education of Witchcraft." *Theoria* (Pietermaritzburg, South Africa, (13), 1947.

Kurewa, Zvomunodita J.W. "Who do you say that I am?", *International Review of Missions, vol. LXIX, No.2* (April 1980).

Lawrence, J.C.D. *The Iteso.* London: Oxford University Press, 1957.

Leadingham, E. *Discover the Word: Reading the Bible for all it's Worth.* Kansas City, MO: Beacon Hill Press, 1997.

Leatherman, J.Artley. "The Decline of the Class Meeting" in Samuel Emerick, ed., *Spiritual Renewal for Methodism,* Nashville: Methodist Evangelical Materials, 1958.

Leclerc, Diane and Maddix, Mark A. (editors), *Spiritual Formation: A Wesleyan Paradigm,* Kansas City: Beacon Hill Press, 2011.

Leclercq, Jean. *The Love of Learning and the Desire for God: A Study of Monastic Culture* Translated by Catharine Misrahi. New York: Fordham University Press, 1982.

Leech, Kenneth. *Soul Friend: An Invitation to Spiritual Direction.* San Francisco: HarperSanFrancisco, 1992.

Lehmann, Edward. "Ancestor – Worship and Cult of the Dead (Iranian)." *Encyclopedia of Religion and Ethics.* James Hastings, Ed., vol. 1:454-455. Edinburgh: T & T Clark, 1909.

Lewis, C.S. *Mere Christianity,* New York: Macmillan, 1960.

__________ *The Four Loves,* Harcourt, Brace, New York, 1960.

Lindblom, Gerhard. *The Akamba,* Uppsala: Apperlbergs Boktrycheri Aktiebolag, 1920.

Longmans, Tremper. *How to Read the Psalms.* Illinois, Downers Grove: InterVarsity Press, 2005.

______. *Shaped by the Word,* Upper Room, 1985.

Lovelace, Richard F. *Dynamics of Spiritual Life: An Evangelical Theology of Renewal.* Downers Grove, Ill.: InterVarsity, 1979.

Luther, Martin. "Luther's Large Catechism" (1529) in Luther, Martin and Wace, Henry and Buchheim, C A. *Luther's Primary works, together with his Shorter and Larger Catechisms.* London: Hodder and Stoughton, 1896.

Malandra, A. "The Ancestral Shrine of the Acholi." *Uganda Journal.* Vol.7, No.1 July 1939.

Manala, M J. Witchcraft and the impact on black African Christians: A lacuna in the Hervormde Kerk in Suidelike Afrika. *HTS Theological Studies 60(4),* 2004.

Marshall, Howard. "The Biblical Use of the word Ekklesia" in *Expository Times* 84 (1973).

Marshall, Walter. *Gospel Mystery of Sanctification* Grand Rapids: Reformation Heritage, 1999.

________. *The Gospel Mystery of Sanctification: Growing in Holiness by Living in Union with Christ.* A New Version, Eugene: Wipf & Stock, 2005.

Martin, T A. *Our Restless Heart, The Augustinian Tradition.* Maryknoll, NY: Orbis Books, 2003.

Marwick, B.A. *The Swazi* London: Frank Cass & Co., Ltd., 1966 (1st edition), 1940.Darton Longman and Todd, 2003.

Mbiti, John S. *African Religions and Philosophy*, London: SPCK, 1969.

______. *Akamba Stories*, Oxford: Clarendon Press, 1966.

______. *Concepts of God in Africa.* London: SPCK, 1970.

______. *New Testament Eschatology in an African Background*, London: Oxford University Press, 1971.

______. "Christianity and Traditional Religion in Africa." *Crucial Issues in Missions Tomorrow.* Donald McGavran, ed. Chicago: Moody Press, 1972.

May, Gerald G. *Care of Mind, Care of Spirit: A Psychiatrist Explores Spiritual Direction.* San Francisco: Harper SanFrancisco, 1992.

Merton, Thomas. *Contemplative Prayer.* New York: Image, 1969.

_______. *New Seeds of Contemplation.* New York: New Directions, 1961.

_______. *Spiritual Direction and Contemplation.* Collegeville, Minn.: Liturgical Press, 1960.

Miley, John. *A Treatise on Class Meetings*. Cincinnati: The Methodist Book Concern, 1851.

Mircea, Eliade (ed). *The Encyclopedia of Religion,* New York: Macmillan Publishing Company, 1995.

Moulton, J.H. *A Grammar of New Testament Greek* 2, London: T & T Clark, 1906.

Mulholland, M Robert. *Shaped by the Word: The Power of Reading Scripture in Spiritual Formation,* Nashville, Tenn: Upper Room Books, 1985.

___________. *Invitation to a Journey.* Downers Grove, Ill.: InterVarsity, 1993.

Muto, Susan A. *Pathways to Spiritual Living.* Petersham, MA: St. Bede's Publications, 1984.

Mwailu, Daniel M. *Christology in Africa: An investigation of the Encounter between Biblical and Indigenous Concepts with Reference to Messianism in two New Religious Movements in Kenya*, Birmingham: Birmingham University, UK, (Ph.D. thesis) 1989.

Mwalwa, Matthews Kalola. *The Power of witchcraft among the Kenyan Akamba,* unpublished MTh thesis submitted to Nairobi Evangelical Graduate School of Theology, Nairobi, June 2001.

Ndeti, Kivuto. *Elements of Akamba Life.* Nairobi: East African Publishing House, 1972.

Nyamiti, Charles, Christ our Ancestor: Christology from an African Perspective, Harare: Mambo Press, 1984.

Olson, Roger E. *Armenian Theology: Myths and Realities*, Downers Grove, Ill.: IVP, 2009.

Otto, Rudolf. *The Idea of the Holy.*Trans. John W. Harvey. Oxford: Oxford University Press,

1923; 2nd ed., 1950 (*Das Heilige)*, 1917.

Pearce, R.V. *Conversion in the New Testament: Paul and the Twelve*, Grand Rapids: Eerdmans, 1999.

Page, Sydney H.T. *Powers of Evil: A Biblical Study of Satan and Demons*. Grand Rapids, MI: Baker Books, 1995.

Parrinder, E G. *African Traditional Religion*. London: SPCK. 1962.

P'Bitek, Okot. *Religion of the Central Luo*. Nairobi: Kenya Literature Bureau, 1971.

Peace, Richard. *Spiritual Journaling: Recording Your Journey toward God*. Colorado Springs, Colo: NavPress, 1998.

Peers, E. Allison. (trans), *The Works of St Teresa*, Vol 1, London: Sheed and Ward, 1946

Piper, John. *The Pleasures of God: Meditations on God's delight in Being God*, Colorado Springs, Colorado: Multnomah Publishers, 1991 revised 1992.

______. *A Hunger for God: Desiring God Through Fasting and Prayer*: Wheaton, Illinois: Crossway Books, 2013.

Pobee, J S. & World Council of Churches. *Towards Viable Theological Education: Ecumenical Imperative, Catalyst of Renewal.* Geneva: WCC Publication 1997.

Procter, Andrew and Elizabeth. *The Essential Guide to Burnout: Overcoming Excess Stress,* Oxford: Lion Books, 2013.

Pusey, Edward B. *The Confessions of St. Augustine,* New York: Washington Square Press, Inc., 1960.

Rack, Henry. "The Decline of the Class-Meeting and the Problems of Church-Membership in Nineteenth-Century Wesleyanism," *Proceedings of the Wesleyan Historical Society 39* (1973-74).

Roscoe, John. *The Bakitara or Banyoro.* Cambridge: Cambridge University Press, 1923.

______. *The Banyankole.* Cambridge: Cambridge University Press, 1923.

Rosser, L. *Class Meetings: Embracing their Origin, Nature, Obligation and Benefits,* Richmond: Published by the Author, 1855.

Salalah, Charles S. "The Place of Ancestral Spirits in African Theology: Evaluated in Biblical Teaching." M.A Thesis, Columbia Graduate School of Bible and Missions. 1981.

Schrage, W. *"Ekklesia" und "Synagogue" in Zeitschrift fur Theologie und Kirche 60, 1963*

Sellner, Edward C. *Mentoring: The Ministry of Spiritual Kinship.* Mahwah, NJ: Paulist Press, 1989.

Shapera, I. *The Khoisan Peoples of South Africa*. London: Routledge & Kegan Paul Ltd.,1930.

Smedes, Lewis B. *Union with Christ*, Grand Rapids: Eerdmans, 1983.

Stanley, Paul D. and H, Robert Clinton. *Connecting: The Mentoring Relationship You Need to Succeed in life*. Colorado Springs: NavPress, 1992.

Steinmetz, D. "Reformation and Conversion," in *Theology Today* 35 (1978).

Stevenson, Robert Louis. *From The Upward Call*. Kansas City: Beacon Hill Press, 1994.

Stott, John R.W. *Christian Counter-Culture: The Message of the Sermon on the Mount*. Downers Grove, Illinois: InterVarsity, 1978.

______. *The Cross of Christ*. Downers Grove, Illinois: IVP, 2006.

The Methodist Church, *Singing the Faith*, London: Hymns Ancient and Modern Ltd, 2011.

Thompson, Marjorie J. *Soul Feast*, Louisville: Westminster John Knox Press 1995.

Thompson, Marjorie J.; Howard, Evan B. *Soul Feast: An Invitation To The Christian Spiritual Life*. Westminster John Knox Press. 2005.

Times Magazine, Friday, May 31, 1963.

Tjernagel, Neelak S. *Henry VIII and the Lutherans: A Study in Anglo-Lutheran Relations from 1521-1547,* St Louis: Concordia Publishing House, 1965

Tracy, Wesley. Herald of Holiness, Feb. 1991.

Tracy, Wesley. et al., *The Upward Call.* Kansas City: Beacon Hill Press, 1994.

_______. *Reflecting God.* Kansas City: Beacon Hill Press Christian Holiness Partnership, 2000.

Uchendu, Victor C. *The Igbo of Southeastern Nigeria.* NY.: Holt, Rinehart & Winston, 1965.

Varughese, Alex. and Hahn, Roger. *Discovering the New Testament: Community and Faith.* Kansas City: Beacon Hill Press, 2004.

Watson, Kevin M. *The Class Meeting: Reclaiming a Forgotten (and Essential) Small Group Experience.* Franklin, Tennessee: Seedbed Publishing, 2014.

Watson, David Lowes. *The Early Methodist Class Meeting: Its origins and Significance,* Nashville TN: Discipleship Resources,

Webster, John. *Holiness.* Grand Rapids: Eerdmans, 2003.

Webster, Merriam. *Webster's Third International Dictionary Unabridged*, Chicago, 1986.

Wesley Granberg-Michaelson. "Where Protestantism Went –Wrong: The 500th Anniversary of the Reformation Calls for Repentance as Well as Celebration." In *Sojourners: Faith in Action for Social Action Magazine*, February 2, 2018

Wesley, John. *A Plain Account of the People Called Methodists*: In a letter to Revd. Mr. Perronet, Vicar of Shoreham in Kent. London: Printed by H. Cook, 1755.

________. *Letters, 3:212;3:94-95; 5:333; 5:87; 5:187; 6:116; 8:158*. San Francisco: Harper & Row, 1984.

________. *Minutes 1:5*

________. *Sermons* 1:272

________. *"The Repentance of Believers," Sermons on Several Occasion*. London: Wesleyan- Methodist Book Room, n.d.

_______. "Our Lord's Sermon on the Mount, Discourse III," *Sermons on Several Occasions*

_______. *Sermons on Several Occasions,* (London: Wesleyan-Methodist Book Room, n.d.)

_______.*Works 8:261*

Willard, Dallas. *The Spirit of the Disciplines*. San Francisco: Harper and Row, 1988.

_______. *Renovation of the Heart: Putting on the Character of Christ*. Colorado Springs, CO: NavPress, 2002.

Wilmon, William H. & Wilson, Robert L. *Rekindling the Flame: Strategies for a Vital United Methodism,* Nashville, Abingdon Press, 1988.

Willoughby. W.C. *The Soul of the Bantu*. N.Y.: Doubleday, Doreen and Co., 1928.

Wilson, Monica, *Rituals of Kinship Among the Nyakyusa*, London : Oxford University Press, 1957.

Woods, Rachel. *Into the Garden: Cultivation as a Tool for Spiritual Formation and Community Renewal.* Cambridge: Grove Books, 2016.

Wood, Robert. *A Thirty-Day Experiment in Prayer.* Nashville: The Upper Room, 1978.

World Council of Churches, Ecumenical Theological Education, Conference in Oslo, 1996.

Yancey, Philip. *What's so Amazing about Grace?* Grand Rapids: Zondervan, 1997.

Zion's Herald, Boston, November 30, 1825. (Designated as a reprint from the Arminian Magazine).

Zizioulas, John D. *Being as Communion*. Crestwood, N.J.: Vladimir's Seminary Press, 1993.

Printed in the United States
By Bookmasters